A Professor's Work

A Professor's Work

Matthew Melko

University Press of America,® Inc.
Lanham • New York • Oxford

Copyright © 1998
University Press of America,® Inc.
4720 Boston Way
Lanham, Maryland 20706

12 Hid's Copse Rd.
Cummor Hill, Oxford OX2 9JJ

Library of Congress Cataloging-in-Publication Data

Melko, Matthew
A Professor's work / Matthew Melko.
p.   cm.
Includes bibliographical references.
1. College teachers—United States. 2. College teaching—Social
aspects—United States. 3. Participant observation. I. Title
LB1778.2.M45 1998   378.1'25'0973—dc21   98-29101 CIP

ISBN 0-7618-1216-4 (cloth: alk. ppr.)
ISBN 0-7618-1217-2 (pbk: alk. ppr.)

To Nelle

Contents

Acknowledgments

I would like to thank Glena Bucholz for her patience in sending, copying, and printing, for advice on computer management, and for otherwise contending with the manuscript for this book;

Lynn Morgan, for handling everything else when Glena was contending with manuscripts;

John Hord for his editing and counsel, and for his willingness to read revisions and proofs;

Mary Brighthaupt for typesetting, resolving problems, and reassurance;

Doug Mitchell for a helpful early read;

David Orenstein for playing the role of Chorus;

Jack Davis and Roberta Monnin for unobtrusively taking the photographs;

Jeanne Ballantine for providing protection and support;

Wright State University for supplying not only financial support for the photographs, but also the Theater.

1

Perceptions of the Professor

The Aloof, Involved, Selfish, Concerned, Indefatigable Drone

Here I was at Dayton Airport, waiting for a flight to San Francisco and the beginning of a great adventure. My hair was combed straight forward, a trifle long. My beard was slightly out of control, sticking out here and there. The only suit coat I had with me I was wearing, with shirt open at the collar, drab gray pants, unshined shoes. In short, I was consciously entering the role of a professor, in this case a professor on his way to a scholarly conference.

While I waited for the plane, I was writing the first notes of my research project in a Stuart Hall three-subject notebook.
It was the beginning of what was to be a year-long study of a university professor's work.

How had I gotten into this situation? Why was I committing a year of my life to study a profession that is not exactly at the center of dramatic action in our society?

One aspect of my normal work concerns occupations. I needed but could not find a participant-observer study of a professional occupation, that is, a study by someone who is both working as a professional and observing himself at work. There were studies in which a sociologist both assumes the role of a worker and describes what that is like for himself and others, as when Richard Balzer worked for five months assembling components at Western Electric (1976). But I couldn't find any study of the day to day work of a

1

professional. I could see that there would be difficulties if Balzer attempted to do a study of the medical profession, working as a doctor, even as a family practitioner. But why was it so hard to find a study of professional examining his own work?

Locating the Study

Whatever the reason, I could find no such study, so I decided to undertake one myself. I chose to study professors rather than doctors, lawyers or engineers. For one thing, professors might be more tolerant of being studied. For another, if the study is to be that of a participant-observer, the participant needs to participate; and probably there would be less danger in his disseminating abstract information carelessly and inaccurately than in giving uninformed legal advice, trying to contribute to the planning of bridge construction, or prescribing drugs he never heard of.

Having decided to study the work of a professor, I wanted to work within a university that was at a middle level, respectable but not glittering. I thought a state university would be preferable to a private one, because students would come from a wider socioeconomic range. An urban commuter university would be preferable to a rural or residential university because the professor would be a member of a wider ranging community, not too much in the company of other professors, in this respect more like a lawyer or a clinical psychologist. I wanted a city that, including its suburban regions, would be fairly typical of the United States as a whole, preferably in the midwest as being possibly less idiosyncratic than the coasts. Ultimately I settled on Wright State University in Dayton, Ohio.

Well fine, but now what? I needed to get funding, to find a place in a department, to be able to practice on clients (i.e., teach in the classroom), to get places on committees, to attend and present papers at meetings. In the end, the administration at Wright State University was very supportive and willing to provide a "line" for a year's study and even funding to support the work. But where should the line be? I had to teach where I could not do irreparable harm to the students and where it would not be obvious to them that I didn't know very much. Finally it was decided that I would be assigned as a sociologist to the Department of Sociology and Anthropology, since my project was perceived to be either sociology (participant-observation) or anthropology (field study). Besides, it is considered normal for a sociologist to say just about anything and contradict himself the next day. I was also to teach two sections of a freshman level history course in the summer because this course covered a century a week and the period of teaching was so brief that someone who knew less arguably had an advantage over someone who knew more.

Wright State is part of the Ohio state system of universities. Ohio State University is in Columbus, the state capital. Each of the other six large cities has a state university and there are four more in rural areas, one in each corner of the state. All the other city universities are named for the city they are in, but there is a private University of Dayton, so Wright State needed a different name. The newest university in the system—it first held classes in 1964—was named after the Wright Brothers, who had their bicycle shop and did their pioneering airplane construction in Dayton.

In the year of the study there were 15,000 students attending several colleges in Wright State, and about 500 full-time faculty members. It was big enough that you would not be surprised to meet someone at a party or civic meeting who turned out to be a colleague you had never seen. The environment was rather utilitarian. The buildings and classrooms tended to be functional, the campus flat and lacking trees. The most striking feature of the campus was probably the parking lots.

The Participant-Observer Conflict

The reason Wright State was willing to give me a line was that I already had it. I had been a professor for 30 years, the previous 13 at Wright State. I'd had my beard for nine years, my dress style much longer. The reason I wanted to do this study is that I taught the sociology of occupations and professions, and for that course had searched unsuccessfully for a participant-observer study. I wanted a professional social worker or nurse to write about her work while it was being done. I wanted it to be at a middle level so students could identify with the kind of work they might be doing in ten years.

When, however, I couldn't find any such study, I decided to study my own work and that of my colleagues. I wanted to look at the work from a day to day level to try to see what it is like. I wanted to provide a study that would differ from literary images, though these certainly have a value of their own. And, if I were lucky, I hoped to stimulate some debate, and some other case studies in other situations. Of course, this was also a situation that was convenient. I wouldn't have to search for a grant, get a line, locate a typical Midwest city or grow a beard. But, as my introduction suggests, the situation has a number of qualities that a sociologist might well look for. My colleague Len Cargan enjoys beginning books and articles with his choice of Dayton as an area of study as if he had spent months in a preliminary search for the Truly Typical American City.

An insider participant has some advantages over an outside observer. He has a better knowledge of the system than the outsider could have and is fully established in it. The meetings he reports are continuations of past meetings; the business of some of the committees is already familiar. Colleagues will regard him as an insider and his presence will be nothing new or special. He doesn't have to worry about trying to blend in as a participant because he is one.

But as an observer he has disadvantages. He gets carried into issues, is outraged by what he regards as "unprofessional" behavior, frustrated by what he perceives to be duplicity in the administration, disheartened by lack of student interest in what he believes to be important. He can easily forget his observer role: the understanding of the perspective of the professor, administrator or student. As a sociologist, I should be able to maintain an observer's perspective, since sociologists are supposed to be observing what occurs around them as if they were not part of it. But that proved to be easier to do when I was studying the nearby community of Millfield than when I was studying my own department meetings.

Another disadvantage for the insider is that he is busy. For the observer, the study is the main thing; for the participant it is another thing. Richard Balzer didn't care as much about how many wiring units he turned out as about the short run skill required and the long run boredom. When I took on the task of making research notes for this book, it was another overload and one that wouldn't reward me. It could have lost out to the "more important" research I was doing, or the preparation of writing guides for the Occupations course, or even another crisis facing the Early Music Board.

What is a Professional?

That's a question we ask undergraduates in the Occupations course. They get their answers from an occupations text book (e.g., Watson 1980, Pavalko 1988, Abbott 1988, Hodson and Sullivan 1990). Usually they learn that two models have been used to define professional conduct and development. The one that defines conduct is called the "attributes model" and is rather flattering; the one that describes development is called the "process model" and is rather deflating.

The attributes model states that professionals usually are members of some sort of associational body that sets standards, that they are expected to be scrupulously honest and ethical, have a strong desire to serve their clients, are intrinsically committed to their work, maintain autonomy from external controls, conduct themselves in a style that commands respect while reflecting humanitarian values, avoid any suggestion of commercial motivation, maintain a perspective beyond everyday emotionalism and irrationality, and make the most of their talents.

The attributes model says that professionalism is a quality of an occupation. If we refer to an occupation as a profession, as we do to the work of professors, we mean this is an occupation that tends to include strong professional standards. Within the occupation, we would expect some people to possess these attributes to a greater degree than others.

A professional is supposed to possess a body of theoretical knowledge. To some extent it is generally shared by professionals within the field; but most professionals also possess some specialized theoretical knowledge.

Professionals tend to belong to associations that have national or world bases. These associations provide situations in which professionals within the same discipline can meet and exchange information, and they also provide ethical guidelines and guidelines for the testing of competence.

A professional, then, is supposed to be both competent and ethical by an explicit set of standards.

He is supposed to be honest. He doesn't lie or mislead. He doesn't seek special favors. He assumes that other professionals are also honest.

A professional is dedicated to service. She has empathy for her clients. She does not condescend, nor manipulate, nor use her authority to take advantage of others.

A professional is committed. He believes in what he does. He is involved in it. He would like his salary to reflect his value, but that isn't a primary consideration.

Somewhat in conflict with concern and commitment is the idea that the professional is cool. Since she is competent, she does not get rattled. When she is attacked, she responds coolly and rationally. Though she is committed, she keeps her long range perspective. Though she may dislike a client or colleague, she does not let that show, and treats the other person courteously and with respect.

A professional has power. She doesn't use it to intimidate others, but she is able to be effective. She is able to influence her environment and to positively affect her clients.

A professional has autonomy. He is not someone else's employee. He operates within an institutional framework but makes his own decisions, develops his own style within his range of competence.

A professional is not a merchant. He does not sell, he does not calculate advantage, he does not withhold information for his own advantage, he is not concerned about material gain or display.

A professional develops a professional style. She conveys her competence, power and autonomy with dignity and without ostentation.

To what extent does the professor manifest these qualities in his day-to-day activities? Let's keep these qualities in mind as we examine the professor's work.

The process model, on the other hand, looks at practice as related to ideal. It has been notably explored by Andrew Abbott, who considered not only individual professions but also their interactions and conflicts with one another. This approach tends to perceive some less lofty characteristics, e.g., tendencies for professions to upgrade themselves in order to command higher salaries, to assume wider varieties of work, to increase standards to make it harder for others to enter the profession, and to continually steal work from each other, all of which tend to help the professional obtain higher status and income.

Professionals tend to value their professions, to upgrade them, to increase the requirements for achieving the status of a professional in each field. This seems desirable, but it does mean that those who are established are raising standards for their successors. And if the status of the profession is raised, so also are the monetary rewards.

Professionals are on guard against deprofessionalization. If they become more responsive to clients, they have to be careful that the clients don't come to regard them as less skilled, less worthy of status and economic reward, which is one reason for the development of arcane professional language. And as they raise their standards, they need to protect themselves against some lower profession or even trade expanding its claims and taking some of its business by charging lower rates.

The process model is less easy to see in a one year study, since these changes take longer periods of time. But we can look for signs of process responses in the professor.

The Dark Side of the Profession

After I had completed my study and while I was organizing my notes, I began to be aware of a series of criticisms being leveled against professors from journalists and scholars studying higher education and from state legislatures. It is surprising, perhaps, that I had not been aware of these before. But they came from literature that wasn't familiar to me, though it would be very familiar to colleagues from the College of Education, which had its offices on the floor below ours.

The gist of this criticism was that professors have cushy jobs and are overpaid. They teach relatively few hours, they are protected by tenure, they travel around the country to conferences on trips paid for by the state or the parents of students. And since, like other professionals, they set their own standards, they protect their prerogatives. Moreover, their political views are well to the left of the average American's, so they bias their teaching; and they pride themselves on being neutral regarding moral issues (Bloom 1987, Sykes 1988, Kimball 1990, Wilshire 1990, D'Souza 1991, Huber 1993).

The legislative argument focused on their easy teaching loads in a time of economic austerity. If they gave more time to teaching, less to research, traveling and committee meetings, wouldn't hard pressed universities be able to reduce their deficits?

While I was taking notes, I had not been aware of these criticisms. So I never had them in mind while playing participant-observer. But though I should have preferred that the critics use a more professional tone, some of what they were saying could be considered with relation to the expectations of the professional models. As the process model suggests, the critics see the professors as protecting their prerogatives and making it tougher for their successors. And contrary to the attributes model's expectation of sharing information and upholding standards, the critics see the professors as engaged in boondoggle trips to association meetings where they stay at expensive hotels. Also, if the critics are correct in their view of professors as lazy and radical, that would violate the commitment, competence and integrity aspects of the attributes model. If being radical means they are presenting their own views instead of weighing the evidence, that would be a serious violation of both the competence and the integrity attributes. Let us keep these critical perceptions in mind and review them again after we have seen the professor at work. Let's keep in mind also that the professors encountered here are not among the elite; they are the everyday professors of a typical city university. But that does not mean that they are necessarily better or worse in their possession of the attributes of the profession.

As for Method

I planned no special activities. My intention before taking on this book had been to reduce my service activities for the sake of coherence. So I did not add activities for the sake of giving a more well rounded picture. I did not schedule an appointment with the university president for the sake of the book, nor with the basketball coach (whom I've never seen). As far as possible, I tried to do what I would have been doing if I were not gathering data so that the year studied would be as much as possible like any other year.

I tried not to be specific about focus. Initially I had the title "The Professor's Profession," which reflected my interest in writing about a profession. But as I got into the notes it became evident that much occurred that had little to do with profession, so the title was modified to the more mundane "A Professor's Work". ("Work?" exclaimed colleague David Orenstein. "Who would think of what we do as work?")

While I tried not to be narrow, I knew from the beginning that one focus would be our objectives and how we go about trying to achieve them. Does the system create new problems, particularly because people have different objectives? But in retrospect I don't think that focus was kept, a sign that the participant may have impeded the observer. Then, what makes a professor a professional? How does he deviate from that role? I did not think I had a clear idea what a professional was, but the taking of notes certainly enriched my understanding even if it did not clarify.

Should the study be overt or covert? Should I let the "subjects" know they were being studied or would that bias responses? From the methodological literature, I concluded that the study should be as overt as possible, that the subjects should be given an equivalent of the surgeon general's warning. This could bias the information somewhat, but the bias might also work toward getting some information that would otherwise be missed.

Most sociologists would be particularly sensitive to areas of norm, role or value conflict, because these indicate some of our unwritten social determinants. One of these is the conflict between professional confidentiality and research objectivity. It would be unprofessional to reveal the content of a private meeting, but it would also be unprofessional not to report fully whatever is relevant to his study. So it would be possible for me first to refuse to reveal the contents of a tenure discussion and then to publish them the following year because I adhered to two contradictory sets of mores.

Some sociologists may consider this book to be weak in theoretical underpinning. If I were more professional, I might have spent a year really getting immersed in occupational theory. Luckily I happened to be teaching the Sociology of Occupations and Professions during the year of note taking, and that did give me at least an undergraduate's level of theoretical material to test against events.

This book is essentially a case study. Like other case studies, it does not deal with large numbers of professionals, cannot generalize about them as, for instance, would Burton Clark's study of 170 professors in 16 institutions (1987) or Bowen and Schuster's *American Professors* (1986). Nor can it do what a longitudinal study could do, showing change over longer periods of time as, for instance, Howard Becker does for medical students in *Boys in White* (1961).

Also, this book represents the perspective of an individual.
If I had been a genuine observer, I might have gotten a better picture of the University as a whole, had more time to wander into the offices of others and intrude on their business. But as participant, I

wrote about my own work; and the work of others came into it as it related to mine.

Topical organization, for all the work it takes, has one disadvantage when compared to a journal. Topical organization gives a false impression of coherence. We see the search for a new department member uninterrupted by preparing classes, grading papers, meetings of the Monster Committee, trips to conferences, worries over the contractor. We try to achieve a retrospective clarity that was not present at the time.

But retrospective clarity is at the core of a professor's work. He comes out of the daze of daily impressions and asks, "What happened?"

Let's see if I can tell you.

2

Inside the Department

*How We Searched for a New Member and
Why the Department Is the Center of Power*

The Search

The Department of Sociology and Anthropology was authorized a new line, i.e., granted permission to create and fill a new faculty position. We got it, Vice President Hathaway told me, because of the total contribution we had made to general education, not only in introductory sociology and cultural anthropology, but also in the Middle East courses from Gordon Welty and Ann Bellisari and my Western World courses.

A Search Committee including Jerry Savells, Ann Bellisari and David Orenstein, who chaired, drafted an advertisement that was approved by the Department, our chair, the college dean, probably the vice president for academic affairs and the affirmative action officer. It called for a person who could teach methods, introductory sociology and a regional studies course, that is a general education course about some major non-Western region of the world.

The new member began to play a part in our department well before being chosen. In early April, shortly after our ad had been published in *The Chronicle of Higher Education*, the Department Curriculum Committee made out a schedule for the following year. They allocated to "New" a pair of methods courses, three Social Lives (in-

11

troductory sociology) and a pair of Regional Studies courses, which would depend on the regional specialty of the successful candidate.

A few days earlier Orenstein had remarked that seven of the first twelve applicants appeared to be non-Western. He wondered if this were an indication that non-Westerners really did not get equal treatment in the application process and took the regional studies requirement as a signal that this was a real job opportunity. Whereas previously he had seen the regional studies requirement as incidental, now he thought it was going to have a major impact on the mix of applicants.

A week later we had 61 applicants. Each of the committee members was putting together a list of candidates whom they thought best fit our requirements. Then they would compare lists and collate one to recommend to the Department.

The following week Orenstein commented that we had a number of applicants from "First Tier" universities, like the University of North Carolina. Ohio State, he explained, was a second tier university while Bowling Green (and therefore presumably Wright State) was a third tier university. It did wonders for my ego to learn, after thirty years, that I labored in a Third Tier University.

On the first of May the committee gave us a prioritized list of seven candidates. I had looked at their list, then at perhaps ten folders in an hour and a half, so had a few candidates of my own to add. So, presumably, did some of the other Department members who were also looking at folders before the meeting.

It wasn't easy to sort them out if you didn't pay attention to tiers. How did you judge a methods teacher if you weren't one yourself? Most were qualified to teach at the general education level, but how well they would do in an introductory course was something you couldn't tell until they got here for interview. The first question was, with limited travel money, whom to invite. So a good part of the selection had to do with whether the candidates had specialties that interested you, subjects they would talk about in the hallways. After all this accumulation of curricula vitae (academic resumes), a lot depended on our subjective preferences, our inattention, how well someone argued at the meeting. Most of us had been selected in a process like this. Most of us wondered how some of the others could possibly have been hired.

At the Department meeting, Orenstein explained that we could invite three national candidates, who would require travel and accommodation money, and three locals, candidates from nearby who could come in for the day. The committee submitted a prioritized list of seven nationals along with three locals, and collectively we added a few more. Before we voted, Tom Koebernick argued for combining the lists, even though the locals were free. He didn't want to interview folks who didn't have a chance. This was a break from previous procedure, but the Department accepted his suggestion.

Now we voted on those we wanted to invite, ending up with two of the top three recommended by the committee along with their first alternate. One of the locals was fourth, so we invited her. The order among these four wasn't important, because each would have an equal chance on interview. If one of the first three declined the interview, we would invite number five. All of those who would or might be invited for interview came from the committee list, none from the additions proposed by Department members.

Of the six, two were East Asian, one African. Three were women. There had been 69 candidates for the position. The affirmative action office required only that minority candidates be considered, but members of our Department were particularly receptive to having a variety of races, nationalities, genders and theoretical backgrounds. It was also known that Deans Perry Moore and Bill Rickert would strongly support hiring of minority faculty.

The Interviews

Now in rapid succession came the candidates. David and I interviewed Linda Dorsten together. This saved time, but perhaps we didn't make a good team. From my perspective he talked too much, told the candidate more than he got. But I felt Linda did not take hold of my questions, which were intended to give her a chance to apply her organizational and sociological knowledge to real problems. She may have been advised to be cautious, but she didn't ask probing questions, didn't provide interesting hypotheses, didn't use her sociological knowledge, and didn't do any better with Orenstein's theory questions.

Her classroom lecture was reasonable, she made no mistakes, but was never dynamic. I couldn't see her taking a large class. After the class, Jeanne Ballantine, our Department chair, shared with us that Linda had another offer, would have to make up her mind before the interviewing process was over. For us, perhaps, that made this visit a practice run.

At lunch I couldn't even get her to talk about herself. Tom finally got on her wavelength talking about data in her research. But there must be methodologists who can talk about themselves and about ideas. I told David later that he was rescuing her from my "tough" questions by filling in what I meant, not allowing silence. He said he felt that was his role as host, but I felt his desire that candidates be comfortable contradicted the interviewer's need to get an indication how the candidate would function as a teacher and colleague.

David and Dennis Rome, our newest Department member, dropped by my office to discuss Linda. David felt she was competent, but hoped someone would be better. Dennis thought she did a good job in class, saw her as one to beat. I wasn't satisfied, would go to candidates 5 and 6 before voting for her.

After the interviews were completed, we would have a secret vote on candidates so that when someone was chosen, he wouldn't know who voted for him. But David held hallway meetings which insured that everyone knew how everyone else appraised Linda Dorsten, so that if she were chosen she would certainly learn that I wasn't impressed.

Next came Abdelrahman Abdelrahman, a demographer originally from Sudan. As David put it, he was the opposite problem from Linda Dorsten. He would make a delightful colleague, really challenging, but would he be able to handle his classes? I wasn't sure he was familiar with how an American sociology course is taught and I wasn't sure intro classes were what he wanted to do. His accent was also difficult for me to follow, less so for David. How would he do in a large class? I didn't hear him because of a squash match, not a very good excuse, and trusted to the collective judgment of Jeanne, Ann and Dennis, who did attend.

At lunch Abdelrahman confirmed my opinion that he would be an admirable colleague, a person with his own opinions and different perspectives. But that was not a sufficient trade off if Jeanne caught too many complaints from students about his classes.

Jerry Savells, Dennis and I discussed him over pizza before an evening class. Earlier I had talked to Jeanne and Associate Dean Bill Rickert about him, and both were doubtful about how he would do in the classroom. Dennis and Jerry, however, thought he would do all right. Dennis, who heard his lecture, admitted his accent could be a problem, but thought it would improve.

I talked to the third candidate, Susan Shoemaker, for only 15 minutes, but I was able to establish that she had experience with large classes and had a good idea what she would do with an Asian Regional Studies course. She was forthright about her research on women in science and had some interesting information about gender socialization. Her comparative interests were not far from some of mine. So I was disappointed that her class presentation was okay, but not a stellar performance. She didn't make use of her intercivilizational or environmental interests until a student question led her to call upon them.

David and History Chair Tsing Yuan had lunch with her, and David told me later he was not impressed, that she did not seem interested. He thought we should go on to the next two on our list if In Soo Son, the fourth candidate, was not spectacular. It seemed as if, after I had interviewed her, she lost energy. I wondered if she got tired. But getting tired isn't allowed when you are interviewing. Len Cargan, one of our emeritus faculty members, suggested that perhaps she had lost steam in her presentation and at lunch because about that time she had decided that Wright State was not for her. We each thought of times when we had made such decisions while being interviewed, but still had to go on with the process.

Last came In Soo Son, who was impressive at breakfast. His research was on comparative minorities, and he himself had been a member of the Korean minority in Japan before he came to Hawaii and then the American mainland. So he would be doing research with an international perspective on an important subject. His classroom experience, however, had been as a teaching assistant. I missed his presentation because of squash, again relying on my colleagues' assessment. His English seemed better to me than Abdelrahman's, so David and I were hoping he would turn out to be the anointed one and we wouldn't have to interview further candidates.

Making the Choice

The crucial meeting began with the information that Affirmative Action Director Juanita Wehrle-Einhorn had been called in because of the comments made to Jeanne and me by Bill Rickert concerning whether we thought Abdelrahman's English would be a problem in his classroom presentation. Had the process thereby been compromised by a dean's verbal participation? After meeting

with David, Jeanne and Liberal Arts Dean Perry Moore, Juanita recommended that the process continue.

Linda Dorsten was quickly dismissed, failing to impress most
of us either in interview or in class.

Abdelrahman was seen as dynamic and interesting in interaction, but Ellen Murray and Dennis disagreed about whether he
would be understood in class. Bob Riordan asked whether his sociology background was adequate and I asked whether he seemed to
be familiar with American introductory sociology courses. Others
may have interpreted that as suggesting that the American Way is
the Only Way. I felt both pressured to accept Abdelrahman as an
alternate choice, so as not to seem racist, and pressured not to, so
that I wouldn't be yielding to pressure.

Relatively little was said about In Soo Son. He was perceived to
be strong in methods and people liked his lecture.

I had no notes on Shoemaker. She must have been discussed,
but I must have perceived that she had taken herself out.

In the vote we decided to recommend that In Soo Son be invited, with Abdelrahman second and Shoemaker a close third, so not
everyone shared my perception about her. Did we adhere to this
vote or did we vote again on second choice? Things got hot. Jerry
proposed we take them in the order of the first vote and lost 6-5.
Things get hotter. Gordon Welty suggested there might be an affirmative action violation if the vote were reversed. Jerry saw a second vote as politics, Dennis as madness. I made things worse by
referring to runoffs in Southern politics, which confirmed Jerry's
opinion that politics were influencing our voting. We revoted on
Jerry's motion and it carried, Jeanne and I changing our votes, and
maybe Bob. An affirmative action appeal could scuttle the search,
and we thought In Soo Son would accept.

I felt bad about the meeting. My reference to runoffs in Southern politics was certainly a blunder, which Gordon used to advantage. After I had already asked about Abdelrahman's familiarity with
American sociology, I really felt like a bigot.

The following week Dean Perry Moore dropped by to ask how
I felt about Abdelrahman. Given my feelings about the meeting, I
told him more, probably, than was ethical, suggesting that it was his
prerogative to veto our recommendation. On reconsidering, my own
vote was surely influenced by politics. I didn't want to vote against
an African Muslim. If the opportunity had arisen, I should have
preferred to vote against inviting him or Shoemaker, and instead

interviewing a couple more candidates. Mind you, all of this was contingent upon Son turning us down, which some of us thought unlikely.

The same day I talked to Dennis. His perception, of course, was that on a second vote games might have been played that weren't on the first vote, the games being the denial of a Third World candidate his (fairly won) second place finish. More alarmingly, Dennis gathered from his meeting with Perry that the question had been raised about whether to invite anybody! That is, it seemed alarming when Dennis said it, though I had myself reminded Perry that he had the option of vetoing the Department recommendation.

Dennis and I had dinner that night before he made a presentation to my Careers class. I now could see the possibility that our delay might cost us In Soo Son, who might accept another offer. Then the Dean might reject Abdelrahman, thus scrapping the search. We would have to do the whole thing over again next year or, worse, lose the line and not get anyone.

And what about the anger and personal attacks generated? Not only was I labeled ethnocentric, but Dennis also wondered about Bob Riordan, who had commented on Abdelrahman's undergraduate work being Sudanese. Bob! An ethnocentric anthropologist? Who could be more stable and balanced than Bob? What hope was there for any of the rest of us?

The next day, before a special departmental meeting, I also talked to Jerry. I hoped I cleared up the Southern politics reference and I inferred that as a Kentucky born Southerner he sometimes felt himself to be a Department outsider .

The Special Meeting

The special meeting was attended and opened by Perry, who gave a lot of attention to the need for the new candidate to teach sections of 200 to 400 students in the Regional Studies part of the general education program. Nothing had been said previously about this. It turned out that on his visit here, Son had taught a small methods class, so it was hard to judge whether he could handle a large one. And I hadn't been even to the small class because I was playing squash!

The meeting now began to tilt toward scuttling the search. Gordon pointed out the advantage of readvertising and stressing the

bly tell you he had very little influence. His best chance would be to suggest that he did not want a course. That would likely produce three or four versions of it.

No, our board member would do better to contact the chair of one of the centers of power, a department curriculum committee. In the year I was studying, one of these powerful figures happened to be me. By what stratagems did I obtain this powerful position? When Jeanne was looking for people to serve on committees, she asked me to serve on this one, knowing that I had served before and either liked the work or didn't mind. In other words, the Sociology curriculum committee, this center of power, was not everyone's favorite assignment. It could meet often and its work of juggling courses for the next two years seemed fairly routine and rather boring. But it also had the fascination of puzzle solving; and it had a central role in determining not only what courses would be taught, but even who would teach them.

These courses were listed in the catalog and could be found in greater detail in a file of syllabi. Included in the catalogue were also "topics" courses, which were new. Even these were assigned, and the lucky faculty members who got them had the opportunity to create a course within very general parameters, such as family or social problems. If a new course were successful and taught a second time, it became eligible for listing as a regular offering in the inventory. But over time, adding new courses required deleting old ones, and the Curriculum Committee proposed which ones these should be. If it did not actually create courses, the curriculum committee had a good deal to say about who would.

So I was a member of this powerful committee. But by what intrigue did I get to be chair? Well, there were three members serving two-year terms. David Orenstein was on the committee the previous year and would normally have chaired this one, but was excused because he directed the Masters in Humanities Program. Dennis Rome was just entering his first year with the Department. He had no choice about serving on this powerful committee because he had been elected to it the previous spring, before he arrived on campus. That the newest and least known faculty member was so elected, and would become chair of the committee in his second year in the Department, said something about our Department members' lust for power. So, as the only other member with previous experience, I became chair by default.

Perhaps you think I am being facetious? After all, this was only a committee of three, and it determined only part of the program for one department. The anthropologists had their own curriculum committee. There were 13 other departments in the College, and who knows how many in the University? And every course in the catalogue had to be approved by college and university committees. But the courses and programs had their origins in the departments. They usually passed at higher levels because the members of the higher level committees were indifferent and because it was difficult to evaluate courses in other disciplines from sample syllabi. So what the departments proposed usually passed and what they proposed originated in the curriculum committees. Therefore, if you wanted to have impact, you wanted to be a member of a curriculum committee, preferably to chair it. The conflicts and processes here described may not seem to have much scope, but they were of crucial importance in determining the quality of our state educational system.

What Would Be Taught?
Who Would Teach It?

In the country as a whole there appeared to be a decline in sociology. Two universities had eliminated their sociology departments. But at Wright State, sociology was booming. It could be because our faculty was so wonderful, but more likely because sociology was more of a concern in urban universities. Moreover, we still had a C-average for an entry level to the major, whereas many other departments and some colleges had raised their entry level requirement to B minus. So many of our problems involved finding ways to teach enough courses to accommodate both majors committed to the field and university students just taking the Social Life required for general education. (We used the noun "major" to mean both the area of study and the student who chose that area of study. Thus a student who chose to major in sociology was called a sociology major.)

We began in September, two weeks before the fall quarter, with a modest revision of the schedule for the next academic year. That schedule had been drawn by last year's committee, chaired by Tom Koebernick. It appeared that we needed to add at least one more class of 400 students in order to accommodate the backlog waiting to take the Social Life course required in the general education program (Ch. 3). We balanced this with a cut in the number of family courses, because of a decline in enrollment in the School of Nursing. The nursing majors were required by their department to take our family course. We hoped these changes would enable us to offer every upper level course at least once this year or next, in accordance with a new biennial schedule that had been introduced by the Koebernick committee.

Now with reference to power, the changes in the general education and nursing situations were outside our control but they offered us an opportunity to carry out a departmental objective. The objective, teaching every course listed in the catalogue at least once every two years, was bequeathed to us by Koebernick's committee. But we agreed with it and exerted ourselves to meet it in the current two year period.

There was another reason for our getting to work so early in the school year. If Jeanne could submit this revised schedule early, we would have a better chance of getting the necessary adjunct teachers, persons with sociology backgrounds but not members of the Department. Adjunct teachers could be housewives wanting to keep their hand in, or business people who liked to teach, or emeritus professors, or graduate students. They were poorly paid but usually enjoyed the work. Often they were perceived to be better teachers than regular faculty, who might skimp on elementary preparations in favor of their upper-level specializations. But there was a limited budget for adjuncts, and competition for money was stiff. So a schedule submitted early might have a better chance of being fully funded.

That our schedule included four general education classes of 400 was a cause of regret. But we had to teach Social Life to 2,500 students a year in some way. We decided that a combination of 400's and 60's was better than 20 classes of 125 students each. In the classes of 60 you could do something about writing and learn the names of most of your students, while in classes of 125 you had to use multiple choice anyway. But Jan Gabbert of Classics and my wife, Nelle, among others, felt there was a powerful negative psychological element when a student found himself in a very large class. These "monster" classes were a subject of concern throughout the year (Ch. 3).

We also had to put together a draft of the teaching schedule for the following academic year. Dennis and I were able to do this in an hour by matching the list of courses scheduled by last year's committee, as slightly modified by us, with a list of course preferences expressed by the faculty. At some point when Dennis and I were meeting and David wasn't there, we decided that in the coming year we could get by with three classes of 400 by sacrificing a few small Department classes. Apparently I never told David, but expected him to read it in the memo I sent to the faculty describing the modified schedule and listing the courses they were to teach.

If that was what happened, I got what I deserved because at the November Department meeting, David surprised me by arguing for returning to the four classes of 400 and reinserting six courses that the reversion would make possible. What happened was that, like most of us, he had brought the memo to the meeting and read it for the first time. After some discussion, the department voted his way 3–2 with five abstentions. The others, apparently, wanted to think about it; and further modifications could be made if the question were raised again. At the time I was annoyed at David, but I should have told him verbally about the change. Bad politics and even questionable ethics on my part, the punishment being yet another revision needed from the Curriculum Committee.

This time David did the revision and the committee accepted it, but then guess what? We learned that Tom and David had been granted quarter sabbaticals from the College and were applying for more quarters from the University, Tom for one and David for two. If they were to get them, we would have to scale back to where we were before David intervened, because he would be one of the teachers of large classes and we probably wouldn't get adjuncts to cover for five quarters. So the curriculum committee had been working hard but spinning its wheels through the fall quarter. It wasn't easy being at the center of power.

Oh No! Not Large Classes Again!

The debate on large Social Life classes resumed toward the end of winter quarter, when the Curriculum Committee turned its attention to drafting the two year schedule. This would be arranged by quarters and was to include all courses listed in the biennial model that had been initiated by the Koebernick committee and modified by ours. This was important not only because it increased the likelihood that all courses listed would be taught, but also because it meant the Department was giving priority to the content of the curriculum before considering what they, as individuals, would prefer to teach. It was easier to agree on the list and frequency of courses a year or two from the present than on who would teach what next spring.

Orenstein drafted the initial proposal and, of course, put in four large classes a year, which would allow six more small classes and make our task much easier. There was also a real possibility that we would need more graduate courses. We were involved in a joint graduate program with two other departments, but there was a chance that in the near future each would get its own graduate program. If that happened, we would be left with the Applied Behavioral Science Program, which could become virtually an applied sociology program with more interesting classes and the research assistants that graduate programs bring.

If we were already scheduling three large classes, why not have four? Was there really that much difference? Well, for our department, there were 2,500 seats a year to fill. If we had three large classes of 400, that would mean 1,200 students in large classes, 1,300 in classes of 60 (which we were now beginning to call "small" classes), about a 50–50 division. If we went to four large classes, that would mean 1,600 in the big ones, only 900 in the regular size classes.Only about one third of the students would have the advantage of the instructor's knowing who they were and the chance to do some writing in take-homes, challenges, or whatever else the instructor might devise.

We decided to present alternative models to the Department, one that had "only" three large classes (mind you, there had not been *any* in the academic year preceding ours), and one with four but also with more graduate and marginal classes. I did not expect that Dennis and I would win this debate. Department members know sociology majors personally, but general education classes usually consist of students never met before. So you would expect the professors to be concerned first about the students they knew, students who were majoring in the field they cared about most.

In the debate, David suggested a method for protecting "at risk" students. We could hold ten places in each class of 60 so that University Advisors could put in students who might get buried in big classes. That might protect the most disadvantaged students from having to cope with a monster class. Despite his suggestion, however, the vote came out 5–2–1 against four large classes. Voting against were Gordon Welty and David Orenstein, an unusual alliance. The three newest members of the Department, Norma Shepelak, Ann

Bellisari and Dennis, were solidly for holding to only three. So was Jerry Savells on the ground that it was in the best interest of the student.

Now the Curriculum Committee would have the task of trying to draw a biennial schedule under the greater constraints of the three-large model as well as meeting the desires of the Department for an adequate number and distribution of upper-level and graduate courses. By the time we had reviewed the biennial schedule for sufficient evening courses, discussed and rejected both modifying distribution requirements and a review of our curriculum by an outside committee, included three new courses, and rejected other proposals for expanding offerings, it was June. The Department faculty, looking forward to summer, passed the schedule without discussion. The biennial schedule? Who cares? By the time they started to complain, the Sociology Curriculum Committee would belong to Dennis.

Afterword

The study of a single year often leaves events hanging. So where appropriate I thought I would add a brief update to complete hanging stories like the failed search, or to show the unraveling of something that appeared to have been completed, in this case the Koebernick biennial schedule.

The Department repeated its search the following year, once again advertising, winnowing candidates, and carrying out interviews, at great cost in time and money, not only to the Department and University, but to all the candidates who applied and all the professors who wrote letters of recommendation. This time the candidate who was preferred was invited and accepted a tenure track position. His name was In Soo Son.

The Koebernick biennial schedule, however, which I saw as a marvelous invention, looks to be lost and gone forever. My guess is that Dennis, being new, assumed that it was to be presented only every two years and that Norma Shepelak, who followed as chair of that committee, was probably unaware of it. When I began writing about it, I noticed its absence, but by that time new computers were being installed and the schedule was left to molder with other minor problems in the middle of an in-box. Its great strength of being important but inconspicuous proved to be its great weakness.

3

How an Intrepid Band of Professors Confronted

The General Education Monsters

While the Department Curriculum Committee may be perceived as a center of power, you could hardly say that about activities that were carried on at college, university or regional levels. There were a variety of permanent and ad hoc bodies whose separate and collective impact was difficult to gauge. Committees formed that had no authority; committee members became invisible; collective actions were so well balanced as to leave no trace; achievements dissolved at another level; the greatest achievement of the year maintained the status quo. That so much of this activity was frustrating if not surreal, however, does not necessarily mean that it was futile, useless or counterproductive.

Mind you, there was nothing extraordinary going on here. I feel obliged to recall the ordinariness of our institution. We were perceived to be a regional, urban institution in a typical American community in a state whose motto was "The Heart of It All," meaning the center of nothing in particular. I also want to confess my functionalist perspective. It seemed to me that most people were trying to do the best they could most of the time and that, as a group, they were above average in intelligence. Finally, I should admit that I rather liked bureaucracy. Coming from a small private college, it struck me that the great advantage of bureaucracy was that you were never defeated. In a small college, if you lost, you lost. There was no other group to appeal to, no other source of funds. But in a bureaucracy, if you lost, you just lost a round. You could take the same idea, with minor modifications, to a different group. Or just wait till next year and take it through the same committee, which would then have different people.

A sample of university debates, rituals and adventures will be examined in the next chapter, but the central tale of this chapter involves a faculty attempt to respond to the perceived menace of monster general education classes, classes of 200 to 400 students, many of them for freshmen just entering the university. Such classes are taken for granted in many universities, but they were new to Wright State.

The General Education Monsters

The General Education program at Wright State was a source of pride to many members of the faculty. It involved replacing a potpourri of more than 100 courses by a required set of about 15, with a few narrowly defined alternative choices. The courses were chosen because the faculty thought they were most appropriate for the education of undergraduate students, and the choices were made without regard whether we had the faculty to teach them. The feeling I had about that was that eventually we would hire the necessary faculty but if we picked courses according to the faculty we had, we wouldn't get nearly as good a program. We had, for instance, a history faculty consisting mostly of American historians. So if we went by faculty, our general education requirement would be American history. But we thought it should cover a wider temporal and spatial range than that, and thus wound up with a full year's Western World course from 3000 B.C. to the present, supplemented by two non-Western courses, one regional, one comparative. So, for instance, a student might take a quarter on African civilization and a quarter on Third World politics and economics. The adoption of the new program represented a great accomplishment for Liberal Arts Dean Perry Moore and Associate Dean Lillie Howard. Lillie had gone on to become Associate University Vice President and had been replaced by Bill Rickert, who directed the General Education Program.

It was an ominous August memo from Rickert, our ever cheerful, ever fair, ever judicious associate dean, that begins the story of the monsters. The memo said that starting in the winter quarter, we were going to have many more large general education courses. Until that memo, we had assumed that the general education classes would be limited to 60 students and have a strong writing component. But now enrollment pressure dictated that we have much larger classes, too large to include writing. I wondered why. How could we lose money if we hired faculty to teach seven general education courses of 60 students each? That would be 420 students a year, 140 students a quarter, about a 35–1 student faculty ratio. Why did we need the large classes?

I should also mention that this was the year in which the Nutter Center was being completed. The Nutter Center, at a cost of more than $30 million, would provide Wright State with a basketball arena as well as a center for graduation ceremonies and various public entertainments. While the University Administration argued that the Center and General Education came from different and unexchangeable funds, it was easy to feel that the more glamorous and less academic enterprise was being well-funded and publicized while the major academic innovation, which affected every student entering the university, was being starved.

A few days after the Rickert memo, I had my first clue on the faculty response. Tsing Yuan, chair of the History Department, observed that the change would mean less demand for teachers. From his perspective, the reduction of writing in courses was outweighed by simplifying the scheduling problem. I might have responded that way as chairman.

The day after I talked to Yuan, Rickert told me that the economic pressure was coming from rising entry enrollments with no corresponding increase at upper levels. Since upper-level courses have higher state subsidies, we were getting more students without a corresponding rise in subsidies. Bill had no expectation that writing would be continued in the large classes. He felt that writing would have to be handled by a "Writing Across the Curriculum" program that was being developed in upper-level classes, so that no one could graduate from Wright State without having considerable writing experience. Such a program, however, was not yet in place.

Another concern I had was that we were an open admissions university, meaning we admitted a considerable number of marginal students who were at risk in their freshman year. Some wouldn't make it no matter what. Others would under favorable circumstances. Certainly classes of 60 in which the professors knew the students and there was some writing would seem more favorable than classes of hundreds in which professors hadn't a hope of knowing anything about the problems of individual students.

One possible advantage Bill did see in the large classes was that we could put our stars in charge of those classes, our most charismatic teachers. They might give a superior performance compared to the marginal teachers who would be added if we taught a much larger number of classes.

In the same conversation Bill told me that visiting professor positions would be phased out and replaced by tenure track openings. There was irony in this, because as a member of the American Association of University Professors Council, I had been opposed to having visiting assistant professors teach nine general education classes, compared to seven for the rest of us, It would create a two tier system. But each of those professors could teach nine classes of 60 students a year, 540 students in all. The tenure track replacements would teach only seven classes, probably not all of them general education. So here was a further loss to general education teaching, brought about because the college was responding to the urging of a group in which I had been strongly involved. The irony, I thought, was not lost on Bill.

David Orenstein, responding to my report of the conversation with Bill, agreed with me that if we had large classes, it would be better to have some of 400 and some of 60, so there could be writing and contact in some classes. This would be better than having all classes of, say, 125. I hadn't perceived that Bill disagreed with this position, but David thought he had. Later, as recounted in the preceding chapter, the question of how many 400's and how many 60's became a source of contention between David and me.

Who Would Bell The Cat?

Who would oppose monster classes? At a fall retreat, Department members agreed that there ought to be a response to the large class proposal. But what were we to do? We didn't have enough faculty to service our majors (students majoring in sociology or anthropology) plus general education and other departments requiring our courses for their majors. Should we limit the number of students majoring in our programs by raising our entrance requirement? We didn't want to do that, because an alumni study showed that some of our majors who were mediocre students have done well in the occupational world. So if we wanted to keep offering enough upper-level courses for our growing number of majors as well as meet the GE requirement of 2,500 students a year, what could we do but offer more large classes? We assumed that similar alternatives were being confronted by other departments that had general education courses.

This was confirmed a couple weeks later by Jeanne, who had talked to three chairs, Jim Jacob of Political Science, Bill Stoesz of Religion and Tsing Yuan. Jim, she said, was willing to have (and teach) large classes to preserve the Political Science program. Tsing and Bill were open to further discussion, but I had the impression Jeanne did not think a response would come from the chairs.

Toward the end of September I met with Lillie Howard, the associate academic vice president who had been associate dean when the new general education proposal was being worked out. She said the Liberal Arts College Administration didn't ask for resources for general education and that Dr. Hathaway, the academic vice president, had responded to what had been asked for. I inferred that there might be substantial differences between Lillie on one hand and her former boss, Perry Moore, and her successor, Bill Rickert, on the other, and that she felt the University Administration's position had been misrepresented. She mentioned that she and Perry weren't on speaking terms for awhile, which in any event suggested that our administrators were not indifferent. According to Lillie, Peter Bracher, chair of the English Department, wrote an item in the English Department newsletter indicating that the college was offering fewer GE classes for more students, hoping that the growing backlog of students who couldn't get into the courses would create pressure to hire more general education faculty. This went to Lillie, who was a tenured member of the English Department.

Certainly there was a feeling among faculty members of the Liberal Arts College that enrollment pressures would force the University to allocate more funds for the hiring of Liberal Arts faculty, but this followed the perception that the University allocations had been inadequate.

If we were to have large classes for the next few years, it seemed important that the Writing Across the Curriculum program be in place as soon as possible. This would designate upper-level courses as writing-intensive according to criteria to be worked out, and students would have to take a certain number of these to graduate.

This was a program that shouldn't cost any money. It would be just a matter of finding the courses that already were writing-intensive and so designating them in the university course schedule. The proposal had been under discussion for a couple of years. Yet from my conversations with Bill Rickert and Lillie, I had the impression that each administrative unit perceived that the ball was in the court of the other.

Lillie suggested that I assemble an ad hoc committee representing general education from different colleges to make a direct proposal to Dr. Hathaway. Given the mixed agendas other possible groups had, I thought that might be an approach to consider, though you hesitate to create another committee when there are so many already. One advantage to an ad hoc committee, though, from my perspective, was that I would chair it.

I saw Bill Rickert over the chess boards in the Liberal Arts Faculty Lounge. He, with as much reasonableness as Lillie, saw the problem as coming from the perceptions of the University Administration: failure both to consider General Education Program as a University rather than a Liberal Arts program, and to accept a universal definition of writing across the curriculum. But he, like Lillie, would welcome the contribution of an ad hoc committee recommending short and long run approaches to the problem of the large classes.

The Ad Hoc Committee

I wanted a committee representing different colleges, even though most of the courses come from our college. And I thought all the members should actually teach GE courses. Those who agreed to serve on the committee were John Blair of Economics, Herb Neve of Religion, Charlie Funderburk of Political Science and Brian Kruger of Psychology. Economics and Psychology were in different colleges, the College of Business and the College of Science. I knew John from a period when we were chairs of our respective departments. He was very much concerned about the monster classes. Herb had chaired the first committee to tackle the problem of revising general education, so his involvement went back a long way. Herb and John felt strongly against the large classes, were concerned about their impact on the recruitment of new faculty, wanted quick action. Charlie, on the other hand, saw advantages in the large classes and would teach one himself. Brian I didn't know at all, which had the advantage of making him a random factor. I expected that he might surprise me, and was not disappointed. The committee consisted entirely of white males, which I had tried to avoid. But Helen Klein of Psychology, whom I was going to ask, did not teach general education courses. The advantage of our committee's composition, however, was that despite the unorthodoxy of having been created without official authorization, though certainly with administrative encouragement, it could not be perceived as antiestablishment.

In recruiting Charlie, I talked to Jim Jacob, Political Science chair, who felt that majors were more important than general education. Better, he felt, to have a less effective general education program than to undercut the major, because the latter would undo the damage done by the former. But Jim also took the view that excellent teaching can go on in the big classes, and he himself was going to teach one of them.

The first meeting of the Ad Hoc committee was unforgettable. I was the only one who came. I had a photographer to take a picture of this historic meeting and he duly took my picture, with attendance augmented by my reflection on the glass top table. Herb Neve had sent me a note that he was ill. Eventually Charlie Funderburk turned up, late from another meeting. We agreed to work over my draft during the week and ask the others to do the same. So, without actually meeting, I would correlate their responses and send back a revised draft. *Then*, perhaps, we could have a meeting. John Blair called the next day: he had forgotten the meeting. In the next week he and Herb Neve gave me revisions to my first draft memo. I would try to get Charlie and Brian to respond also, and set another meeting. Certainly I would expect a need for negotiation between Charlie and the others, and as yet I didn't know where Brian stood. I tried calling him twice during his office hours, but couldn't reach him. Suppose I got everyone else lined up, and then he intervened with major objections?

In the next several days, John, Charlie and I produced a revised memo that said we thought large classes would reduce the quality of education, discourage enrollment by students from suburban schools trying to choose between us and a residential college, undercut our reputation for having general education classes taught by regular faculty rather than teaching assistants, eliminate the writing component from many general education classes, and unfairly penalize untenured faculty members who might suffer from poor

4. Large classes should be so designated in the University schedule.

5. Hathaway or Howard should address the University faculty on reasons for changes in general education and plans for the future.

6. Students should be informed in the same way through the *Guardian*.

7. Large classes should be taught by tenured faculty.

8. Budgets should be modified so that more money goes to general education, working toward teaching classes as originally planned. This should be done over a planned period, hopefully not more than five years.

At our January committee meeting, John and Charlie showed some willingness to modify the program, head a bit back toward cafeteria style (a wider range of classes acceptable for general education). John said he had wanted his daughter to go to Wright State, partly because of the GE program, but with the large classes, he was not so sure. Charlie and I agreed that if the class is over 60 you can't do much writing, so Political Science, like Sociology, was going with general education classes of either 60 or 400. But Charlie said Political Science wouldn't be able to keep doing that. Their smaller classes would have to go to 90 or 120 if the department wanted to continue to prepare their majors for law school, government, and other careers. John and I agreed that a large part of the faculty probably shared Charlie's view: the needs of present majors must have priority over the needs of possible future majors. In the end John and Charlie supported my memo. They particularly approved labeling the class size in the calendar.

I typed a memo to Hathaway, summing up our recommendations, and set about the tedious process of getting it signed. Herb Neve, who had not been able to attend the committee meeting, was not satisfied with the first point. He didn't want the departments to have control of GE, precisely because he thought they would favor their own programs. John Blair, in signing the memo, said he really didn't care if too many freshmen were assigned to large classes, because then there would be more complaints about the program. In walking the memo around, I finally met Brian Kruger, because the memo had gotten lost for a time in the Psychology office and I needed him to find and sign it.

Meanwhile, Bill Rickert reported at the University quarterly faculty meeting that the monster classes had better student evaluations than the mean of the small classes, with no difference in retention. Was this because stars had been chosen to teach the large classes? Or did students really prefer not being bothered by teachers and not having to write any sentences?

At the Liberal Arts College quarterly meeting the next day, Dean Perry Moore said the new General Education Program was not the cause of the problem. The cause was a 30 percent increase in the number of freshmen. If we tried to cover with new professors teaching classes of 60, we'd need an additional million (dollars, not professors). He acknowledged that big classes had problems: more absenteeism, no writing, maybe more cheating. But we had to go this way.

On the other hand, the large classes made possible some substantial faculty rewards. A faculty member who taught two large classes would receive a course reduction plus $3,000 in research money. No doubt that was a substantial compensation, and would cause some faculty at any rate to look on large classes with a new perspective.

Confirming what Bill had said, David Orenstein and Jim Jacob, in their classes of 400, had higher than average evaluations and an average completion rate comparable to the classes of 60. While one-on-one discussion with the instructor was lost, Jim and David had discussion groups run by student tutors. That might be a reasonable trade off considering that in a class of 60, I probably had a dozen students who talk in class, fewer who actually visited my office. On the other hand, Mary Frost-Pierson, who I would have thought would be one of our better adjuncts, was refusing to teach at all if she had to teach a class of 400 for adjunct wages. Would we lose other good adjuncts for this reason?

I also talked with Rickert about our proposals to Hathaway. He agreed freshmen needed to be protected from having too many big classes, but that we would have to find a different way to protect them. He agreed Writing Across the Curriculum should start as soon as possible, but he was waiting for a lead from the University. He agreed that the University should address faculty and students about GE, but said we couldn't have only tenured faculty teach large classes. But the College plan to compensate faculty with course reductions and student help should protect them from any disadvantage in the pursuit of tenure. He did not think we could make long-term plans for restoring small classes. He didn't think that large classes, having come, would ever go. The faculty wouldn't let them go because they opened up other possibilities for compensation and upper-level classes. The Administration, of course, wouldn't let them go either.

As it happened I also had a preliminary exchange with President Mulhollan on general education because I was a randomly chosen faculty member invited to have breakfast with him and Hathaway (Ch. 4). Mulhollan reiterated that Wright State had been losing graduate enrollment while picking up more undergraduates, which meant less state funding for the same number of students. So any solution to the General Education situation would have to come out of internal adjustment, not additional funds.

The Meeting with the University Administrators

On the designated afternoon in March, the Ad Hoc Committee met with Hathaway and Howard. John, Charlie, Herb and I were there, with only Brian missing.

Hathaway pointed out, as we knew, that the Administration could not actually give instructions to departments on size of classes. This would be an invasion of department autonomy, which John and Charlie would certainly oppose, Herb and I might countenance. The only place where departmental autonomy did not exist was in areas like Regional Studies that had not existed before the new General Education Program and which therefore were not assigned to a particular department. He was not enthusiastic about trying to program computers to prevent freshmen from entering too many large classes. He foresaw conflicts with students who would feel they were being unnecessarily hassled by being closed out of a time they wanted. But he said he would talk to Lou Falkner, the registrar, and Judy Roller, the director of University Advising, on what might be done to get upperclassmen into big classes and save space in the small ones for freshmen.

The discussion of writing across the curriculum seemed to support the perception of confusion between the University and Liberal Arts College. Definitions differed about what writing across the curriculum should be. There was $100,000 in challenge money to be appropriated by the University, but I wasn't clear about when or what for.

We had a confusing discussion on the proposal to list classroom size in the schedule, with Ad Hoc Committee members pointing out some problems and administrators sometimes pointing out advantages. Bill Rickert had argued that since seniors and juniors registered first, they might grab the small classes, forcing more freshmen into big ones. But there was also some agreement that setting big classes at prime times would attract some of the upperclassmen.

There also was agreement that Dr. Hathaway would communicate with faculty and students through university publications. Hathaway agreed with Rickert that big classes couldn't be taught entirely by tenured faculty, and also that exploitation of junior faculty could be avoided. He did not think the problem could be solved in five years. The demand would fluctuate; all segments of the University would be participating. But I didn't feel he thought we would ever have a GE program consisting entirely of classes of 60 students.

Hathaway also expressed concern because we had about 12,000 full time equivalent students (i.e. if you divide the total number of classroom hours taken by 15, as if all students were full time), and of these 5,000 were "marooned" in University Advising because they couldn't get admitted to a major. They didn't have grade point averages high enough, or the major they wanted had requirements they couldn't meet. So you could have a grade point average of 2.2 (C+) but not be able to get into a major that required a 2.5 (B-). The department faculty set these requirements for majors in order to maintain manageable numbers in upper-level classes. They could admit more by lowering the required grade point average and increasing the size of upper-level classes, which implied less writing at that level or, of course, by teaching more monster classes and thereby freeing faculty to teach more upper-level classes. All in all, this pool of marooned students did not bode well for combatting monster classes.

Lillie and Hathaway also discussed provisions to make the large classes more effective. Equipment was being brought in; rooms were being made available. But, I was thinking, once we have these, we would have an incentive to teach more large classes. We wouldn't want to allow those big rooms with state of the art equipment to sit idle.

Another worrying comment. The Administration insisted that all new faculty members be qualified to teach general education. They needed to be good at teaching introductory courses and to be assigned to teach them. But once they were hired, they had other skills in the major field that their departments wanted them to teach, and perhaps other agendas of their own. So after a couple of years, the number of general education classes they taught would begin to decline. Even when our sociology candidates were being interviewed, some of us were telling them, you'd start with three introductory courses, but we have topics courses. Perhaps in a couple of years you would be able to introduce your favorite specialty through those, and eventually make it a regular course. So, thinking ahead about possibilities for the Department, we were already undercutting general education.

Provisional Outcomes

I wrote a summary memo to the committee, to see if we could come up with a common perception that we could send back to Hathaway as our collective understanding. I thought we had agreement in principle that something should be done to limit the number of large classes taken by freshmen, and on communication with faculty and students. Everyone also agreed, I thought, that we should move ahead with Writing Across the Curriculum, so the problem was to find out what was holding it up, or possibly to get the University and College Administrations to talk about it. We didn't get anywhere on our departmental autonomy proposal, partly because we didn't agree among ourselves and, therefore, could not make a clear proposal. It didn't look as though there was likely to be a limiting of large classes to tenured faculty members. Nor did it look like the monsters were a short-term problem to be exterminated as soon as budgets allowed. For many they were an opportunity, unopposed by students, not contributing to attrition, saving money, providing faculty research opportunities. Hardly monsters, just great big warm fuzzy teddy bears.

Before I could get agreement on my draft Hathaway sent me a memo indicating that it was possible to print the class size in the schedule, and that the University would move toward making this information available by winter of the following year. When the time came, he added, it would also be possible to denote intensive writing classes. That meant that once we had agreed on the definition and number of intensive writing classes, there could be a university requirement that needed to be filled for graduation. If a student survived the monster classes, we would be sure that she take a certain number of upper-level classes that included a healthy dose of writing.

As for limiting large classes for freshmen, Hathaway pointed out that there was an Enrollment Management Task Force working on that problem, and concluded, sensibly enough, that the committee be permitted to complete its work and submit recommendations.

Encouraged by this, I wrote a revised memo to the Ad Hoc Committee, updating them on Hathaway's reply, with copies to Hathaway, Howard and Rickert. This did not require committee approval, with the inherent disagreements perhaps re-emerging. It did leave a record that could be referred back to in six months or a year, so that we could check on the implementation. I felt that if we had not slain the monsters, we had at least done something to protect the freshmen. And we had an important ally in the Enrollment Management Task Force, which had been appointed by the University Administration because enrollment had leveled and our only hope for increasing state subsidies was to improve our retention rate.

It really seemed as if the ramshackle, unofficial Ad Hoc Committee had made considerable progress. At the end of March I wrote: "I'd have to say the GE Committee had some success. It's one committee that was better existing than not existing."

A False Dawn

My mood at this time is indicated by my note to an advertising firm, Media Networks, that had been advertising its success in promoting neighboring Wilmington College by creating an image of a "Lemming" student who followed everyone else, had to park a long way from the classroom, and attended huge classes with other lemmings. The alternative was to go to Wilmington College, attend small classes and become a leader.

"We at Wright State," I told them, "Home of the Lemmings, are disconcerted to learn that you are advertising that we are fictitious and that you invented us." Not only were we real, but we took

Meanwhile, we had an excellent general education program, but students were experiencing multiple large classes. In our Social Life course, the choice between three and four large classes soon became history: the monsters expanded to six, consuming all small classes except one for honors and one for evening students.

Students could take small general education courses at Sinclair Community College for less money, and a survey of city high school graduates going to Wright State (Ch. 4) indicated that two-thirds of the students in the sample were indeed doing this. But that only added to the budget woes of Wright State, which was a factor in diminishing faculty raises, which was a factor in an AAUP drive for faculty collective bargaining (Ch. 4). Consequences have consequences.

Overall, you had to hope that students taking general courses in history, political science, economics and psychology would have a better understanding, would be better prepared for life, than they would have been if they had been permitted to take any elective they chose. But we don't know that. We have no control group to compare to our students taking the current program. We could probably apply for funds to make such a study, but no one wants to. We rely on our hunches and prejudices and, as Katie Dvorshak said, tend to be more critical than outcomes would really warrant, were we disposed to study the outcomes.

Oh, and remember the day, trying to get a memo signed, that I actually met Brian (Swing Vote) Kruger? That was the only time we ever met.

4

University Encounters

*How Jim Jacob Defeated Semesters. What About City
Schools? The Peace Studies Disaster. Defending the Faculty.
The Ten O'Clock Bus. Farewell, Wright State! The Games
Professors Play. Nor Heed the Rumble. Important Work.*

Before going on to the actual teaching of classes, I'd like to finish
with a few of the more interesting encounters that occurred during
the study year, because they show something about university dy-
namics.

The Semester Watch

In Ohio, every now and then, there will flash on your television
screen a note that Montgomery, Greene and Preble counties are having a tornado watch. For a couple of months it seemed like Wright
State was having a semester watch, with people looking up and
down the halls to see if the semester system was coming.

I first heard about it early in the fall quarter, when Jeanne, coming out of a chair's meeting, thought President Mulhollan might
announce a switch from our present quarter system to the semester
system at the Convocation, which began the academic year. This
was very distressing to me, given my concerns about general education, because such a change would almost certainly force a complete revision of the General Education program.

The semester system is probably the more common in American education. Students have two terms of 15 weeks a year whereas in the quarter system, they have three 10-week terms. (Both systems also usually have summer sessions.) When I first came to Wright State, after 17 years of teaching under the semester system, I thought the quarter system inferior. Obviously you couldn't get the depth into your upper level courses in ten weeks that you could in 15. But over the years I changed my mind. It seemed to me that ten weeks was a better length for undergraduates, with less slack in the middle than there had been in 15-week courses. And for a commuter university, it seemed a better system because if a student ran short of money, she might have to drop out for only one quarter of a year rather than for what amounted to half a year. Also, the quarter system allowed for a much greater variety of courses. When I first came, I couldn't believe that all the department courses listed in the catalogue were really taught. But they were.

Still, there is no doubt that there is academic justification for a semester system. And a university that is trying to upgrade its image may well consider changing to the semester system: it implies greater depth. If some courses had to be given up, they would be the less important ones. The basics would be maintained. Also there would be one less registration, which would be less inconvenient for the students and for the bursar's office, which would also save money.

The president, as it turned out, did not make the announcement at Convocation, but the subject was in the air. It was on the Department agenda for October. It happened that at the same meeting I had told members about this book, so they knew I would be taking notes for it. You might have expected us to be a little more altruistic than usual, that besides considering the effect on summer school and winter vacation, we would also discuss effects on students. None of us did. It looked during that meeting as though the faculty would accept this momentous change without too much protest, perhaps with favor.

The next day the subject was raised at the fall Liberal Arts College faculty meeting, and this time the discussion was lively. Jim Walker of Political Science presented a motion opposing the semester system. Charles Larkowski of Music thought we ought to go slowly, explore costs and implications. Jim Jacob, Chair of the Political Science Department and a former faculty vice president, thought the faculty controlled the calendar and the president would have no right to make a determination. Dean Perry Moore thought that whether he had the right or not, he would pay a lot of attention to what the faculty thought about it. Perry favored the semester system academically, but saw heavy costs in terms of money, classrooms and faculty stress.

The majority seemed to agree with Charlie Funderburk that the needs of the undergraduates called for a maximum number of courses taught at the widest possible variety of hours. But Larkowski, History Chair Tsing Yuan and Art Chair Jerry McDowell mentioned advantages of the semester system for graduate students and the performing arts. Finally the College faculty voted for the Walker motion as well as for a motion by Jacob affirming the right of the faculty to determine the calendar.

A couple days later Jacob followed his successful motion with a public memo of his own to President Mulhollan. Jim's memo was certainly saltier and more crowd pleasing than the group memo on general education we were preparing for Vice President Hathaway (Chapter 3). Would it also be more effective? I noted that Jim and I were in agreement that kicking up a fuss is a good idea. Jim's memo, I thought, might have the effect of getting Mulhollan to indicate that he had no intention of switching systems by decree. Our private memo, on the other hand, might lead to some quiet reform, some dialogue between College and University, some long term planning.

But, I note, I was jealous of Jim for grabbing the spotlight while I worked behind the scenes. And, I admitted, might I also have been a tad regretful because Jim, perhaps, reminded me of myself 20 years ago?

Mulhollan sent a memo of his own, dated three days after Jim's memo appeared. He said the only reason he was looking at the semester system now was that a triumvirate of past, present and future faculty vice presidents said he had to. I presumed he meant that Al Smith, Jim Sayer and Rudi Fichtenbaum were saying that uncertainty about a future semester system would interfere with university planning. A few days later Mulhollan followed with another memo saying that he was not presently considering the semester system. The question had come up a few years earlier, and there had been a great deal of opposition then. So he may have decided that, given other plans he was carrying out, a fight over the semester system was not worth the trouble at present. But on the evidence you would have to say that Jim Jacob's memo may have played an important if not a decisive part in the president's decision.

It is also worth noting, perhaps, that the year's most spectacular and decisive result of faculty action was that the status quo was maintained.

What About City Schools?

More than a decade before the year studied, members of the Department, along with the social workers, had visited the high schools that contributed the most students to our college. This was part of a larger project that Social Work Chair Phil Engle had called "Total Advising," because we were looking at our students from the time they were in high school and wanted to stay in touch with them when they became alumni. This was possible to a greater extent in a commuter university than it would be in a residential college.

The high school visits suggested to us that students from suburban schools were much better prepared for college than were students from city schools. This was no surprise, of course; but if you read the reports of the visiting faculty, you couldn't help but be struck by the degree of discrepancy. The suburban teachers were greatly concerned how many of their students went to college and where they went. But for the city school teachers, college was far down their list of concerns.

In subsequent years we did a great deal about Total Advising, including a major restructuring of our advising system, development of a newsletter for majors and alumni, and two alumni surveys that gave us a great deal of information how our students were doing after graduation. But we had not gotten around to dealing with the city schools, probably because it was more difficult and promised the least return. After all, we were not trained to develop support systems for high school students.

But for the coming year I had asked Jeanne to put the subject of city schools on the agenda for our Department Fall Retreat. Talking to my wife, Nelle, at Saturday breakfast, I was telling her I thought we would want to engage in a kind of triage. There were students from those schools who would get to college because of something in themselves or because of strong family support. There were others who wouldn't, no matter where they went to high school. And there were students—our prospective target group—who would have gone to college if they had lived in the suburbs, but would not because they lived in the city, lacking support from either families or school. The families, not being college educated themselves, had other problems that seemed more pressing than whether their children should go to Sinclair Community College or Wright State. So what we needed was to engage a group of education and family sociologists in making the proposal. We would want to do something that would involve the families as well as the students, and involve the families sufficiently that they would stay involved.

It seemed to me that to address the problem we would need a broader committee than the Department could provide, though a broader committee would be more cumbersome. Obviously the condition was not one of high schools alone, but a systemic disorder that needed to be addressed at several levels. In fact two Wright State social workers, Jewell Garrison and Vernon Moore, were entering new jobs that would involve helping children at elementary and middle school levels. But supposing there were a broad category of city students who could make a success of college if given appropriate support? It seemed to me we needed to find out if there were such a category, and if so, what kind of intervention would be meaningful and necessary to make such help possible. A daunting project.

At the September retreat I didn't push anyone to join the project, just presented the problem. Someone, possibly it was Tom Koebernick, thought that an awful lot more was being done about this than had been the case a decade ago, and that we should first find out what was happening both within and outside the University. It did seem that a wider committee, perhaps a multi-university committee, should be formed.

Early in the fall quarter I wrote to Larry Dalzine, Chair of the Sociology Department at Central State, and Walt Shirley, Chair of the Sinclair Community College Sociology Department. Central State is only ten or 15 miles from Wright State. It began as a state adjunct to Wilberforce, a black college and though admission had long been open, it was still a university to which many black students preferred to go. Sinclair was Dayton's community college, better placed in downtown Dayton compared to Wright State's peripheral cow pasture location, more interesting in architecture and spiffier than Wright State. One would guess that many city school students would begin at Sinclair, taking advantage of its lower tuition, and earn a job oriented degree in two years. The more academic of these would then transfer to Central or Wright State and pursue a four-year degree.

By the middle of November I had replies from Larry and Walt. A luncheon meeting was set at Wright State for December, with Larry to represent Central State, Ellen Rosengarten and Donna Fletcher Sinclair and Jeanne and I, Wright State. Larry Dalzine's coming himself suggested that he was no more successful than I in raising volunteers for this first phase of the project. At the meeting Larry favored expanding the project to all areas, not just social sciences. Donna Fletcher wondered if our target population was just core city or if it included graduates of city schools in the satellite cities of Xenia and Springfield. Larry, Ellen Rosengarten and I favored gathering more information from the Admissions Offices and other sources. Larry thought whatever research we did would be valuable to both the universities and the schools. Jeanne wanted action: visits to the schools, bringing students to the colleges, perhaps a plan that extended from middle school to beyond college graduation. Jeanne and Donna both favored working with a pilot school in the city, whichever one was weakest in percentage going on to college.

Ellen envisioned a middle level of students, particularly girls, who were quiet, never said anything, did what they were told, and never saw themselves as going on to college. This was similar to what I had been comparing to triage. How wide was this middle band? Ellen thought it quite wide.

How were we to translate this range of perceptions into action? It would be tempting to go with Jeanne and Donna's pilot idea: at least something would be done. Toward the end of January Ellen Rosengarten called to say she had found someone at Sinclair who was doing something: working full time with city school children from grades 8 through 12. We decided it would be worth meeting in February to talk with her. So we held another lunch time meeting, this time at Sinclair's beautiful facilities. We learned from the outreach person, Veronica Watkins, that she was bringing 300 students a year from the five city high schools to visit Sinclair, providing minority students who enrolled with student mentors, then working with them to help them get through. We also learned in passing that the Sinclair faculty saw Wright and Central State as institutions with sour faces. They said it was harder for students to move from Sinclair to one of the universities than it was for them to go from high school to Sinclair. Apparently the Sinclair staff who directly meet students, admissions people and bursar's clerks, were given special training in interacting with people.

This changed our perspective on the problem. Jeanne thought we might put off visits to high schools and begin by concentrating on the junior level transfers from Sinclair, providing mentors for them and seeing that as many as possible graduate from Wright State.

But one evening in the spring, I was driving Keith Hudson (see below) home after class, and realized that he was a city school graduate who had entered Wright State directly. It didn't make sense to be providing peer advising for juniors and not for freshmen. I also realized that though we had a better idea about what we wanted to do, we weren't going to be ready to do it by fall.

In June, after the year studied had ended, I contacted Ken Davenport, Wright State's Director of Admissions, and (via Wayne Peterson in Student Services) he sent me a list of prospective students from city schools who were planning to enter in the fall. It contained over 100 names, far more than we had expected or remembered from the Department faculty visit to high schools during the previous decade. It now became clear that we had more than we could handle just trying to deal with the problem of retaining city students who chose Wright State as freshmen. That came before providing peer advisors for transferring Sinclair juniors, not to mention visits to high schools to encourage still more students to try for college.

With the wisdom of hindsight, why did it take a year to learn what our problem was? We could have had the enrollment information any time we chose to ask Davenport. But we had been blinded by a sociologically generated image that dreary schools and lack of family involvement had discouraged students from even applying.

If triage were envisioned, it could now be seen as involving those who would graduate without special help, those who would drop out without help, and those who would never enter. In helping those who needed it, we would be still dealing with a middle band, but it was a different middle than we had been thinking about the previous fall.

Was the City Schools Committee successful in its first year? The crucial information for Wright State had actually come in a flash from Wayne Peterson's computer. But it took us the year to know what we wanted to ask. Meanwhile we had also gained valuable information about how Sinclair perceived us, and the Sinclair sociologists learned about the work that Veronica Watkins was doing in their own institution. And who knew what future outcomes would owe their origins to the meetings of members from the three sociology departments?

The Peace Studies Disaster

Late in July, Reed Smith looked into my office and asked if I wanted to see the final draft of the Peace Studies brochure. This was the product of a long period of committee work and production delays, so it was something of a triumph that it was finally going to the printer.

Reed was the founder and steering committee chair of the Peace Studies Association, a group that organized an annual community peace conference and invited a yearly distinguished speaker on the subject of peace. I had been the chair of an education committee that had produced material for a brochure that told students how to add a peace studies concentration to their major. We did it in question and answer style and thought it kind of cute. What we really liked was that it could be done without any cost or involvement with bureaucracy. Students chose from a cafeteria menu of courses according to their own preferences, and wrote the concentration into their resume.

A concentration differed from a minor. A department might grant a minor. A sociology major, for instance, who took a a certain number of acceptable anthropology courses, could receive a certificate confirming that the requirements for the minor had been met. A concentration, on the other hand, was created by the student and carried no certificate. The student would be simply pointing out that besides majoring in sociology, she had concentrated in anthropology, that is, taken a number of anthropology courses. On a resume, there was probably little to choose between a minor and a concentration. Our brochure told students they could create a concentration in peace studies (there was no such department) and gave them a list of courses that appeared to be relevant.

But it had been delayed when Frank Dobson couldn't get to a PSA meeting at which he was supposed to present it, and then again when Peg Kane's Printing Office challenged both the design and style of the brochure. This challenge came from a general directive from President Mulhollan that more attention should be paid to the quality of brochures produced under the University's name. Her challenge meant that I had to battle for the color of the brochure and the Q and A style, even though the brochure was being paid for by funds the Peace Studies Association had raised on its own. I was annoyed by Peg's objections, particularly at her view that Q and A was tacky. But it was a Peace Studies group, right? So we should set the example by demonstrating patience and willingness to compromise. I put up with further delay, therefore, and gave Peg's office a chance to propose some modifications. After all, they were the experts in public relations and we did want to produce an attractive and effective document.

At this point I was taking a quarter sabbatical, so I asked another member of our committee, Alice Swinger, if she would be willing to complete the negotiations with University Printing. She said she would, but warned me that she was not as committed to the Q and A as I was. I thought that just as well, because it would be a more communal process. Besides, Alice would be stronger on the art side than I was.

Reed chuckled that the University had managed to get in a paragraph on its new Nutter Center, and asked if I wanted to read the revision. I declined, figuring that if I made further objections, the draft would be held up again and wouldn't be ready in the fall. Reed mentioned, in passing, that the design was so beautiful, and the list of peace courses so impressive, that he had upped our order from 1,000 to 4,000 copies, because the brochure could be used to publicize the Peace Studies Association as well as the concentration.

A month later the brochure was out, 4,000 copies in a beautiful blue, with a dove on the cover. Since Reed had retired and no longer had an office of his own, several boxes wound up in my office. They stayed there a few days and then I had a look at one, intending to write Alice a graceful thank you note. The Q and A was gone. I was disappointed about that, but Alice had given me fair warning. As I read it, however, I realized to my horror that in the editing, the original idea had been lost. The free advertising for the Nutter Center was achieved at the cost of explaning how to write a concentration! There was no way a student could do that from the information given. It did say that "we" would help you, but "we" were not identified. The brochure was useless. And there were 4,000 copies, most of them in my office.

I was really depressed. All that work and all that time, and nothing to show. The conflict was resolved, to be sure, but what an outcome! And to make it worse, the revised prose was bland, the Nutter Center a gratuitous insult. Reed was soothing. He really liked the look of the document and the list of courses relevant to peace studies. If the document was weak as a heuristic device, that was probably secondary for him. I realized, too late, that probably neither Reed nor Alice, and certainly not Peg, had internalized the idea of a concentration. Worse, Reed had given me the opportunity to proof-read the document and I had declined.

But coming home that night I had a relapse of anger, like you get from long-acting hay fever pills that every so often send another blast into your system. I was angry at Alice for allowing the Q and A to be dropped, at Peg for contributing to the making of a useless and expensive brochure, and at Reed for wanting to get it out, regardless of its inanity, because we had spent the money.

When I had cooled enough to be rational, I decided to call a meeting of Peace Studies members who happened to be around in the summer, to decide what to do. Perhaps we were not as damaged as I thought. Perhaps my ego was getting in the way because of the style change and the damned Nutter Center.

Then came the regrets. If Frank Dobson had made that meeting. If Mulhollan hadn't articulated his policy. If I hadn't been going on sabbatical. If Peg hadn't interpreted the policy as she did. If I had taken more time to discuss the brochure with Alice. If I had accepted Reed's invitation to proofread!

And writing more than a year after these events, it occurred to me that the total cost of this disaster was only $1,200. About 20 percent of the PSA budget, but a drop in the bucket for the university. I could have gone to Mulhollan and said, "Look, this needs to be done again and you ought to pay for it." But Reed would never have let me do that. The University's goodwill was worth more than $1,200.

Anyway, the meeting was held. Reed and Tim Wood of environmental studies represented the Peace Studies Steering Committee. Also attending was Jerome Clemens, who advised students who wished to create their own major and who would, according to the original brochure, advise students who wished to add a peace studies concentration. I was representing the Education Committee, which had proposed and designed the original brochure. By the time we met, I thought I had a partial solution to the problem of the uselessness of the brochure. We agreed, after discussion, to have my name pasted on a blank area of the brochure as the contact person. If contacted, I would give the student a copy of the original question and answer sheet we intended to circulate in the first place. There were 4,000 copies of the stupid flier, of course, but work study students could paste on the contact note 200 at a time as needed.

The following month, Paul Ogg came in, the first student to inquire about the Peace Studies brochure. It turned out he was really looking for a major, so I sent him on to see Jerome and Donna Schlagcheck, who directed a possibly relevant program within the Political Science Department. After that, nothing. There were no further pastings after the first 200. The boxes of fliers remained in my office. No students came for the retyped Q and A. The Peace Education Committee never met again. Writing this section led me to send a memo to Barbara Eakins-Reed, the new chair of the steering committee, asking that the matter of the fliers be put on the agenda for fall. Perhaps we could have a farewell ceremony at the Fairborn Landfill. Peace Studies types like ceremonies.

Defending the Faculty

One self-imposed duty was membership in the American Association of University Professors. Members, fewer than five per cent of our faculty, had the responsibility of helping preserve the rights of faculty members, their academic freedom, their participation in university government, and their compensations and benefits. For the privilege of having this responsibility, dues in most cases were something like $100 a year, certainly one factor in the small membership.

The activities of the AAUP were mostly informal: quiet, behind the scenes efforts to help faculty members in trouble or to improve conditions of interaction within departments or colleges. The behind the scenes aspect, I suppose, was another reason for our small membership.

At a joint lunch with University of Dayton members, we learned that they didn't have a university faculty meeting in which they could publicly address the president. We, on the other hand, didn't have a faculty committee that met on a university level with the president, though we had an Academic Council that included faculty, administrators, staff and students. We also had our three elected faculty vice presidents, past, present and future, which U.D. didn't have. I had the feeling, which I'd had at other AAUP meetings with other faculty members, that the Wright State faculty was more involved in university governance than those at most other colleges and universities in the state, whether public or private. And this could be another reason for lack of faculty participation in AAUP: it seemed to add still more governance work where there already was perceived to be too much.

In January we had a faculty case, an assistant professor in the college of business who was on a "rolling" tenure track, something I had never heard of. I passed the information on to Don Swanson, who chaired Committee A on Academic Freedom and Tenure. I never knew after that whether we were of any help, because Committee A worked behind the scenes. What bothered me was that there was no committee. Don was chair and sole member, handling the business himself. My opinion was that there should always be a committee of several members, including a carry over member from the previous year, someone with experience, who should chair the new committee. I expressed that opinion at our January Council meeting, our first of the year, but felt that I did not impress. On the other hand, Mark Sirkin, chairing an also nonexistent committee on governance, did follow up on the work of Jim Runkle's committee of two years before, and reported an improvement in the governance documents of the Colleges of Education and Nursing. The next thing, in a future year, would be to see whether the improved documents were being used.

In March we had the case of a female faculty member from the College of Education who had been asked to resign in mid-year and did. She now had a better job at another university. Chapter President Alan Barclay asked what I thought, and I said Committee A should discuss it with the College Dean Gies and express concern. The deposed faculty member didn't want her job back, but we should make the Dean aware of our existence. Alan then wrote a letter to the teacher, advising her to contact Don Swanson. I doubt she did and we therefore had little impact. In the end Alan did send a letter to Dean Gies expressing concern.

I thought the Dean should have been visited by members of Committee A, representing several colleges, who should express concern about the dismissal of a tenure-track faculty member in midyear without due process. Otherwise, why should the College not turn the practice into policy and continue to fire faculty without due process? Letting such a matter slip because it had worked out all right for the dismissed faculty member could mean allowing a freedom-limiting precedent to be established.

A major concern at a joint spring meeting with the University of Dayton AAUP was a court decision that universities be required to turn over papers involved in tenure decisions in cases in which racial or gender discrimination is claimed. But for protection of committee members and free discussion, such records were usually not kept in my experience, though apparently they were at UD. The absence of written records protected the members of the tenure committee, but the candidate was given reasons for rejection only informally by his dean or department chair. So, was it more important to protect the committee or the person?

The most interesting and revealing episode of the year in AAUP was surely the case of Don Moloney. A Jesuit with a remarkable range of talents, Don had been teaching as an adjunct in different departments in two or three colleges. Because he was teaching in multiple colleges, no one realized for awhile how many courses a year he had been teaching. But for the current year, counting summers, it was 12 or 13, as compared to a normal faculty load of 7 to 9. And for this Don was being paid adjunct wages which, for all those courses, would have come to less than the lowest paid instructor in the university. Moreover, Don's evaluations were sparkling, whether he was teaching history, religion, language or science. What a bargain for the University!

But wasn't he being exploited? Well, compared to others, he was. But he was no longer a practicing priest; he had a dual career marriage; and though he had the credentials, he did not have the publications to win a full time job. So he preferred to do what he was doing, even if underpaid. He seemed to like the challenge of a variety of courses; and from the viewpoint of several department chairs, he was the preferred utility infielder.

The University was worried, however, and with justification, that if Don continued to do what he was doing, he could acquire de facto tenure. After teaching a full load for seven years, he might claim that tenure had been implicitly granted. Not that anyone thought that he would, but the University had had a suit on this subject several years before, and was sensitive about letting the situation arise. The solution would be not to employ Don for two years, then allow him to work again.

There was no doubt where the National AAUP stood on this issue. It was opposed to full time adjuncts, on the ground that a university could load up on those instead of hiring more expensive full time faculty members. Even if Don or others in his situation didn't see themselves as exploited, AAUP had plenty of cases in which this practice did lead to exploitation.

I talked to the national office in Washington and they said that if an adjunct taught no more than a two-thirds load, the question of de facto tenure would not arise. I passed this information on to Dean Moore and he worked out a four course schedule for Don, all in Liberal Arts. Don, then, would be free to negotiate additional courses at other colleges and universities in the area.

This turned out to be useful information to Ed Rutter, AAUP Vice President and chair of the Math Department. He had been hiring adjuncts for years for introductory classes, then not rehiring them after six years because of the danger of de facto tenure.

It was the one accomplishment in a not very impressive year for AAUP, and we hoped that effective and happy adjuncts could now return each year to teach without giving the university further fear of de facto tenure.

The Ten O'Clock Bus

I mentioned driving Keith Hudson to the city after evening classes. Keith was a social and industrial communication major who needed either my Occupations or Industrial Sociology course to fill his major requirement. But both courses were offered at night and ended at 9:50, whereas the last bus from campus to the city left at 9:30. So Keith elected not to take the Occupations class in the fall (Ch. 5). I told Jeanne about it and she wrote a memo to Vice President Hathaway asking if the Regional Transit Authority couldn't be induced to supply a ten o'clock bus. The great majority of students drove or carpooled to school, but a minority could not. Some of these worked during the day and could come to class only at night. It would seem, therefore, that if we were going to run our classes until 9:50 we should be obligated to supply a ten o'clock bus or, failing that, at least a University bus that would take students a few miles to the nearest city bus stop.

Jeanne's memo was sent in the fall, and I believe Dr. Hathaway indicated there was some discussion going on with the Transit Authority. Months went by. In February I reminded Jeanne about the bus and she again contacted Hathaway, who told her he thought it improbable that RTA would run the bus. But he also sent a copy of a note he had sent to Ed Spanier, the Finance VP, asking if the university could run a bus at that time, either to the nearest city bus stop or downtown. Again, silence.

Spring went by without a bus, hence my driving Keith home. There was no word about Spanier's reply to Hathaway. But in June I heard from a bus driver that RTA would start running a 10 p.m. bus in August and weekend buses as well. A problem that we hadn't addressed in our letters was that some students who were residents on Wright State's campus could not get to the city on weekends. Many of the apartment renters drove, but a sizable proportion of the residents of our one dormitory were disabled, They had been marooned on the campus for the weekend.

I would like to present this as the one great faculty achievement of the year, not just a preservation of the status quo but the addition of something new and valuable that came about because two members of the Sociology and Anthropology Department persisted in badgering the Academic Vice President. But I'm afraid the evidence suggests that our efforts had little to do with the outcome. RTA had decided for reasons of its own to extend its service in many outer areas, adding both later and weekend buses. The fact that they added weekend buses without being asked and that they began in August, when summer quarter was almost over and buses were least needed, suggests a correlation rather than a cause.

As David Orenstein says, when people eat more ice cream, sailboats appear on the lake.

Farewell Wright State!

In June I attended two graduation ceremonies, the big semi-annual blast at the new Nutter Center and a small one for graduates of the Professional Psychology Program, because my mentee, Francis Padinjarekara, was graduating,

The Professional Psychology Ceremony was charming, the class being small enough that Dean Ron Fox could honestly conclude: "I shall never forget you!" Ron began by saying that he wanted to say something they would remember more than two minutes, but his conclusion was all I remembered. There was a great deal of hugging among the psychologists, including deans. Did they have bumper stickers that ask: "Have You Hugged Your Dean Today?"

At the main ceremony, with more than 1,000 graduates, they actually handed out the diplomas with much throwing of confetti and releasing of balloons. When the nurses rose, the doctors rose and applauded them and everyone applauded that. Very moving.

Also moving in a different way were the two lines of students whose every name was read alternately by the voices of Wright State, Jim Sayer and Bill Rickert. I timed them at 35 a minute, less than two seconds of glory per student. Still, many of them were the first in their families to graduate from college, and it was a big occasion. They deserved those two seconds, the chance to wave the diploma, the chance for their Dads to take their pictures. And we, the faculty, in our mortarboards and colorful hoods, needed to be there to help provide an impressive and colorful background.

The Games Professors Play

By games I mean games, not quirky verbal interactions. One at Wright State was chess, played only by men in the faculty lounge. We played move a day chess, four or five boards going at a time. You looked at the boards when you had to go to the bathroom, which was nearby. It was perfectly acceptable to take advice from others, and the same kibitzer could advise both sides. It was also permissible to change your move if you returned to the board, your opponent hadn't moved, and you saw something better.

It was play, of course, but men play pretty seriously. Helping me clear my files, my daughter Ellen discovered I had actually saved the moves of the only game I had ever won from Ron Hough. Was chess a metaphor for life? For what it's worth, in chess styles, Orenstein was opportunistic, Hough devious, Peter Taylor blunt, and our House Conservative, Martin Arbagi, always chose black. Rickert, the epitome of style, had no discernible style in his chess game.

One day Rickert dropped by to tell me he had beaten Orenstein, David's first loss in two years. We also talked about large GE classes, so arguably chess was a social device that facilitated other business. Or the other way round?

We also played squash. I was playing Dan DeStephen on Tuesdays and Charles Hartmann on Fridays. Dan and I played pretty even but I beat Charles only twice all year, once on the day, unknown to both of us, that our pictures were being taken for this book.

In the winter Rickert began playing again after a year's absence. Normally such a quiet, mellow person, Bill was the only player I knew who dove on the squash floor. Well, Dan dove occasionally but Bill not only dove, he got up and hit your return. Dan waited until you pulled him up.

There seemed to be little in my record about it, but we spent too much time discussing sports. One day, coming in to discuss the Giants, David Orenstein speculated that maybe ballplayers discuss which academics have the best style. Parsons is ponderous, Mead is deft.

One winter night we held our annual Hot Stove Meeting, with beer, pretzels and other baseball food at Paul Burgess' house in Fairborn. We watched a baseball film, traded stories, did a trivia quiz, predicted outcomes for the coming season. The group consisted of professors mixed with others from the community who shared the addiction.

Also, and less forgivably, I did some writing for the Baseball Newsletter, an occasional in-house publication. During the year I wrote a review of Tony Kubek and Terry Pluto's *Sixty-One*, the year Maris broke Ruth's record, an unidentified statistical article that came out with a column of figures misplaced, and a silly article about Ping Pong Keller and Chevy Trucks, two mythical players in the Fantaserie League. Did the taxpayers know what I was doing on their time? And my syllabi not done? (Allen Hye would want me to add that the Newsletter was self supporting, though it probably bootlegged some secretarial help.)

One other activity also should come under games, though its academic justification was a little more obvious. I kept a cartoon board on my door, which as the year began contained the cartoons of the Wall Street Journal on economics and those of Somebody Wilson on great moments in history. I had five up at a time, rotated one a day, sending the one taken off to the most appropriate person or keeping it for my classroom bulletin boards. By winter the cartoon display paired Charles Addams (1970) and Jim Williams (1943), thus combining the macabre humor of the sixties with the clean humor of previous decades. Williams got comments from faculty, never from students.

I also served as assistant director (we had no funds for a director) of the BevRon Gallery, which featured exhibits taped on the white wall outside my office. The gallery was named after organizational communicationists Bev (Bunny) Byrum and Ron Fetzer, who shared my section of the hallway and put out a BevRon journal. In the summer there was the art work of Mary Ridgway, who transformed ugly rough drafts into compelling charts. Mary's charts, done on cardboard, kept falling down until she directed my attention to some amazing substance ("this is serious stuff"), which you rolled into little clay-like balls, and they stuck to both picture and wall, coming off both easily when you wanted to remove them.

In the fall I had an exhibit of human activities in organizations. One particularly worth noting was of two organization men playing a "brown" in Saudi Arabia, since it is cheaper to wet down the sand with oil than to try to maintain a green. In the winter we did pictures in world history by period, and in the spring, pictures of famous sociologists accompanied by characteristic but boring quotations and then, the same for sociologists in our department.

While these activities had some academic justification, mostly they were simply play. You could say that the same faculties that are called forth in creative efforts, spill over into play. Or the other way round?

From that perspective, an absence of play could be a cause for concern.

Nor Heed the Rumble

I had a fairly substantial pile of notes on Wright State University. But honestly, as I tried to organize them, what struck me as most interesting was that the University beyond the College of Liberal Arts, was a distant drum. Take, for instance, President Mulhollan. In the fall I filled out a form evaluating his first five years. But it was just the duty of a bad university citizen trying to be good. Basically I said that his appointment of Hathaway as vice president seemed competent, that his priorities on the Nutter Center and Division I basketball were not mine, that I wished he would do more for general education in terms of intervening and publicizing, that his advocacy of the semester system had not been helpful. Generally I thought of him as a stronger advocate than our previous president, Robert Kegerreis—why do our presidents have such difficult names?—but maybe there wasn't much to choose when it came to action, except that Mulhollan was more likely to do what I don't want done. But I suspected, finishing this evaluation, that Mulhollan was not going to be a major character in this book.

Charles Hathaway, whom we met in the General Education chapter (3), was the vice president for academic affairs, and therefore the top ranking official for matters that most directly concern the faculty. In my notes I had an assessment of him by Jim Runkle, but only as I later relayed it to Charles Hartmann in the locker room. I summed up Jim's appraisal that Hathaway didn't listen well and passed up opportunities to be conciliatory. Jim gave the example of a discussion of writing across the curriculum. The biologists told him that it was going to cost some valuable biology. Hathaway, in Jim's opinion, stonewalled, said it wouldn't when he could have said it would but we think the sacrifice of some content would be worthwhile if students were better able to express what they did know. Anyway, Hartmann said he thought that was a fair assessment and added that he thought that Hathaway, without malice, liked to argue. (Faculty Vice President Jim Sayer, at some point, made a similar observation, contrasting him with Mulhollan, who didn't.) A few minutes later Hartmann added, of course, when you put together "likes to argue" and "doesn't listen," that could be a problem. He then added that Hathaway struck him as a man who felt he knew more than most other people. I asked if that might not be a common shortcoming of professors, and wondered if it contributed to most of us not listening as well as we should.

I saw the president occasionally, at the quarterly university faculty meetings, once at a breakfast to which I was randomly invited, and twice in the locker room.

He was in the locker room twice within a week in the fall, and not seen again. He explained that he ran but couldn't play squash or racquetball, because his schedule was too uncertain. I didn't want to talk to him about the hot issues of the moment, general education or the semester system, because he might be jogging to get away from those things for awhile. So we wound up talking about the joys of teaching in a small liberal arts college.

My one informal meeting with Hathaway came in the spring, when he poked his head in my office. He was taking the day off to wander around and visit faculty. (Had he heard the criticism that he doesn't listen?) We talked about Stephen Hawking (Hathaway is a physicist) and the physicist's view of the universe as compared to the social scientist's. He expressed surprise that I should perceive the social scientist as so deterministic. Hathaway started out as a theater major, then switched to physics. It was interesting to consider that we had a vice president who believed in and said he contributed to the second law of thermodynamics.

In the winter, Jim Runkle and I happened to be randomly invited to the same breakfast with Mulhollan and Hathaway. We went
round the table, and Jim asked about his department's expanding
enrollment without new equipment. Mulhollan said that equipment,
new faculty and salaries come out of the same pot, so that raises in
salary reduced money available for other purposes. It was the same
with insurance benefits. So if insurance benefits went up, as they
probably would, we had to choose between raises and adequate
student support. Another reason for the biology problem was that
we were losing graduate enrollment while picking up undergraduates, which cost us because the state subsidized us most for graduate courses, least for general education. So if Sociology made room
for half a dozen graduate applied behavioral science courses by
having one more GE class of 400, we were helping biologists get
equipment, and us, new faculty or raises.

Mulhollan and Hathaway were proud of the new, expensive
Nutter Center, which they saw as contributing to community visibility. They were proud of the basketball team that played in it. They
believed the team's victory over the University of Dayton greatly
enhanced our local image. They believed the Center would greatly
enrich student life and bring income to the community as well as
the university. The President went so far as to say that the victory
over U.D. was worth more to the university than if I had won the
Nobel Prize. (He didn't know that I joke yearly with Bob Pruett and
Jim Jacob about losing the Nobel Peace Prize to some less deserving
person, e.g., the Dalai Lama.) (Bob and Jim don't know that I'm not
joking.)

I had to sympathize with Mulhollan and Hathaway. As they
pointed out, most of their jobs were concerned with problems. We
didn't go to Hathaway to tell him things were going well. Talking
about it later on the bus, Jim Runkle and I were inclined to believe
the administrators when they said that most faculty members
weren't interested in absorbing information given and that many
would prefer to use all the money in the pool for faculty raises, never mind equipment or new faculty.

Oh, and one last vision of the president from the Bus Crowd.
Jeff Vernooy, Jim Runkle and an entertaining lady student were re-
counting the filming of a clip for the opening of a television program called "Good Morning America." It seems the Quad was
mobbed. Professors canceled classes so they and their students could
be there. Apparently it took 45 minutes to film this five-second clip

in which everyone shouts the program's title. The entertaining lady said it was the first time she had ever seen Mulhollan. Must have been like finding Waldo.

During a locker room conversation between Charles Hartmann and Larry Crum, Chair of Computer Science, Larry remarked that education and research were the major purposes of the University and that University staff existed to support the faculty in carrying out these functions. This was what most faculty believed, and it probably accounted for the somewhat condescending view they seemed to have of staff. Whenever there were budget problems, and usually there were, faculty believed one solution would be to cut staff and administrators. We were "bloated" (too many staff members) or "top heavy" (too many administrators).

Charles responded that faculty members were too ready to assume the staff wasn't any good. He wondered if there were a staff locker room where everyone was assuming the faculty wasn't any good?

I did get some of the staff perspective from time to time on the bus from Elmer Hesse, computer specialist and long-term planner. He felt that faculty and staff didn't interact enough, that faculty might benefit from staff input but—guess what?—tend not to listen. He mentioned, for instance—guess who?—Larry Crum's resistance to suggestions that it wasn't reasonable for the Liberal Arts College's required computer courses in research methods to be so hard that a substantial number of students couldn't pass them on several attempts, even though they could pass everything else. He also felt that the University Budget Review Committee, which we looked at as a defender against administrative dominance, was actually a faculty raise protection committee.

Not surprisingly, Elmer didn't think the University was overstaffed. But perhaps the staff was in need of some redistribution, e.g., computer services and television might be low, student services high. I had no way of evaluating, since most of this was invisible to me, although Elmer's appraisal was mildly alarming. It suggested shifting more advising and registration to departments. That would mean more advising for me, perhaps more work for secretaries, more delay on processing my manuscripts.

Speaking of Elmer Hesse's work, there was a letter in the *Dayton Daily News* about the ugliness of the power lines and the metal fence separating the Wright State campus from Interstate 675. The writer thought these were ugly? Hadn't she looked at the campus itself? Flat, neofascist buildings with narrow windows that could be used for crossbow defense against an attack by the University of Dayton. Baby trees that never grow. Elmer Hesse was working on the problem of campus beautification, and sometimes I asked him what he had done during the day. The campus looked the same in the evening as it had in the morning.

Important Work

This was a charming adventure, an example of absolutely unnecessary but important work. Intended as a bonding mechanism for Western World General Education teachers, it actually had very little to do with teaching or research. It was the closest thing we had to a Friday Afternoon Social.

The Western World Symposium was created out of a grant secured by Lillie Howard, Associate Vice President and Professor of English. It seemed demeaning that a $600 honorarium should have been required to get a group of professors engaged in a common enterprise to discuss books of common interest. Some of the books chosen might have been used in general education courses, but that didn't seem to be a central requirement. For me there was a bit of grace involved, because with the development of large classes, my services would no longer be required in Western World courses.

We opened with Shakespeare's *Julius Caesar*, Ceil Cary presiding. I was the lone social scientist among historians, English professors, philosophers, classicists, and religionists. There was a feeling of being among nice, clever people, none of whom would have been a conspirator, would kill for any purpose whatever. They did love words and ideas, and it was pleasant to end the week sitting around a table discussing a play.

What I remembered most from this session was Jim Gleason saying he'd known more real people in fiction than he had known at Wright State. True. As he was saying that, I was thinking that I knew Maureen Howard's (1982) fictional Maude Dowd, her history, her fantasies, better than Jim Gleason, whom I had "known" for 13 years, but only as a fellow walker of hallways and shopper at Dorothy Lane Market. And he, in turn, knew me in the same way.

In October we discussed Thomas Kuhn's curiously influential *Structure of Scientific Revolutions* (1962). Bill King commanded the most attention by arguing that the earth really does go around the sun. This produced a great effort from the rest of us to demonstrate that this was a conception appropriate to our present outlook, didn't fit the Medieval outlook, might not fit future outlooks.

But when Carolyn Stephens suggested that Kuhn's view represented only a candidate paradigm because it did not include feminism, we argued that was irrelevant. Kuhn neither included nor excluded feminism. We were as sure of that as we were that the earth didn't "really" revolve around the sun.

While this part of the discussion was provocative and enjoyable for me, still I came out of the session with reservations. I wasn't sure that a dozen bright people sitting around a table could make any collective contribution. Nothing was building. We didn't seem to be resolving anything. We just kept moving.

But a few weeks later, Bob Thobaben commented in the hallway on the relative absence of casual interaction among faculty members as compared to English institutions. We rarely have dinner together, not even lunch. We eat in our offices or, in my case, not at all. And we are sometimes impatient with David Orenstein because he behaves as if Wright State were an English university. So perhaps the Western World Symposia helped fill that gap. If so, it said something that Lillie had to get a grant before it happened. (She, by the way, didn't have time to attend it, needing Friday afternoon time for necessary administrative matters rather than for her important professorial role.)

At the November meeting we discussed *Moby Dick*, Bill King having suggested crucial chapters for those who felt they couldn't read the whole novel. We had a literary visitor: Carolivia Herron, who earlier in the afternoon had made a presentation on the epic qualities of Black story telling.

Bill made the mistake of asking about the nature of evil. Nobody could come up with a concept others would accept. Comes out of nowhere said Carolivia. Jim Hughes said evil requires intentionality. I said, if so, *Moby Dick* wasn't about evil. Jim quoted D. H. Lawrence as seeing the whale as white civilization. I said Ishmael saw every possible meaning attached to whiteness. I wondered if the book was about whaling? Bill said some students thought it was about the evil of people killing whales. Jim said at least Moby Dick never came into Nantucket looking for Ahab. "I keep thinking about ignorance," said Chuck Taylor. No one let him. Discussing the swearing on the quest, Carolivia said that was what a tyrant did: got peo-

ple to swear to their own destruction. Jan said a good tyrant doesn't
need to do that. (Only an evil tyrant?) Carolyn Stephens offered a
feminist interpretation: a group of men in a female ship under female skies hunting female whales ("Thar she blows!") which they
penetrate with male harpoons. Jim Gleason said, suppose Ahab was
persuaded by Starbuck? Yeah, we'll get that damn whale if he comes
along; but if not, we'll just hunt whales for profit.

Jan Gabbert said the book was rich in possibilities for represen-
tation, but it seemed to me that it was we who were rich in interpretation. In one sense we played a game at which there were many
good players and no rules. When the sessions were over, I felt as
though I had been to a party.

The December session on Nietzsche was held as Peter Melko
and I were climbing out of the Grand Canyon (Ch. 9), but driving
west I had a chance to read *The Use and Abuse of History* and hold a
two person seminar uninterrupted by the rude and distracting comments of my colleagues. Nietzsche opened with the happiness of
cows, which we saw all day as we drove, though I couldn't swear
they were happy. Anyway, we humans had problems because of
our historical remembrance. Nietzsche observed that life didn't need
history; but history was helpful to the active person (he said "man"),
the lover of history, and the critic who, I suppose, kept us realistic in
our reverence.

Generally I found historical perspective helpful and didn't worry,
as Nietzsche did, about an overdose of history leaving us superficial, subject to fashion. Whatever the German problem may have
been, we could benefit from a sense of history. I would have liked to
see our students looking at the present with a historical sense. On
the other hand, in our time as in Nietzsche's, we did see ourselves
as both epitome and epigoni. But couldn't you say this comes from
insufficient historical perspective?

Trouble for the January meeting began when Robert Sumser gave
us a formidable looking set of chapters by Haydn White (1978). Pages
and pages of turgid looking stuff and 15 of us at a two-hour session,
so there wouldn't be much chance to say anything. Was it worth the
time? When I tried the first chapter on tropography, even though I
was reasonably familiar with Freud and Piaget, who were used as
examples, I made no progress. It was essentially worthless reading
for me. I didn't have the patience or interest in levels of abstraction
that I had when young. I didn't care about why I ask what I ask.
Nor was there motivation in the Symposium format. It was like a

book club. You spent two hours, then went on to something else. There must be a better format.

The meeting itself was surprising in that the group seemed to agree that history was a fictive form. There was no historical anybody. Historian Peter Taylor went so far as to say there was no difference between history and literature, both bound only by what they have created. Quite a relational group!

Octavio Paz's *Labyrinth of Solitude* (1989) was seen as poetry by Jan Gabbert and Don Swanson because it provided insight and made you respond emotionally. But from Jan that was a criticism, because the book contained too many contradicted generalizations, which may be permissible in poetry. Chuck Taylor saw it as a philosophical interpretation owing much to Hegel, Marx and Nietzsche. Peter Taylor, on the other hand, saw it as fundamentally Mexican, though that wouldn't preclude Western influence. Tsing Yuan pointed to the dilemma of seeing another civilization. When a German and American visited China together, they were perceived as Westerners, though they couldn't see themselves that way. Were we better at seeing Mexicans than Mexicans were?

Carolyn Stephens and Cynthia King were upset by Paz's description of the Mexican view of women. They saw description as endorsement.

It was Carolyn's turn next and she introduced *The Feminine Question in Science* by Sandra Harding (1986), partly a counter to Kuhn. But once again the book seemed so opaque to me that I couldn't get through it. The discussion, as it turned out, focused on conflict versus functionalist perspectives, and whether science was white male dominated (perhaps Asian male soon?). Then we considered the possible influence of women on science. Jim Hughes recalled how science was interesting when he was younger, about growing and nurturing, but in high school it became a lab assembly line, statistical, cutting up dead things. This was the point at which male teachers replaced female.

Ron Hough and I observed that in our respective fields, women would soon dominate. But if they did, would they bring growth and nurturing to philosophy and sociology, or would they be the women who can master the abstract thinking aspects of the field?

Ron offered the next book, Stephen Hawking's *Brief History of Time* (1988). I enjoyed the book, but being a macrosociologist, seemed to prefer cosmology to quantum theory. The former I felt to be marvelous, awe-inspiring, important for how we think. The latter I didn't understand, perhaps didn't believe, in any event didn't want to make the effort. It was the old *Scientific American* experience of getting half way through the article, then bogging down. In trying to formulate a framework for the study of war (Ch. 7), I didn't seem to have any desire to unify a theory to the extent that it explains both war and family abuse. There was considerable discussion of the book in the hallways. Jan Gabbert and I discussed whether there had to be a beginning, and why we ask what we ask (which, I said a few paragraphs ago, I didn't care about). Over the chessboard, is Hawking serious about religion, or is the whole scientific enterprise a metaphorical game? No wonder I lost so many chess games.

Yet the session itself was flat. Either Ron had too much of an agenda and interfered with the discussion, or we had each brought something to say and didn't want to listen to the others.

There were conflicting views of Machiavelli at the April seminar. Jan Gabbert saw him as a staff officer in the direct tradition of Thucydides. Henry Limouze saw him as a Renaissance Man involved in diplomacy, philosophy and history. Paul Lockhart and Peter Taylor agreed he was a Republican. Finally, Robert Sumser asked if *The Prince* were a Great Book. Consensus was that it contained middle level generalization with middle level support. It gave us hypotheses from which we took off. Perhaps it was a great book. Perhaps: but I thought we could take off from any television soap opera, or a stop sign at the street corner.

For May Bob Reece gave us Langdon Gilkey's *Shantung Compound* (1975). We had, Jan Gabbert pointed out, people in an artificial situation, imprisoned in a compound in which they distributed but did not produce. They also knew that the situation was temporary. Of course we spend much of our lives in situations we know are temporary. (Life is Temporary.) Jim Hughes said the book reminded him of *Moby Dick* as written by Starbuck. It strikes me that we had a situation not uncommon, in which moral sanction isn't enough because not everyone desires to appear moral and will be influenced by sanctions.

The criticisms of the book, which I liked, stung because they could also apply to *A Professor's Work*. I was also studying people bound by space and time. Gilkey organized as I would, by topic, and therefore didn't recognize personality development. He was criticized at the seminar for shallow characterization. The only person who was well characterized was Gilkey himself, and that by unconscious revelation. But this was in the nature of topical books. He could have asked about development and drawn conclusions about that, but none of the characters were explored sufficiently to do that and his notes weren't taken that way. As I hoped to explore work, he explored ethical dilemmas, not characters. Carolyn Stephens saw chauvinism in Gilkey, as she might in *Professor*, in my finding Harding opaque, in reporting without comment on our dismissal of her perception of chauvinism. When Bill King described the book as interesting and thought provoking, but not Great, I thought I would be satisfied if he were to so describe *Professor*.

For the final session on favorite poems, Jim Hughes led off with Emily Dickinson.

> The Brain—is wider than the sky
> For—put them side by side—
> The one the other will contain
> With ease—and you—beside—

a good poem for sociologists.

The Kings gave poems that seemed somewhat opposite their personalities, Bill's Leander swimming the Hellespont, sputtering and dying; Cynthia's Horace enjoying life while he can.

Ron Hough gave us limericks including the lady who

> . . . started one day
> in an Einsteinian way
> and returned on the previous night.

Ceil Cary preferred Lear purging himself by exposing himself to the poor. Maybe I should have put that differently.

Henry Limouze gave us a Miltonian sonnet in which he worried at 23 about not having done very much. As a Calvinist he left it to God, all his life spent searching for God's Will, whereas we search for Ultimate Meaning.

David Barr gave us Cummings seeing Humanity putting the secret of life in its back pocket and sitting on it.

Tsing gave Taoist poetry, all in harmony with all, like a Modern Presbyterian God.

Dave Robinson offered Dorothy Parker, death of the spirit worse than death of the body.

Don Swanson gave us Auden on robins who didn't lie, didn't know they'd die, leaving language for us who long for letters or have promises to keep.

Katie Workman chose Ozymandias, king of kings, who told us to look on his mighty works and despair, but all we had was the inscription and his stone head in the desert. Well, that might make us despair.

Carolyn presented, not her own poem about coming unemployment, but a recital of Wordsworth's "Daffodils."

I wasted quite a lot of time trying to write a verse about each of the presenters in James Russell Lowell's anapestic tetrameter. My best stanza was on Moby Dick.

> Here's King with a paradox thirty feet high
> Three-fifths of it blubber, two-fifths of it lie;
> Is this about mania, hubris or wish?
> Or just an old guide book on how to catch fish?

That was my *best*, mind you. Did the state of Ohio know what it was paying for?

Chuck Taylor chose Loren Eiseley, on how we had once thought ourselves the center of the Universe, but not any more. Like the Cebus monkey, we could arrange patterns but could not construct. Chuck's poem came close to our seminar. We could arrange patterns but not construct.

At a final meeting we tried to assess the year and consider the future. Chuck Taylor and Jan Gabbert liked our format, didn't worry that everything didn't get read. Others wanted to get the NEH grant tied to the GE program. But some of us were happy that the connection with teaching was never closely established.

Jim Hughes was pessimistic. He felt the structures of our work prevented Symposia from happening. He noted that individual presentations lost audience over time.

David Barr felt that if we were to continue we needed some continuity between assignments, because group history was a factor in participation.

Could we meet at our houses rather than in a committee room? Difficult in an urban university. There were recollections of outside meetings of this sort dropping off over time. Jim Hughes thought this tended to be the pattern of such informal meetings, outside or inside. Bob Thobaben's perceptions came to mind.

We ended with a few participants agreeing to serve on a committee to try to recreate the group the following year.

Carroll Quigley makes a distinction between necessary and important work, the former being what you have to do, the latter being what concerns matters of lasting importance. This is the only section in the three chapters on university work that concerns important work, even though the exchanges may have been superficial and achieved no visible outcome, no program, no monument, not even a rule to put in the college catalogue. Beyond Lillie's grant proposal, which was in some file, this may be the only record that the Western World Symposium ever occurred.

And yet the exasperation that each of us must have felt over the perceptions of others, or of the authors themselves, the stretching of the mind over such questions as the nature of reality, the realization of the limits of our capacity to see others, surely all of these are necessary for professors, or what prevents them from becoming bound by the necessary work and by the further exploration and refinement of what they think they already know?

What Had We Done?

From my perspective, not much. The Monster Committee may have increased awareness of monsters, but scarcely deterred them. The Liberal Arts meeting and Jim Jacob's memo appear to have preserved the quarter system for awhile. The efforts of two faculty members and a vice president were followed by a ten o'clock bus, but the former probably did not lead to the latter. The three-college City Schools Committee did find out some valuable information that might produce results in future years. The Peace Studies Brochure was a disaster from my perspective, but others might disagree. Committee A may have helped adjunct professors, and the Western World Symposium may have provided some perspective if not bonding. The results were indecisive, hard to gauge, depended on what happened in future years.

Considering all these "service" activities, the failure to select a new faculty member, the continued onrush of the general education monsters, the failure to act on city schools, the Peace Studies fiasco, a state legislator might well ask whether it wouldn't be better to leave such matters to the University Administration. Use this

5

But Don't Professors Also Teach Classes?

The Professor Plans a Course,
Teaches and Evaluates It, and
Gets Evaluated Himself

One image of college professors is that, since their route to fame and fortune is research, teaching is only an incidental activity to which they give as little attention as possible. I did not encounter much evidence for this image at Wright State, but lots of evidence to the contrary.

In fact I should be an example of the irresponsible teacher. I switched from journalism to college teaching because I thought the latter would give me more time and a better environment to write books. And it did. Teaching, on the other hand, I considered to be the work you did in exchange for the time for scholarly research.

The Contexts of a Teaching Year

Certainly teaching was the most difficult part of the work, the root of most anxiety. There was no denying that each day at 12:15, when I had finished my summer classes, I felt a feeling of exhilaration. The hard part of the day was over. Now all I had was research, preparation for the next day's class, and whatever time was left over for "service" work. It was particularly hard to go back to teaching after a break. I have a note on July 4, about a week before the beginning of the Summer B session, that "as the day of return to class grows nearer, my anxiety begins to rise. It's going to be hard getting up at 5:45 for that 8 a.m. class." And David Orenstein, who always seemed so relaxed, told me he could never sleep on the night before "opening day."

My attention to teaching was no better than average. From hallway conversation I would guess that Jan Gabbert, Ellen Murray, Amin Islam, Norm Cary, Chuck Taylor and many others gave more time and anguish to teaching than I did. It is also fair to say that members of my department did not single me out as a great teacher when the time came for merit evaluations.

I should also mention that this topically organized book doesn't reflect the day to day chaos. In one 24 hour period, for instance, I finished preparations for my evening class, prepared notes for the class the following morning, taught the evening class, reviewed evaluations for a class taught two quarters ago, ordered books for a class to be taught the next quarter, taught the morning class, graded papers from the class of the evening before, worked on a syllabus for a next quarter class, and prepared for the next morning class to come.

The courses I taught in the academic year were two sections of History 102, The West in Transition; Soc. 200, Social Life, (two sections, one an honors class); Soc. 204, Careers in Sociology, (two sections) Soc. 201, Modern Society; Soc. 350, Occupations and Professions, Soc. 441, Industrial Sociology. Hist. 102 and Soc. 200 were general education courses required of all students in the university.

The regular Social Life course and the history course were classes of about 60 in which we gave objective examinations mixed with some writing. Ideally about half the grading was to be for writing. Objective exams consisted of multiple choice, matching and true-false, and did not require writing except that in my classes students always got an opportunity to make a written challenge if they thought there was another way of looking at the question. The honors class had only 15 students, all with B or better averages, and all grading in that course was for essay writing.

"Modern Society" was a social problems course, generally required at the sophomore level for sociology majors. It was also taken to fill major requirements for students in other programs or simply as an elective. This was also a class of 60 with mixed objective and essay exams or papers. There was, however, more freedom to organize this course. I wasn't bound to a general education overview.

The Careers course was also required for all majors, but it was all essay, had 15 students in one section, 25 in the other. Unlike other courses, it was graded on a pass-fail basis. And unlike Modern Society, I was the only member of the Department who taught it.

The Occupations and Industrial Sociology classes were for upper level students majoring in Sociology or in Social and Industrial Communication, the latter a dual major in the Sociology and Communication programs. These courses also drew a number of management majors, since they filled a related elective requirement in the management program. Examinations were entirely essay. All my examinations in all courses, whether objective or essay, permitted use of text books and notes. I figured I used books and notes in my work. Why shouldn't the students?

As mentioned in Chapter 4, at Wright State we used the quarter system, ten-week courses taught three times a year instead of 15 courses taught twice a year. (There was also a summer quarter.) This meant more preparations and a shorter time to teach each course.

What is the best way to describe a year's teaching from the teacher's perspective? I wanted to describe the whole year, from the planning of courses to the student evaluations. It was fascinating to see how I handled the different levels of courses, moving from large classes to small, racing from one activity to another, working late to keep up, trying to learn the names of the students, helping them through various crises. At the time it seemed challenging, heroic and exciting. But on paper it seemed chaotic, repetitive and tiresome, just an expansion of the 24-hour period described above.

So I shall describe the planning and teaching of one particular course.

Choosing the Books

In the winter of the year studied there was a column in *Newsweek* by Michael Shenefelt, who taught in Columbia University's general education program. He felt that most middle-class people, including professors, don't have enough breadth. We don't read enough Great Books, must bluff because we don't know what Marcus Aurelius said. I don't know that I would go that far, but I did feel that my students and I didn't read enough books, So as far as possible I tried to use real books, as distinguished from textbooks. If I couldn't get Great ones, at least there was a selection of good ones in paperback. It is worth noting that if I had been well organized, I could have drafted the syllabus first, then chosen the books that would best suit that organization. But I had never done so. The Campus Bookstore had an early deadline, which meant that my book choices already limited the possibilities of the course.

In the general education courses I used a textbook that would give "coverage," would deal with areas with which teachers of following courses would expect students to have some familiarity. Then I would try to supplement with paperbacks that were both challenging and readable. For the upper-level courses there were textbooks, but one could choose to let them pass in favor of a set of paperbacks, since there were no expectations from other instructors about these courses. So the choice was between exposure to a variety of subjects or to a narrower range explored more fully and coherently.

For ordering books I kept files for each course, and when it came time to order I looked them over, checked the books in the library, then decided whether to change. I usually did change something, because that expanded my reading and because teaching one course provided new ideas for the next. The problem was to avoid changing too many books and thereby leaving more reading for me than there was time to do.

I got the books for the files mostly from *Contemporary Sociology*, a journal of reviews, and occasionally from *The New Republic*, from references in other books, from colleagues, from fliers sent to us by publishers, or from the University Library Approval Shelf. The Approval Shelf contained books, organized by department according to a computerized formula, that we could look at and choose to retain if they pleased us. Sometimes in reviewing books in the library, we found others under similar call numbers.

Now which course should I describe? Perhaps "Occupations and Professions," since it was the absence of a book describing the work of a professional that caused me to take notes for this one.

For the Occupations course, despite my resolve to change no more than one book, I wound up with a completely new set. The preceding spring sabbatical had given me more time to look; besides, my evaluations for the previous class had been low and I may have wanted to make a fresh start. But mostly it was because any switch affects the relationships of all the books and calls for compensations.

In place of a text I used Sar Levitan and Clifford Johnson's brief *Second Thoughts on Work,* which gave coverage without trying to be exhaustive. Then I added Peter Drucker's *Frontiers of Management,* because it tells a lot about the underlying framework of occupations as well as giving some practical perspectives on choosing and being a manager. Next I chose Charles Sabel's mistitled *Work and Politics,* which gave a historical framework and also reinforced Drucker's view of the importance of the entrepreneur even in an organizational society. Finally I decided on a reader edited by Patricia Voydanoff called *Work and the Family,* which got to the problems of the dual career family. I had the feeling that the relationship between work and family was neglected in both occupations and family courses.

Of course, before choosing a book, you are supposed to read it. In fact, if it were a new book, usually I would look at the table of contents, skim the book, and read a middle chapter. Selecting the book, of course, insured that you would read it, which is something a professor ought to do. Tony Watson (1980) mentions how academic reading shades off into non-work. This was true. I would carry the book I was reading around, check half an inning on television and read some more, read while waiting in the supermarket line, evenings, on the bus, always working against the deadline of the next quarter. And this is how I came to perceive that Sabel's book was probably too dense and repetitive for undergraduate use. Oh well, I didn't have to use all of it. And the students needed to be challenged.

It's in the Syllabus

When I taught at a private college, I didn't even use a syllabus. At state universities I found they were expected, and using them, found they provided guidelines for me as well as the students.

After information about telephones and office hours, I provided course goals, books, approaches, special projects, grading procedures and a calendar that indicated when exams would come and papers were due.

The goals, I suspect, were ignored by many students, whose vision of results was based more on what they had to do to get a desired grade than on any concept of overview. It would be up to me

ties would range from students who were just passing, or perhaps
not quite, to students who had very nearly a straight A grade point
average. Students not doing well could drop the course quite late
in the quarter, but dropping out often could delay graduation and
raise costs to the point where a student would give up. So the syllabus encouraged students to hang in there, to read exam comments
carefully, and to talk to the instructor.

Each faculty member would have his own standards, a conception of what is good or poor. But these standards could erode if too
high a proportion of your students did poorly in your first exam or
dropped your course. On the other hand you might get tougher if a
class did unusually well. You might not have an explicit curve, but
there was likely to be one in your head.

Just before fall quarter began, Charles Hartmann and Phil Engle addressed both sides of the problem. Charles said we don't grade
rigorously enough in upper level classes. There ought to be a drop
out rate of 20 percent. There ought to be F's. (Would you want to
play squash with this guy?) I wondered if the students dropping or
failing ought not to have flunked out before getting into that situation. Phil was looking at the other side. Here you have a junior with
a low B average and he couldn't write. How could you flunk him
now?

University Media Distribution had a large supply of films, but I
used only those with actual situations and people, not recreations. I
would like to have scheduled more short films to help vary the pattern of a three-hour (7–9:50) evening class, but in Occupations this
was a problem. So many films marketed for management courses
used amazingly bad actors to show how you Motivate the Workers.
The real films would show you what actually happens at a meeting,
or what a lawyer does outside the courtroom. But such films were
virtually nonexistent possibly because they were difficult to do without being boring for the outsider.

In upper-level courses there would be a fourth hour paper or
project, a special assignment of some sort for which no class hour
was scheduled. These were usually intended to carry the student
further into a particular area. Sometimes it might be a research paper, but in Occupations it would be a series of interviews with three
area people currently involved in occupations that interested the
students, e.g., local business men or women, executives, or professionals in a career area. This year I was developing an innovation.
The interviews were to be collected, copied, covered and sold by
one of the local copying establishments to the students. That way

students would get to read the results of their own interviews as they related to those of their classmates.

The use only of purchased books for the writing assignments combined with interviews for the fourth hour meant that library assignments were being neglected. This is a cause for regret, because I like libraries more than many professors. But in a quarter system, you couldn't do everything you wanted in every class. It was a university, and I had to hope that other professors would give library assignments.

Each syllabus was being prepared from the previous one. I tried to recall what had worked and what had not. I usually looked at my previous student evaluations to see if I could shore up areas in which the students had been critical. Reviewing the evaluations reminded me each time of my shortcomings, particularly how students see me, which is an important factor in my capacity to reach them. Though past experience hardly supported the expectation, each time I prepared a syllabus I really believed that this time the course would be a tremendous success in every way. This time, I would think, I'll really do it.

And this year, with notes for the book being taken, I thought the Hawthorne Effect should kick in. The very knowledge that a participant observer was looking over my shoulder should keep me on my toes, goad me to a stellar performance.

Well, let's see.

Class Time

Beneath the goals of any course was a deeper set of assumptions that had developed over time. In all classes I tried to get students to look at their lives in sociological perspective, to get them to think more clearly, to seek greater depth, to reflect underlying causes. Clarity, I thought, was the route to depth.

The need to teach content, in this case our cumulative sociological knowledge about occupations, was less important, though it weighed heavily. When you were working on other things, there was always a residue of guilt about having insufficient content.

Getting depth through clarity required organization. The capacity to organize, I thought, was strengthened if you had the ability to focus on the problem you were addressing. Students should be able to answer a question at least tentatively, to support that answer logically and specifically from data they had from assignments and classroom presentations, to distinguish between the relevant and irrelevant. They should also be able to do verbally, for instance at a committee meeting, what they could do in writing. And they should have the capacity to find their way to information they needed in order to frame and support the answer.

The desire to utilize class time efficiently often got in the way of achieving the goals because something was always being sacrificed to achieve something else. And students had personalities, problems and goals of their own (Ch. 6); what worked for some might not for others. It wasn't reasonable to expect success from every student. It was a university, and if I failed to reach all of them, they would have many other teachers. But it wasn't easy to accept failure to progress (according to my conception of progress) either. I wanted to take the goals worked out and try to reach them through the teaching process, then test the students to see how well they were learning, tests also being a means to further the learning.

The goals themselves seemed to fight for class time. You wanted the student to learn to see in a certain way or to be able to write in a different way. The writing assignments needed logical thinking and support from valid data. All of these took much classroom time. The more you could get the student to do, the better. But at the same time you also had a content goal, the conveying of certain levels of knowledge one ought to have. You shouldn't spend too much time conveying that kind of thing by lecture, however, because it could be read in the carefully selected, content-laden books. On the other hand, you felt it needed some kind of direction from the lectern.

I wrote a revealing note on the eve of the first Industrial Sociology class that would have applied as well to the Occupations class. "Right off the bat we'll go to work. I'll get them to write and answer questions. Willing to share my answers but most important that they develop their own. Lots of discussion, necessary to develop listening habits. Necessary to think in group situations."

Oh yeah. But when those discussions took place, there was underlying dissatisfaction because we covered only the first of the four points I had intended. Or, I covered all four, but some of the students looked pretty sleepy. What good did it do to "cover" points if they were not internalized?

Evening classes made you particularly aware of the use of class time. These classes were valuable because they enabled people who were fully employed to continue their college educations. Moreover, they were apt to be good classes because they contained a higher percentage of older students. But a class lasting from 7 to 10 p.m.

made a long evening even for motivated students, especially if they had just worked a nine to five day.

When I was working on the Occupations syllabus, I remembered from my previous evaluations that the students didn't think I had made my objectives clear or used sufficiently stirring examples. The objectives were listed in the syllabus as means by which the goals would be achieved, and these objectives were underscored during the first night of class when the syllabus was reviewed. But after that the class met only once a week, and in trying to make the evenings interesting and varied (i.e., stirring), I may indeed have forgotten to reinforce the objectives. Students broken down into small groups to discuss a question may well have asked, what the hell are we doing this for?

The need for stirring examples was probably greater in an evening course. You couldn't lecture for three hours, so you had better lecture early and not only use great examples but also be sure that those examples are to the point. I often chased examples too far, entertained everybody, but failed to link the entertainment to the lesson. This from the professor who was trying to teach students to focus and not be distracted by the interesting but irrelevant.

Because of the length of the class and the weariness of the students, class time in an evening course was likely to be segmented: some time for lecture, some for discussion, some for films, perhaps some for returning exam papers and discussing them, with a break somewhere in the middle. Time was also used for reporting and discussing the fourth hour project, as students returned from interviewing Dayton's occupational community. This involved not only the individual interviews but the group project of organizing them into a reader. Since we did have more discussions and the class contained older and more articulate and demanding students, it follows that there must have been less lecturing, less elucidation of material, more dependence on the students to get it from the reading or to ask questions if they didn't. It would seem, therefore, that the design of evening classes ought to be more conducive to learning than the 50 minute day classes.

Okay in Theory, But . . .

In sociology more than in many subjects, there is a direct relationship between what we teach and life experience. This could be both an advantage and a problem. It was an advantage because everyday applications and immediate examples were widely available. It was a problem because a student was likely to think he already knew the subject, which is, after all, human life. Instead of looking at everyday experiences in a new way, he translated the concept or theory he was studying into perceptions he already had. So I wanted to relate the theory or concept to the familiar and get students to think through the implications. In Occupations, for instance, I asked a take home question about the problems confronting dual career families, and used that to get students to confront the dimensions of a problem many of them would face or were already facing.

In any class, a substantial majority of students either planned to be or were in a dual career marriages. Men expected their wives would have careers of their own, and women expected that they would do so. At a broad level of generalization, you could say that older students, already in such marriages, tended to blame the opposite gender for problems. Women thought men as a category were immature and selfish. Men thought women were unreasonably demanding, didn't understand the work situation, were not really in comparable situations in their own careers. Younger students thought that love and understanding would carry them through as problems arose, and that each would be more than willing to sacrifice for the other.

So on one hand I wanted to get them to address these practical problems in their lives. If one partner were offered a promotion and transfer, did he take it? Did she? If children got sick, which parent was to be called? Why? Did a good day care center solve your child raising problems? How did you know? How did the dual career affect household division of labor?

On the other hand, I also wanted the problem understood in a deeper context. Were there more dual career families than there used to be? Was there any precedent, either recent or in the more distant past? If there were more, what were the forces that were bringing this about? We needed to look at feminism and women's liberation in historical context, and to relate them to other changes in perception of civil liberties. We needed, also, to examine whether there really were economic causes, or whether social changes affected perceptions of economic need. We needed also to look at social stratification. Dual career families, after all, were middleclass. How did what was happening to them relate to what was happening to the working class?

The sample in an evening Occupations class was skewed, since the majority of sociology majors were women and a high percentage were already married or divorced. They were taking these classes as part of a plan to develop a career that they would share with a present or future husband who had a career of his own. This gave evening classes a bit more bite, with differences of perception between men and women on one hand, and older marrieds or divorced vs. young lovers on the other.

Depth of discussion required student preparation, and that was often a problem. Consider the student's perspective. Do you read before class? Or do you wait for the instructor to clarify, point out important parts, make your reading easier? Almost a rhetorical question. Consider also that in the Occupations class, of 28 students responding, 13 had full time jobs, ten part time. Fifteen had worked during the day before coming to my three hour evening class, 17 had another evening class besides mine. Twenty-one were taking more than eight hours, more than half a load. So for many of these students, discussion might be something to break up the evening, but hardly something you had extra time to prepare for.

Another consideration about a discussion was that it not only used more time but was unpredictable. These judicious observations about what happened in the gender discussion don't reflect my notes at the time. I noted that it was chaotic, created some heckling from the men's side which I didn't think was in the objective spirit I had hoped for. I found myself interfering too much, providing statistical support. In the end it was a good discussion in terms of percentage participating, but I didn't think it had been very useful in helping the students craft a well supported, judicious answer to a question about the problems of dual career marriages.

Depth and Clarity In Ten Weeks?

Since I aimed at developing a capacity for depth and clarity, my method in upper level classes was to get the students to write often, to answer questions I had asked, and to support these answers specifically and logically from the data in the course. The method could be used in any upper level course I taught. Only the questions differed.

The questions were usually chosen with relation to the homework assignment for the following week, in which case there would guilt feelings that the simplification would seem laughable to an economics professor. But this was a cost to be paid for using real books rather than text books, a cost all adults pay in reading difficult books. Getting over her head is something an educated person does.

Networking the Urban Environment

I have alluded to interviews in the "Fourth Hour Project." I would never persuade Charles Hartmann, who taught law in the College of Business, that this non-classroom Liberal Arts fourth hour was anything other than a boondoggle that gave teachers credit for more hours than they deserved and made the student's path to graduation easier. But many of us thought the fourth hour encouraged the teacher to expand, to create something that would enable students to go further in a particular area by writing a paper, carrying out a participant observation study, or interviewing people who know something about the subject.

In Occupations and Industrial Sociology, I liked to take advantage of our urban environment and get students out to meet people who held positions to which they might aspire, or who could tell them how the industrial system worked from a local perspective. While I wanted the students to get the feel of how a particular occupation fit into the structure, I also encouraged them to try to learn something about how various positions were reached and what the work would be like if the position were attained. I also wanted them to use the interviews to begin to form networks of acquaintance, leaving their resumes behind, and hopefully taking up further interviews on their own as they neared graduation.

How the position was reached was important because if you were aiming to be a personnel (AKA human resources) director, you wanted to know how other personnel directors got where they were. When the student asked what the work was like, he was likely to get a job description, what the work was supposed to be like, unless he could ask a timely follow up question that opened the floodgate. One suggestion made to the class was that they ask whether Mondays were preferred to Fridays. Lisa Holiday tried that with Diane Jennings, general manager of a box company, and this is the response she recorded:

I asked Diane if she had any distinctive feelings regarding Fridays versus Mondays and she stated that she did, but the response was quite unexpected. She stated that she did not particularly like Fridays as they are quite hectic with the phones ringing off the hook for those people who want boxes to be delivered for Monday or for those doing their last minute, end of the week advertising. Mondays, she stated, are preferable to Fridays as they are not as hectic, but she said that some of her personnel can be more difficult to get along with on Mondays though. The other aspect that she shared with me was her feelings of lack of freedom that she believes that most other General Managers have, in that she is still responsible to the owners, and she is closely in contact with them and to some extent even under their control, where she feels that she does not make as many major decisions or even some smaller ones that other people in her position would be making.

Ah, so. Here we do get a feeling of what the position is really like, of problems a manager actually has. Over three interviews, most students did get better at eliciting more revealing responses.

The Occupations class really came alive when we talked about class interviews that might lead to job interviews later on or about salary negotiations, both ethics and amounts. I'm afraid it wasn't sociological perspective that intrigued them. They weren't asking about the meaning of negotiation rituals, nor considering them from functionalist, conflict and interactionist perspectives. They were asking, how do I get "real" interviews? And if I'm offered a job, how do I know what to ask for, how much time have I got to think about it, what is permissible for the negotiators to do?

Examinations:
The Professor's Perspective

While comments and questions from students may give an indication of how things were going, each professor established his own means of evaluating students. The most common method, however it may be described, was the examination.

Students, naturally, viewed examinations with trepidation. We all did. Sometimes we tried to help reduce the anxiety by giving shorter examinations and calling them quizzes, or by giving take-homes that didn't have to be done in a room full of other students in a specific span of time. But however we packaged it, the measure of performance was the examination.

Exams were as much a subject of debate among teachers as among students. How well did they reflect what the student learned? If the students were tense, did the tests accurately reflect their abilities? And to what extent did writing answers in a room with a group of other students over a timed period reflect real work? We ourselves may work against deadlines, but except for journalists and a few others, we didn't have to produce something in 50 minutes. Did the examination reveal understanding, or just knowledge?

In choosing these questions out of many, I am revealing my own biases. Over time I had concluded that the possession of in-head knowledge was not as important as knowing how to find the appropriate knowledge when needed. Sometimes work is done in a work situation, sometimes we take it home. We should be comfortable doing both, though separating the home and work situations is an important professional problem (Ch. 10).

If there were no other constraints, probably I would have preferred all essay exams involving answering important questions from available data. Some of these would be done in an office situation, assigned and returned on the same day. Some would be taken home and done over time. But there were constraints. Students had to do their work in the classroom, not an office. And take homes had to be limited in consideration of the fact that the majority had to manage both studying and jobs.

As mentioned, in preparing the syllabus for Occupations, I thought I'd try to take some pressure off the students by scheduling a quiz every week and allowing them to submit any six.

One night, for instance, this was the question they were asked: "What are the implications of Peter Drucker's world analysis on the occupational field that currently interests you?" So if the student were interested in personnel work, and Drucker's analyses suggested more interaction with other countries or the need for a different kind of knowledge, how would this affect the selection of personnel?

Or, "Why is the dual career family so difficult to maintain?" And here they might combine the family literature with the literature on the demands of organizational careers. They might.

Or, more difficult perhaps, "How does the changing world economy affect Americans?" Sabel and Drucker on this one, plus perhaps what they have heard from local managers about markets, labor costs or competition.

Or, on a more general level, "What seems to be the relationship between business and government?" Here they could cull information from at least three of their books, plus the interviews.

What Did the Students Learn?

That's the critical question, isn't it? Teachers tended to play "Ain't it Awful" in the hallways, a blown class has been described here and there are notes about exams in which the point had been missed or the work hadn't been done. But there is still more evidence that on quite a few occasions, the examinations suggested that something had been learned.

Certainly I often complained about the inadequacy of the students, or of my teaching. I was disappointed that more than half the Occupations class missed (what I had intended to be) the point of a film "The Business of America," failing to relate it at all to the literature they had been reading. I knew perfectly well that people don't automatically relate what they read to what they see every day or in a film. That is why teachers exist. Students learn to relate data after someone shows them how. I knew this from experience, yet failed to put it in that perspective when I was looking at a particular set of papers.

The same kind of thing happened when I raised a problem from the contemporary world. Many students responded as other people would, including teachers and public officials: from the gut level. A student needed to learn to write a more thoughtful, better grounded paper by getting back criticism and helpful suggestions on papers that had been based more on feelings than on data. But still I expressed amazement and disappointment when they based their responses on emotions and saved the worst of them for the next hallway game of "Ain't it Awful." But wasn't my response also emotional?

I clipped for my office door a Calvin and Hobbes series on Calvin doing a paper on bats, about which he knows nothing. "You could do research," Hobbes suggests. "Research! Give me a break!" says Calvin. That's how it seemed with some of the papers. Support tended to come from logic, what one would expect to be the case, rather than from data that would have come from the reading. But the appeal of Sam Watterson's cartoon suggests that Calvin's response was deep in many of us. I know it was in me.

I made several comments suggesting dissatisfaction with the quality of my teaching. After getting superficial and poorly supported answers from one set of papers I commented: "I need to make better use of my class time. To get them to clarify their answers. . . . I'm not pleased with the work I'm getting. I'm not *teaching* students to work out their answers from the data of the course."

Or: "What I need to learn is how to get students like Brad Carpenter, who really want to do it, to learn what specific support really means. I need some written device that I can give them as models." Was this a realistic self appraisal or a longing for an overly simple solution not so different from "getting tough on drugs?"

"It is so important to answer the question!" I exclaimed, Then I added: "But even faculty are easily led from the question to side issues."

Or reading a third set of Occupations papers: "Now I'm cracking down. They need to answer, then support logically and specifically. Answers tend to run across the tops of paragraphs. . . . Support doesn't make use of the definite information given by numerous studies in their reading. If they are specific, they can learn to harness the support. If not, they can remain logical and wrong indefinitely." And so the process went on. Reward the clear answer with specific support, punish the scattered answer lacking support. But keep the punishment mild and praise the positive. Don't make a lot of red marks along the margin, just a positive green comment at the end, with a suggestion of what needs to be done further. This you have done well; this you need to work on. When the student becomes confident of the answer, the place for the support will become apparent. The paragraphing will improve, then the punctuation, and even the spelling. So all those early critical notations of comma faults may have been, not only unnecessary, but even discouraging.

And then came a set of final examinations in which the majority of students answered and supported better than they had in any previous examination, a reward we had all earned. Was this an acquired ability that would carry into other classes in future courses? I hoped so.

The interviews also produced interesting results. Most people interviewed seemed to enjoy the process, tended to be upbeat. Most people seemed to like their work. The range of work found in the city was intriguing: desk top writer, geriatrician, special education teacher, public relations specialist, advertising entrepreneur, personnel director, city manager, CEO, electrical contractor, social counselor, clothes buyer, judge. The students did very well writing about work when they cited the book of interviews they had done themselves. Here was intelligible material rich in specific examples.

Overall, while it is easy to be cynical about the enterprise, and we do lack information about our long term impact, there was also more than a scattering of evidence to indicate that some approaches appeared to have produced favorable results, at least for some students. It is probably unrealistic to hope for more than that.

What Did the Students Think?

There was another kind of evaluation. The professor evaluated the students from A to F, and he also evaluated his own courses. How well did the students learn? How well did I achieve my goals? Meanwhile, at the end of the quarter, the students had a chance to evaluate the professor. Did they think this was a good class? Would they recommend it to their friends?

I should mention that this scale was the same as the student scale. Faculty are rated from 0 to 4, whereas students were rated F to A. But when the letters were translated to numbers for a grade point average, the ratings were identical. Students were more generous, usually rating their faculty over 3, while their own mean was well under. If the faculty had not discovered this, more of us would be content. I'd probably think myself, well, I'm a B minus teacher as I was a B minus student.

I must have been apprehensive about the Occupations evaluations, because I dreamed I was teaching a closing class, almost certainly Occupations. The dream had a heavy feeling. I was working hard, not getting a response. I called on someone and a blond, male student said they should decide if they wanted to stay before anyone got called on. Then he packed up his books and left. Everyone else was packing up as they do at the end of a class. I heard someone say outside the door: "We shouldn't have done that." I realized I had no class evaluations.

On the other hand, Occupations was an upper level evening class, where there were more mature students who were likely to appreciate the subtlety of my approach.

Enough stalling. What did they say? The envelope, please.

Clarified Responsibilities?	2.6
Organization	2.5
Communication	2.5
Stimulated Interest?	2.9
Work Level	2.7
Availability	3.6
Evaluation Methods	3.0
Recommend to Others?	2.7
Grand Mean	2.8

Same old lows: organization, communication and interest. Many wouldn't recommend to others. Typical grand mean. Lower than usual in clarifying responsibilities. Above 3 only in availability (being approachable, keeping office hours) and evaluation methods. Actually these lows and highs were consistent with other courses taught this year, whether introductory or upper-level, elite or regular, using objective exams or essay, bigger classes or smaller classes.

I had thought, from my years as Department chairman, that evaluations tended to be holistic. If students were not enthusiastic about instructors, they would not rate them high in anything, though some ratings might be higher than others. But my ratings for availability provided some contrary evidence. Here students consistently rated me high in almost every class. So if I got a different evaluation there, could I not, for instance, work on organization, so that I was not only well organized from my perspective, but seemed well organized to them?

On the upper level courses, one commented under organization that I seemed like a typical absent-minded professor; another said, "I always had to ask someone else what was being said in class." No, that's a communication comment. See, I'm not organized. There were other comments about vagueness including a kindly "instructor left material vague to try to bring out class participation." So they thought I was vague and disorganized when I was trying to teach them to organize and support specifically. Under suggestions from the industrial sociology class: "He tests us on content, but says *nothing* in class!" And "Answer questions with *answers* not *questions.*"

The comments on work level were clear enough, not vague at all. "60 ch. of reading is entirely too much!" "TOO MUCH READING" And there was a general comment under suggestions that seemed pretty bitter:

If this is a class in sociology lit writing, the class description should say so!!! I think Melko could be a better instructor if he gave more direction regarding the class objectives and tried to be more open minded to student's opinions. I think I speak for the majority of the class when I say I didn't have a clue what the expectations were in the assignments or the class outcome. I also felt Melko was very critical of students' opinions and seemed to enjoy correcting students' answers (even when the answer was based on personal opinion). I have never had such a poor professor in all my years of college.

There were some favorable comments. "Good use of interviews. Very helpful." "Made you think somewhat." "Writing assignments stimulated thought about subject." "You made me confused but this was due to making me think in a different way. You showed me another approach to looking at questions." "Very open minded and patient." "Learned a lot from this course." You had to notice these, too, if you were to maintain perspective.

I recalled that in the 1960's a college dean, Lou Menand, told me that no instructor was likely to have a great impact on all of his students. If you think back on your own college career, he said, only a few professors really mattered. That was before evaluations, but these evaluations would confirm what Lou would expect. I might be content if I didn't know that many other faculty members, among them the brightest and most interesting, had consistently high evaluations across the board.

What My Colleagues Thought

Well, okay, so I wasn't a star to my students. But perhaps more mature people would be more supportive. I would also be judged by my Department colleagues. Their assessment of my teaching was to be part of an overall judgment on three areas of our work—teaching, scholarship and service—that was made by a committee of the whole. Each of us, sociologists and anthropologists, was evaluated by all the others. Preceding the committee evaluation, which was done in the winter quarter of the next calendar year, we each prepared a report on our year's work. Included in this was a report on our teaching, including all student evaluations as an appendix. You may have noticed that the last line of the student numerical evaluation of Occupations was a "grand mean," the average of the other means for each item. Many of us did not consider the grand mean a meaningful category, since it combines scores for unequal and disparate topics. Well, for the yearly report we listed the grand mean for each of our courses, and then averaged those for what was called a grand grand mean. One could argue that this was meaninglessness compounded, since you were now averaging dubious figures for classes of different sizes, with an all essay honors Social Life class with 15 students counting the same as a monster Social Life class of 400 students. Yet it did mean something, because popular teachers got high numbers, at least half way between 3 and 4 (i.e., B and A), regardless of what they taught.

This cumulative mean, then, was a crucial number. Regardless of what else you may have done, it was the departure point for evaluation. In evaluating one another, we used a scale of 1–7 for each of the three categories. In the previous year I had a 3.2, very high for me, which earned me a 3 for teaching on the l–7 scale from my colleagues. So you can see, a 3.2 didn't rate very high in a department in which several members scored regularly between 3.6 and 3.8 in their teaching evaluations. Nothing I could say about how innovative my courses were, or what good finals my students turned in, would very much modify the evaluation.

For the year in question, however, my cumulative mean turned out to be 2.9. In only two courses all year was I over 3. In fact I was the only member of our Department to be under 3. So it was with some trepidation that I opened the Department evaluation. It turned out that my colleagues were very kind, suggesting in their collective comment that my efforts were not always reflected in my evaluations. They gave me a 4, a middle rating in teaching, higher than the previous year when I had achieved an unusually high number for me. Perhaps last year my middle level number looked just mediocre, whereas this year my lower number caused some to think, oh, come now, he isn't bad!

Jeanne's cover comment, as expected, was generous. She thought I might be good for some students, puzzling to others. Her prescription for improvement was step by step clarifying and visiting other classes to see what others do.

Was it gross hubris to wonder if it mattered that I didn't thrill all my students if I got good results from them? I knew I was teaching something. Was it crucial to be popular? Perhaps it wasn't crucial, but it would be desirable to improve student perceptions of the classes without compromising on objectives. As long as I failed to do that, it was hard to know whether I was rationalizing.

Burnout?

In the middle of the fall quarter, struggling with Occupations and Social Life, I wrote: "At this point I'm discouraged about both classes, feel I've been vague, don't have an overall purpose, haven't taught critical thinking, haven't taught writing either. What is discouraging at this point is that I've been teaching for 30 years. A couple years ago, even though I didn't get good evaluations, I thought I was an effective teacher. At the moment that's in doubt. How can I tell Katie Workman how to teach (Ch. 6)? How can I send articles to *Teaching Sociology*? Why, when I am a good organizer, even tempered, humorous, am I having so much trouble in the classroom?"

Looking back at this comment, I note that my perception of myself as organizer was contradicted by the students. Whether my self-perception was accurate or not, apparently I was conveying disorganization to them.

All in all, I seemed to be intrigued by the problems of teaching, but I no longer liked them. Over the years, as methods had become more complex, as solutions to problems had created other problems, as summer school has left activity almost unbroken without adequate opportunity to read and reconstitute, feelings of anxiety had increased. One of my after-class notes said I felt relieved coming out of the classroom, maybe like a surgeon who had finished an operation. He didn't know whether he had been successful, but at least he was done for the day.

6

And of Course There Were Students

Of Different Genders, Races, Ages, and Backgrounds,
With Worries and Agendas of Their Own,
Without Whom the University Would Have—
Well, Run More Smoothly, Actually

When I described how incoherent my day was before being topically arranged for these pages, it would have been well for me to consider that the lives of my students may have been even more chaotic than mine. The students typically had more courses than the instructor, and besides were working and trying to deal with love lives and families often in crisis. One night, coming home on a 9:30 evening bus, I heard a student tell another he was working 30 hours a week but needed more money for rent, so he was looking for a midnight to ten job on a Sunday morning.

"But when do you study?" asked the other student.

"Well, you know me," said the first. "I don't until just before the exam." He went on to say he needed to keep his grade point average at 3.4 (high B+) in order to maintain his two financial scholarships.

So however well organized the teacher may be, he would have to realize that individual students were likely to have priorities that were not ideal from his viewpoint. There was no typical student. One was taking my course because he needed the credit to graduate, and a D was good enough. For another it was crucial to get a B to maintain financial aid. A third might be moved to major in sociology or history as a result of this course. A fourth would never take history or sociology again if she could avoid it. A fifth thought it was required, found out it wasn't, but by then it didn't pay to withdraw. One of my students, Beth Adler, told me she wanted to become a cosmetologist, but her parents insisted she go to college first. Well, I thought, of course astronomy would require a college degree.

Knowing Students

If you did know something about student lives, it could make a difference. In honors class, Melissa Hedden asked me how I could pick on her for her language (me and him) when I didn't say anything to Scott Stemley, who came from Patterson Co-op, a city school. After class Scott had come to me because he had a D average, was depending on a scholarship, and should he drop the class? I told him to hang in there, that he obviously belonged in an honors class, that I was sure he would get a C. I found I was quite emotional, tears in my eyes, because something in him connected me to Perth Amboy, N.J., where I come from. I was never Scott, but some of my friends were. He was majoring in electrical engineering, and a total revamping of his grammar might not be necessary. I did identify with his uncouthness, his lack of culture, which I had at his age, even though my grammar was mostly middle-class. Melissa later told me that she also had gone to a city school, but she was certainly suburban by the time she reached college. Perhaps Scott triggered different memories for her.

The possibility of knowing students individually depended on the size and length of class. It was tougher in the five week summer session. I noted in the last week of summer, when I had about 70 students in two classes, that I could identify more than three-quarters, but partly from where they sat. If I looked at the roster, I could recognize them. If I went around the room and tried to name them, I would do less well. If they came to my office, chances were I couldn't identify them. And the next quarter I wouldn't even realize they had been in one of my classes. At least I think that must be so, because I often saw my students in the hallways and on campus when I had them in class, but the next quarter they disappeared. Often they didn't expect to be known, explained that they had me for a course a couple years ago. But if I asked which, they rarely remembered.

One day when Nelle and I were shopping we met two of my former students. One, Mike Stewart, who was graduating in two quarters, had taken a Social Problems course from me. When he remembered me, I remembered him because he was the boyfriend to whom my only German student, Anna Schultz, had switched. Oh, do I remember that class. What a toothache I had! As you can see, Mike Stewart had not deeply penetrated into my life.

Can I Help?

Students had a variety of problems. I did what I could to help, but often didn't go far enough, or else wasted too much time where I couldn't help anyway.

There was Aimee Slocumb. She attended the history class regularly, never spoke, and failed decisively. I asked her (on her paper) to see me after the first exam, but she never did. Usually, you never know anything more. Why didn't she drop the course? Were all her courses going like this?

As it happened, her father dropped by after the course was over with a late paper from Aimee. I told him that she had failed the course and that the paper wouldn't make any difference. He told me she was the oldest of four, the only girl, possibly neglected. I felt mild guilt for never taking her aside, but I rarely got to students who didn't get to me.

It appeared that Aimee would not succeed at Wright State. But looking at the records of older students, there have been many like her who have returned when older and done quite well.

I think, by the way, Mr. Slocumb was the only parent I talked to during the entire year.

The evening following Mr. Slocumb's visit, an older student, Melanie Aper, called. She was late with her take-home, with a reasonable excuse, but wanted to drop her history project—a scavenger hunt at the Dayton Art Institute—because she wouldn't need it to get a C. I calculated she would indeed need to do the hunt and gave her a week's extension.

Did Melanie deserve more consideration than Aimee? Both were weak history students, though they may have been good at something else. But Melanie was ready to look out for herself, to persist, to ask, so there was a good chance she would fight her way through to a C. Aimee took what came, never interacted. If Melanie behaved like that, and perhaps once she had, she would get an F too. For me, there was something admirable in Aimee's fatalism, in that she accepted my grade without asking for special consideration. And sometimes I was exasperated with Melanie's persistence combined with what could be perceived as denseness. But if Melanie could fight her way through to a degree, I didn't doubt she would persist until she got a middle class job she could learn to do well enough, and she would have the tenacity to fight through problems. She might be perceived as nettlesome sometimes, but so are a lot of people who are nevertheless effective at what they do.

Occasionally a problem would come up that I felt was out of my realm. To what extent should you spend your time exploring the bureaucracy? Cindi Carlson, one of the students in the history class, told me she had just got into the learning disability program, but would be dropped from school if she didn't get a C and a B in her summer courses. And she had gotten a D in her first exam. I was skeptical. Why would she be dropped when she had just gotten into the program? Was she trying to con me into easing up on her grades? Well, this time I gave Disability Services a call.

Pat Schlaerth, who was in charge of learning disabilities, confirmed that Cindi was right. She was on probation as a regular student and would be discharged if she didn't get at least a C and a B in summer school. Her grades were low, of course, because she had the learning disability. So Pat decided to talk to Judy Roller, director of University Advising, to see what could be done. But on this occasion I went to more trouble than I normally would have; and I have to wonder, if I hadn't been looking at the event as a participant observer and being perhaps a little more curious than I would have been otherwise, whether I would have made the call to Pat.

Keith Hudson (Ch. 4) dropped by to ask if he could leave the evening Occupations class early because the last bus left before evening classes ended. I had tried years ago, without success, to get a 10 o'clock bus from the Regional Transit Authority. So I asked him in class what his address was, and if anyone would be going that way. No one volunteered to take him home. I said I would, but he left class before it was over, and dropped the class. No wonder! Wouldn't you be insulted if your teacher asked for a volunteer to run you home and no one did? That was a ham-handed risk I took.

In the spring Keith took Industrial Sociology, and this time I took him downtown (an alternate route, for me, but scarcely a detour) most weeks. Keith was an interesting person, and I wondered why I hadn't offered him a ride in the first place. Was it a need to keep a distance from students or perhaps a desire for privacy from an introvert coming out of three hours of class? In any event, it got me to renew my efforts to secure a 10 o'clock bus.

A tragicomic intruder in the Occupations class was Ron Flint. My first note on him was that I had better warn Terri Limbert, the chair of the Class Committee assigned to produce an edited book of interviews. Ron was a Vietnam veteran who wore a Vietnam cap, who appeared to have been drinking, possibly was drunk.

But before I got around to it, I became aware that Ron seemed to be managing all right on the committee. He was assigned to pick up the interviews after they had been copied, so that I could grade one set while the committee was organizing the other. He seemed to be carrying out his duties responsibly, and students did not complain about him. Nor did they object when he asked time consuming questions in class.

He dropped in at the office often and I came to understand that he was getting some counseling from the Veterans Administration and was not drunk but on medication. He seemed to have very low self-esteem, wondered what he had done for society in his 42 years. So the Vietnam cap, though it singled him out, was a good thing. Moreover his work seemed to be competent.

Life is tough for lots of people. Ron had already made the decision to come back and, whatever doubts he may have had, he was hanging in there and passing his courses. Other students seemed to recognize and respect that.

Occasionally I got the feeling that I had helped students academically, and not only because they wrote better essays at the end of a course than at the beginning. One day Dr. Robert Lowry was preaching in church on the menstrually bleeding woman who was helped by touching Jesus's garment. It made me think of Karen Gary the previous Friday—she's going to love this analogy—when, talking to her about the history class, I felt she'd gotten something from my power, learned something about sociological perspective, was challenged to give this general education course more time than she had intended to. I must admit, however, that this is the only Jesus experience I can find in my notes.

Because I taught Occupations and Careers, I often got requests for help from students in their job hunts. James Edwards, usually rather somber, was smiling as he told me that his interviews had gotten him a new banking job at a higher level. And, incredibly, Rhonda Matthews-Hunter, who often seemed to court the image of airhead, called to ask for advice in following up a successful marketing interview. And I had to realize that Rhonda, whom students tell me came late into an exam asking why everyone was writing, might all the same be competent at what she did, able to make wise choices in the purchase of clothes, able to persuade others that she could do so. It was probably well to remember, also, that I would appear to be extremely odd if I attempted to do either.

It was rare for students to talk to me about personal problems. There were only two occasions when I recorded conversations of this kind. Jason Christensen told me his girl friend had ovarian cancer and this was causing stress between them. Listening to him, a high extrovert in the Myers-Briggs test, it was obvious that he was the kind of person who solved problems by confronting them and she apparently was more private. I couldn't get him to relax. I gave him Psychologist Dennis O'Grady's phone number, told him to take care of himself first; and perhaps he could then help her. Probably O'Grady was beyond his pocketbook.

Then Leanne Clare came in to ask a question, wound up giving me her life story. This included receiving and spending a considerable fortune, leaving her in the position of establishing herself as independent from her family and poor enough for financial aid. It seemed that you needed to be two years away from your family and in that time to have made at least $4,000, enough to establish financial independence.

I don't want to forget Paul Barrett coming along to discuss why some countries fail to develop even though they have resources and industrial transplants. He needed to have the answer for a coming exam, but what was striking was that he had one and was pleased with it. A student might come to discuss an answer because he was having trouble or wanted reassurance, but not just because the question was intrinsically interesting. Probably I didn't encourage this kind of question. I mean, I had too much work to be bothered by students' idle surmises about why the world is as it is!

Many of our students were classified as non-traditional, meaning that they were older than the 18–24 age category of the majority of the students. Eric Barton, for instance, had dropped out of college, but was returning now as one of my advisees to complete his degree. He had half a dozen "X"s to make up, X being the grade we gave to a student who signed up for a course, never attended, but neglected to drop. When a student had many of those, that suggested it was a hectic or stressful period in his life. Now Eric had a middle class job, needed to complete his degree in order to gain promotion.

Susan Lippencott, another non-traditional student, came in to ask if she could take an independent study to substitute for a Social Problems requirement since she had a scheduling conflict. She hoped to graduate in June, but in order to do so she needed to take two courses that were scheduled at the same time. In that situation I could have given her a directed study option, which would mean she would read the books and take the examinations but not attend the classes. (Some students very nearly do that anyway.) But since this was a sophomore level class and she had considerable education and experience, it was probably better to help her design an independent study that would give her some special insight into social problems.

This was something we did a few times a year, and I think it is a measure of faculty professionalism. The student would take the independent study, the faculty member would read the material, make suggestions, and the student would rewrite. There was no extra pay for this service, but sometimes it just seemed to be a sensible, unbureaucratic solution to a student's problem.

Susan's study took an interesting turn. She was interested in homelessness; and Charles Hartmann, who was on the Salvation Army Board of Directors, knew of an internship available at Booth House, which was established to deal with homelessness. The internee would screen people who came to Booth House, selecting out those who could be helped to find housing and a job. While they were being helped, Booth House would take them in for 30 days. It was for the screener to make the initial decision on whether a person should be admitted, whether the person had other sources of help, or whether his situation was such that Booth House could not help. In other words, a kind of triage was being practiced, a very responsible position for an intern. Susan handled the position very well and at the end of her internship was offered a permanent position, which she declined. Given the amount of work she was doing, instead of assigning her a written paper, I asked her to talk to my Social Problems class on what she had learned about homelessness.

Ethics and Values

In discussing Cindi Carlson's problems trying to avoid dismissal, I mentioned that I wondered if she were conning me. This thought
probably occurs to faculty members too often. For instance, both
Leanne Clair and Courtney Holmes said they had turned in their
Erasmus-Luther take homes, though I had no record of receiving
them. I carried all the exams in the same section of a folder, so it
didn't seem likely that I would lose two of them. But I was inclined
to believe both. Courtney's performance was so strong on the regular exam that she didn't seem to be the kind of person who would
not do her take home. Leanne said she had put it in my mailbox at
the direction of Patrick Jones, one of our work study students. Her
willingness to take an immediate oral and her identification of Pat
seemed to confirm that she had handed it in.

And sometimes it happened that the improbable was so. Take
the case of *Henry V*. For the history class I had ordered separate
volumes of the Henry IV and V plays. Perhaps because Henry IV
has two parts and hence two volumes, the Bookstore never ordered
Henry V. Oh well, it was available in every local library and since
our students come from all around the city, there should be plenty
for all, right?

Wrong, apparently. Students said they couldn't find it in the local library or on the family bookshelf. But the next day a student
from another section said there were about eight copies in our own
University Library when he looked a few days before. So I checked
and immediately found four, two more in obvious collections, and
undoubtedly more still if I wanted to hunt.

What did this say? Had I been conned? Perhaps by one or two
students. But probably most told the truth. One student remarked
that she just had no time to get to the Wright State Library. She
probably had back to back classes and then was off at noon to get
to her job. Others, like me, probably thought our own library was
hopeless because everyone would look there first. Others wouldn't
know that the particular play would be found in a volume of collected plays, and the local library wouldn't catalogue them by individual plays.

So I rode with it, giving extensions without penalty. There are
problems with that, too but it's impossible to be absolutely even
handed. Different people are in different situations. In the end, nearly
everybody read *Henry V* and the few who didn't lost a letter grade.

But had I given an inaccurate lesson about the world? I hope not. The world offers many responses. Sometimes people will be accommodating, sometimes not. If I had tried to figure out who was conning me and who not, I would have used a great deal of time that should have been given to the problems posed by *Henry V.* Such as the fate of Bardolph, who conned once too often.

And sometimes what appears to be outrageous cheating turns out to be genuine innocence. Monica McLendon complained that she received a lower grade than Tye Rome Smith even though she turned in the exact same paper. They worked together and turned in two identical copies. One could cry plagiarism and fail them both, but consider the context. One weakness of commuter universities is that students don't interact enough, and there is lots of research to indicate that students learn more from other students than they do from their teachers. (We all say so, anyway but I hope you don't ask me to cite the research.) So I encouraged students to cooperate in doing take homes. I also said that each should write her own but you can see that that particular point may get lost, especially if a student hadn't been socialized against plagiarism. So I explained about the concept of plagiarism, and told her that she could get in trouble, get an F on a paper, even fail a course, if she and another student submitted identical papers, even in different courses. I said I thought it valid to study together, but that I had penalized them each for their similar reports (taking two-thirds of a letter off pretty good grades). I might have taken off more had I not known they were innocent but I knew they were before Monica had complained, because they turned their papers in together. So the reduced grade was for failure to follow instructions, not for moral deviance. (Why did two identical papers receive different grades? My notes don't say.)

Part of a student's socialization is learning to become a professional. We model best if we treat them as professionals. Did this mean that some students would cheat and get away with it? In the short run, possibly, in general education classes that were mostly multiple choice. But when they reached the upper level, they would have to fend for themselves and hopefully the professional role would begin to have its effect as they encountered other students who didn't cheat and as they had more personal interaction with faculty members. Could a student cheat his way through general education, then reform when he reached the upper level? Possibly, but you have to assume a penalty in that he would be less well prepared for the upper level courses. If, despite cheating instead of studying, he weren't less well prepared, maybe there was something wrong with the introductory level courses.

I noticed that in the Occupations class, I often treated professional honesty as a pragmatic matter. What is the trade off for honesty? You hated to be in the position of arguing (as I did) that honesty pays, that you ought to be honest because your reputation is valuable.

Student Perceptions of Shakespeare and Mozart

Shakespeare. Some students liked him, some hated the language. But you had Shakespeare in high school, I said. Couldn't understand him then either, they replied. Sometimes they did miss the context. When Falstaff says "Banish Jack, Banish the World" and Harry says "I will," many thought he had acceded to Falstaff's request.

But often they were more perceptive than I. There was considerable discussion about who told Northumberland of Hotspur's death. My official answer was that no one dared tell him, and he inferred it from the context of their replies. But Travers is told that Hotspur's spur was cold and later Northumberland asks, "Said he his spur was cold?" John Williams thought this might have been a euphemism for death. At another point Morton says Douglas lives, but as for your son—"He is dead!" cries Northumberland. Considerable discussion among the students about whether Morton gave some nonverbal indication. How were we to settle nonverbals in written plays?

Sometimes student perceptions were truly amazing, as if from some other culture and yet they made sense if I could make the cultural leap. I played Praetorius, Bach and Mozart one morning to show change in style and instrumentation in music from the 17th to the 18th century. Melanie Aper, whose persistence I have commended above, asked (if I understood her) how 18th century music could be recorded.

She was not a traditional student, was probably in her thirties. But she had been sent to see paintings at the Dayton Art Institute, which after all was done by 17th- and 18th-century painters, and

had heard only music played or recorded by 20th-century performers. So it seemed logical to ask how they could make recordings of
earlier performers when the technology for recordings had not yet
been invented. On the one hand it seemed remarkably dumb but on
the other rather perceptive. If I had been writing fiction about college teaching, I never would have had the imagination to give a
student such a question.

In the regular Social Life course I had a Chinese student, Li Xue,
who would ask questions about, say, the Jane Jacobs take home.
What is a landmark? What is a border vacuum? Jacobs' *Death and
Life of the Great American City* is a pretty long book, and I had assumed that students would do some skimming between finding the
answers to my questions. I suggested to Xue that she might try that,
skimming the chapters. It must have been a revelation to her. From
preference or culture or both, she did the assigned reading completely and when it was supposed to be done. The result was that
she always had lots of questions while the American-born students
did not, probably because they waited for the lecture to guide them
in the reading. I found I had become confused about what I wanted.
I wanted them to read ahead of time, as Xue did, but I wanted her to
skim, as they did.

Tye Rome Smith came in one day to ask some sensible questions about studying for an exam. More students, I thought, ought
to do this. Yet I didn't really encourage it, didn't repeatedly suggest
that they come in, because it would be like asking for a run on the
bank. How could I get anything done if students kept bothering me
during office hours? So I compromised. They were given rosters
listing their classmates' names, addresses and telephone numbers,
and encouraged to contact each other, study together. All this was
consistent with theory about students' helping each other, but might
it have suggested that I didn't want them bothering me?

Discussing registration for the next quarter, Ed Swann told me
one day that on the first day of registration, students came in the
wee hours of the morning, as if they were lining up to buy tickets
for a rock concert. I had been at Wright State for nearly 14 years and
had never known that. When I was at a private college, I participated in the enrollment process. Now it had nothing to do with me,
except when I needed to help one of my advisees get into a class
that had been closed.

The Careers course often provided interesting insights into students' lives and personalities. One evening we were discussing an

exercise on complex tasks and matching them with Myers-Briggs preference profiles. John Gibbs, an ISFJ, an introvert who preferred to make decisions from feeling, gave a very complete account of what is needed to coach a young soccer team, with a lot of consideration for how it felt to be a player. A good coach, possibly, for a young team, but not for one that had to win? Chris Viola, a total extrovert, chose to describe learning to play a guitar, an individual activity, but also one that leads to performance. Don Barnette, with an ESTJ, described with considerable enthusiasm the work of a cashier foreman. He had interaction with others, a job that required accuracy, thinking and closure, exactly what the profile suggested. Suddenly his enthusiasm was explicable.

Was there consistency between work and the rest of our lives? The students also tried to examine their personal values. It was interesting to compare the values that never marrieds like Joan Beddies and Beth Patterson were looking for in a husband—sensitivity, intelligence, love, honesty, faithfulness—against those of a married like Janet Hall: does he have a degree, a good job, car paid for, willingness to help with housework and, as an afterthought, even some shared values?

Joan, a paraplegic who was not far from being quadruplegic, also gave us some insight into her life in a very positive way. She told about achieving independent living: this Tuesday her apartment, next Tuesday her van!

About My Grade

Melissa Heddon stopped me to discuss a C she got in an honors writing quiz. She told me how hard she worked over the weekend and I worked on socializing her against that argument. It will never carry in organizational situations to respond to a criticism by saying that you had worked very hard. That is taken for granted. Then I tried to help her on reorganization, which she agreed was needed, toward writing a better paper with less work next week. But you may have noted elsewhere that I rarely miss an opportunity to complain about how hard I work. Given the value we place on hard work, we really don't want to make it look easy.

Tim Jerome came up one morning to ask what he would need to get an A in Industrial Sociology. It turned out that he'd need an A in both his fourth exam and the final, whereas there was very little chance he'd not get a B. I suggested he go for the A in the fourth exam, and if he didn't get it, relax in the final, just do a decent job. Was it good education to give that kind of advice? I suppose it was in the sense that students with many responsibilities have to decide how they are going to use their time. But there were contextual factors. Tim was an older student. I might not have responded in such a matter of fact way if it had been an 18 year old.

On another morning Brian Coy came in to express concern about a 79 final grade he got in the Social Life course, which translated into a C. An 80 would have gotten him a B. He had sent me a note saying he needed high grades to get into law school, that he usually got A's, and would I reconsider his grade. I explained to him why I could not raise a grade soley because a student thought he might need it. Brian's questioning the grade came from different faculty and students' perceptions of general education. Faculty members tended to perceive that general courses were important to liberal education. But a student focused on law school perceives he must get the best grades he can, and this makes a course like Social Life seem an irrelevant obstacle. What was perhaps more surprising is that Brian was the only student all year to argue what lots of other students must be feeling: if we must have general education requirements, keep the courses clear and easy.

It sometimes happened that because an introductory sociology class stressed perception rather than a clear-cut set of answers that you can learn, a student who generally did very well in upper level courses found herself faltering in an introductory class. Aprell Evans, who participated actively in the class and was unquestionably intelligent, got what may have been her first college C. She challenged often but ineffectively, demonstrating beyond question that recognizing the example was not easy for her. To a student who rarely gets a B, it must have been highly frustrating to get a C in this required general education course in which the game seemed different from that played in other courses.

Worst of all was the fate of Tye Rome Smith, who has already been noted as a diligent student who asked intelligent questions. Even his studying with Monica McLendon was following the suggestion of the teacher. In my conversation with Monica I mentioned that Tye had not challenged the final, and that was not like him. Later that morning I found on my desk a note from Tye saying

"No Challenges." Too late. I made my comment to Monica because I felt for Tye, knowing that the failure to challenge had cost him a letter.

It got worse. Tye came in and I explained that the grades had been calculated, there was always someone who just misses, but over the four years those things even out. You don't notice when you just make the next highest grade, only when you just miss it. Then Jeanne came in, said Tye had been in to complain that I'd revealed his grade to a fellow student. True, it was a violation of confidence, though of course I knew that he and Monica were friends, studied together. So I felt terrible that I had made the situation worse. In fact, there wouldn't have been any situation if I hadn't been open with Monica.

Why, then, not give Tye the higher letter since it was so close? I guess because there had to be a point at which the next grade is given, and the criteria had to be the same for all. There may be another student with an equal case who stoically accepted the verdict as fair.

Luck was otherwise for Rhonda Matthews-Hunter, the future adjudicator of fashion. She came in on the day I was going to convert her I to an F. An I is an incomplete, and when you give it the student gets a form that gives the date on which the grade will be converted to F if the work is not completed or negotiated. The date had gone by for the Careers course, and I had the form in a file for action. But it took several days to get to it, and on the day it reached the top of the pile, Rhonda breezed in—that's absolutely the verb—and we were able to set in motion whatever needed to be done to complete the course. I had not been aware of it before, but Rhonda, the epitome of irresponsibility, was not penalized while Tye Rome Smith, always responsible and conscientious, was. Wait till he sees that! (There is a good chance Tye will read this, very little that Rhonda will.)

Was I always fair? Of course I thought I tried to be. One day I noted, in the interest of fairness, that I had given Ron Flint a D+ because that's what his paper deserved and he needed to be kept on the mark even if he had extra handicaps to fight. But then I noted that I had given Terri Limbert a C for a poor effort. Why not a D? Because her paper was better than Ron's? Or because even a C would be a shock to her? Or because she had managed the Fourth Hour and I felt a debt? Or worse, because she was prettier than Ron? Would the D have been good for her, the C good for Ron?

Future Careers

Much of the work in the Careers course, naturally, concerned future careers. One exercise was to write about an ideal job, what the student hoped she would find in the job, get from her work. Carleton Harris wanted power. He wanted to have significant influence on the prison system. What a monumental ambition! Carole Durcynski wanted respect. No (more?) doing thankless work, a very realistic and important expectation. Vicky Lewis had real dissonance between her training to be a school social worker and her strong desire for freedom from economic worries. Michael Netzley wanted to be in control of the pace. How I sympathized with that, though I never would have thought of it at his age.

On another day Michael made the observation that he wanted a helping position, but not under extreme conditions. Exactly. How did he know this already? When Mike Pratt, who had wide experience in the juvenile offender field, discussed the narrow area between case hardening and burnout, I thought how lucky I was to have a job in which I could help people who have a reasonable expectation of benefiting from that help. Our students may not always write profound thoughts in concise paragraphs, but they were likely to go on to middle class jobs and live productive lives.

Lee Anne Clare reported on an interview she had at Booth House, where Susan Lippencott had practiced triage. She discussed how stressful it would be to play God and decide whether a person would be admitted, with a chance for housing and job. It was interesting that Lee Anne, who wanted a low stress position, nevertheless would have been willing to take the position if it carried a higher salary. We are all fearful that if we turn down a job, there may never be another offered.

Another day, Cynthia Swinger dropped by and we discussed her future as a prosecuting attorney. I could see the articulate, red haired Cynthia as a prosecutor and wondered if it would come to pass. Lots of times you never knew.

I had a chance to talk further with Carleton Harris about the prison system. How would you make a significant impact? What could he do in his life to shorten terms and uncrowd the prisons? Should he aim to become a legislator, a prison official, a criminologist, a journalist, a judge? If improving the system is what you want to do, and you are graduating from a third tier university with a decent but not spectacular grade point average, what would you aim to be? Again, I wondered what would happen.

Most students, like most people, would probably not reach the level they hoped to reach or achieve what they hoped to achieve. Some would do better than they ever dreamed. Is it better to have high ambitions, achieve something but less than you hoped, and be disappointed? Or to have low aspirations, achieve more than you expected, be generally satisfied, but still have achieved less than you might have?

How did you advise? I thought of Malcolm X's high school teacher giving the best advice he could. Be realistic. Consider your situation. Forget being a lawyer and think about being a carpenter. You are likable and articulate. You'd get a lot of business.

Graduate Students

I had relatively little contact with graduate students, except for two graduate committees. One of these involved Patti Myers, a nursing student whose thesis concerned the attitudes of patients toward male nurses in maternity care. I was the outside member, invited because Patti had taken the graduate Occupations course from me. My contribution at the preliminary review of her proposal was possibly of limited value, because much of the time I didn't know what they were talking about. What on earth is Cronbach's Alpha Coefficiency Test?

I chaired the committee for Humanities major Peg Regan, who was exploring the Mexican worldview. The other members of the ommittee were Charles Berry, who taught Latin American History, and Dave Petreman, a poet and member of the Modern Language Department, who was interested in Latin American literature.

Charles reacted very strongly against Peg's first draft of her thesis. Dave and I were more accommodating, seeing it as a reasonable beginning on a subject that is difficult to demonstrate in detail. When I responded to Peg, however, it was amazing how well Berry's criticisms blended with our more supportive approach. Charles, of course, was not unaware that I would do this, so he could fume a bit to me, knowing that my version of the committee response would be more euphemistic.

Discussing the memo with Dave Orenstein, who chaired the Humanities program, I inferred that Berry and Petreman had had differences on a previous committee and that each might be chary of further encounters. Whether or not that was the case, it turned out that each was willing to accept my written version. Neither thought a committee meeting necessary at that stage or, as it turned out, any other stage. Peg completed her thesis without ever meeting her committee.

Tina Garrison blew the class away. I had invited her to speak to a Careers class because, as an alumna, she had written an article in the Department News Letter on using a sociology degree to enter a career. Her presentation was dynamic. Like many other graduate students, she was already involved in a career, about which she was committed and excited. What particularly intrigued us was her unusual interview experience. She was involved in a group interview in which the candidates for the position met one another. So she had a chance to size up her competition, to see who really was competitive for the position, and ultimately to know whom she had beaten. Then she had another interview in which she alone was interviewed by a panel of 20. It was a fascinating presentation and it showed that even though there may be a large number of applicants for a position, if you choose carefully you should be one of the few who *really* is a candidate.

And then there was Francis Padinjarekara, a graduate student in the Professional Psychology Program, for whom I had served as mentor as well as committee member. In August he left for his internship at the University of Wisconsin. I had learned a great deal from this intelligent Jesuit from Kerala. (Yes, Jesuit. His family, he said, had been Catholic since the mission of St. Thomas.) I felt I hadn't provided much guidance as mentor, but he was a person who ministered, so that wasn't necessary. Though Christian, he was much interested in and possibly influenced by the Indian philosopher Krishnamurti, who felt we needed to stop striving, stop thinking, stop meditating, stop worrying about our identity. So here was this Jesuit, having completed his education in a college that emphasized self esteem, going into the world to tell people to cool it, not to worry so much about who they were.

How the Students Felt

I have referred to the student evaluations of the Occupations class. Besides numerical evaluations, there were also spaces for comments and some of these provided a great deal of insight. For instance, in the Social Life class, there were three comments on "communication of subject":

> "Need to work on giving direct answers when question is asked."
>
> "He eluded everything and every question."
>
> "You're as bad as Jacobs when it comes to simply answering a question—by the time you get to the answer you've confused the hell out of me."

These were revealing comments. Nelle had remarked with exasperation that I don't answer her questions, but go off on a tangent. As I saw it, I was backgrounding context for the answer. Could this be why, when I asked for questions, even if I counted to six, often I didn't get any? Were they thinking, what's the use?

There was no doubt that the honors class was my favorite. The class had done more in ten weeks than any previous introductory class I could remember. But would the students realize that? After all, they didn't have other introductory courses for comparison.

Honors evaluations didn't have numbers, just comments. And I had never seen such a skewed set of responses.

> Does the course belong in the Honors curriculum?
> "Nope. No. No. No. No. What were you people thinking anyway?"
>
> "This honors course was great compared to regular courses."

> Chief Benefit?
> "The value of a bad example."
>
> "Being able to adjust to using my thoughts by voicing them."

> If one thing were to be changed?
> "More structure would be the first step. (You know, one small step for Melko, one giant step for teaching . . .)"
>
> "It is the time for experimentation and Dr. Melko did an excellent job."

Describe the atmosphere of the class.

"Most of the students were confused about most everything."

"Wonderful—Excellent—couldn't ask for anything more."

And so it went, from awful to wonderful, with the class about evenly divided. What was I to make of it? Could it be that I was so original that many students didn't understand what was happening? Could they benefit even if they didn't understand? Or could it be that I was just not facing up to reality? What was wrong with appearing to be organized? What was wrong with clarity of communication?

And yet, I have to admit, I was really delighted with this evaluation. Just what you would expect from such a feisty class. I thought it was one of my best classes ever!

How the Teachers Felt

We often talked among ourselves about our students and certainly faculty members played "Ain't it Awful?" Al Spetter told me at the elevator that in the general education history course he had directed his students to choose and read a biography, which he had to be approve. He was disconcerted by the number of students who were bringing in eighth grade biographies from their local libraries. Now we ought, perhaps, to have talked more about our outstanding students, but "Ain't It Awful?" probably helped preserve our perspective. For one thing, it helped morale to hear that you weren't the only faculty member encountering students for whom studying was not a first commitment.

When Dennis Rome worried about the amazing excuses he was receiving from students who failed to hand in assignments, I managed to take the pompous high road. We had an open admissions system and some students were going to fail. It isn't possible to succeed with everyone. Don't worry about being conned; pay attention to what is effective. Easy to say. You would think I never worried about reaching all or being conned.

Similarly Katie Workman, another new teacher, pulled a long face when I asked her about her first quarter history classes. She felt she was getting hostile questions, wasn't seeing much evidence that students wanted to learn, she'd just have to tough it out. Probably it was most difficult to come out of graduate school, surrounded by smart people, and return to freshman classes where the majority of students were ordinary.

One summer day, Orenstein and I were talking about ordering books and we agreed that probably most faculty did not pay too much attention to the cost of books. This turned out to be one time I violated my planned method (Ch. 1) and did a survey that I'm sure I wouldn't have done if I hadn't been taking field notes. I asked seven other faculty members (Henry Ruminski, Bill Irvine, Ellen Murray, Don Swanson, Cynthia King, Jan Gabbert and Spetter) how much they thought a student should pay for books for each class and all had immediate answers ranging from $25 to $50 per course. So within the Liberal Arts College, at least, the faculty did care about book costs.

There are many notes that suggest there were a lot of concerned teachers in the university. I attended a fall meeting of the general education history teachers in which there were enthusiastic discussions of what works. They read each other's student essays and discussed how to grade them. Marvelous! They graded for improvement, meaning they had to remember or have a record of earlier performances. But they had high standards, were shocked at the writing. I was embarrassed because I thought the writing was adequate. Had my standards of acceptability eroded over time?

There were differences in standards. Jan Gabbert argued that ultimately it was performance, not effort or improvement that ought to be the criterion for judgment. When the student reached her occupation, that would be the criterion. Martin Arbagi said he gave a good grade for a gracefully written empty essay because it was a pleasure to read after a series of clumsy, content filled efforts. Using Jan's standard, perhaps empty grace is sometimes rewarded in life as well?

Then the real world intruded. How did you feel when confronted by 180 essays (60 from each of three classes)? If you took six minutes each, that would be ten hours' work. Peter Taylor, who was running this session, concluded that all you could do would be to say what should be maintained and what should be worked on. No remembering past performances in that situation.

Often Orenstein would drop in with a new breakthrough. He had finally figured out how to teach Weber: *Protestant Ethic* last instead of first. He went on to explain why this worked better, and I punctuated with what tried to sound like intelligent assents. But I was really responding more to his enthusiasm and remembering again what it was like to be a student in a theories course, wondering why I was there.

Perhaps the greatest impact from a young teacher came from Carolyn Stephens (Ch. 4). Arriving at Wright State in the summer as a Visiting Assistant Professor, she was to begin teaching history classes in the fall. So she prepared herself by attending Dave Robinson's summer class on the Ancient World, then mine on medieval and early modern European history. She went with me to hunt slides and tapes for a class on Baroque aesthetics and she was so delightful, so enthusiastic. I don't suppose I was ever that enthusiastic, but watching and listening to her recalled how wonderful it seemed when you first began teaching.

Even when we went to academic conferences, we often talked about teaching and students. Sociologist Midori Rynn of the University of Scranton, at a California meeting (Ch. 7), told me she was happy that she was a teacher. She always tried to give her students her best. By contrast, when the same association met the next spring in Illinois, Larry Wolf of Cincinnati and Art Iberall of UCLA entertained us with memories of New York's City College where students couldn't afford to buy the books, battled to read them in the library. Teachers, Ibby asserted, hated the students because they reminded them where they came from.

But in the 1990's, perhaps we had a different problem. We went to prestigious graduate schools, were at least a generation away from the city streets, could no longer remember or never knew where our parents came from. So we were having difficulty understanding both city and suburban students of ordinary ability who were not socialized to love learning and whose parents perhaps took a more pragmatic view of the value of higher education.

Afterword

Ron Flint did graduate, and called me occasionally. He never was able to secure a regular job, lived apparently on a government disability pension, a casualty of the war in Vietnam. I've advised him to explore the Graduate Humanities Program. He seems to thrive best in a university culture.

Some time after he graduated, Norma Shepelak discovered Don Barnette bagging groceries in the supermarket. While this may have been an excellent job for his Myers-Briggs profile, we didn't think it appropriate for his education. We got him to take two Corrections Internships from Ellen Murray, so he would be able to apply for a position in the Corrections field. He would make more money (well, somewhat) and have more prestige, but he wouldn't get the closure he got from bagging groceries.

After graduating, Susan Lippencott worked in the Family Service Department, out of which my wife also worked. This was after she had become Susan Rickert, wife of Bill Rickert.

One unexpected change that came within a couple of years was the end of long registration lines. It became possible for students to register by Lemming, oops, that is by Raider Express. You phoned a Computer that sounded just like Jim Sayer and arranged your class schedule. Humph, older Wright State graduates would be able to say, in my day we stood in line all night long to register for classes. You kids have it so easy!

The problem of how to read 180 papers from three classes soon disappeared. Within a couple years, no one in the History Department was teaching a general education class smaller than 90, and the problem had become how to get maximum value from multiple choice exams.

In reading the final draft, I can't find any place in which I ever explained the Myers-Briggs profiles. These were short tests given in the Careers and Occupations courses, perhaps others, that gave a quick profile on student preferences. They roughly measure a person's tendencies toward:

- introversion or extroversion (I or E);
- sensing or intuition (S or N) i.e., a preference for overview or for a hands-on approach;
- making decisions based on thinking or feeling (T or F);
- judging or perceiving (J or P), i.e., preference for closure or for remaining open for more information which also relates to a tendency to plan or to go with the situation.

These preferences were often considered in relation to the kind of career a student might consider.

What happens to students in the long run? We don't know, of course, but the Careers class had a "Happy Birthday" exercise that allowed them to project their future careers. They were asked to imagine it was their 70th birthday, and they were to look back on their lives.

On careers, these reports were disappointingly empty. They had been successful, but didn't know how. But when it came to families, they could be specific. Susan Makowski was the mother of the ambassador to Sweden. Robert Brun was married to a third wife. Melissa Peltier was widowed. Heather Rossler had twins when she was 48.

7

The Scholar

Writes War and Peace, *Participates in the
Scientific Enterprise, and Receives a Call from the East*

It will be interesting to make a note of what happened to the various articles and books in the course of a single year. Well, interesting to me.

A cautionary entry for November 23.

For many professors, research is one of the perks of the job.
But there is no doubt that I am more interested in my research
than anyone else would be. I have tried to keep that in mind, but it
has not been easy. Writing was what I did first. It is an integral part
of the profession. Doctors and lawyers are not expected to write
books and articles, but professors are expected to be scholars. For
some of us, this was a major factor in choice of profession. What we
would have done as an avocation, we are actually encouraged and
paid to do!

Usually I tried to set aside two morning hours for research. Most
of the research I did could be organized around book manuscripts.
If I were writing a book, I was also giving papers from it at meetings
so I could get feedback from other researchers. The papers, in turn,
could be developed into articles. Except for an occasional article on
teaching, there was very little I wrote that was not related to a book
manuscript in progress or recently completed.

Peace in Our Time

Perhaps I can illustrate some of this by focusing on a book that happened to be coming out in the year studied. In July I received a call from Ed Page, copy editor of Paragon House, wondering if I had received the proofs for *Peace in Our Time*. They had been sent to Wright State, and in this period I was extending my sabbatical, working at home, so I didn't realize they had arrived. I had to drop everything else, go in to get the proofs, and read them in a few days, less time than I would like to have had. It happened at the time the proofs were sent that I was reviewing John Nef's *War and Human Progress* (1968) in relation to another manuscript. Writing about World War II, Nef saw a moral decline in the 20th century, an inability to distinguish right from wrong because of the development of relativism. For example, he thought the nonsense of abstract art made people less able to see Hitler for what he was. There was a loss of proportion, a loss of a sense of beauty.

In the fifties, when Nef was writing, I was inclined to see the problem as he did. But early in the 1970's I began to think, rather, that the period Nef was writing about was a crisis time. There was more irrationality because an older set of values was being replaced. I began to make the case for this idea in the manuscript that became *Peace in Our Time*. The present period, then, I saw as an age, like the Victorian Age, but with a different set of dominant premises.

This was not the kind of idea you could prove. You could only say, suppose this were the case. If it were, we should expect to find certain phenomena, ideas, ways of seeing. Then you looked for them and, of course, found them. Once I had invested a certain amount of time gathering evidence supporting my idea, I'm sure I began to look at contrary evidence not as what it was but as a problem to be disposed of.

In the period in which I was reading the proofs, I noticed that in the coming International Studies Association meeting Jack Levy was doing a session on what he called "The Long Peace." That was *my* peace! I had discovered it 20 years ago, when I began work on what would become *Peace in Our Time*, but editors told me I was simply wrong. In a way it was gratifying to find others agreeing; but in another way it was disappointing, because I didn't get credit for it. Telling this to Nelle, I said if you are going to work cooperatively with your colleagues, you can't expect to get credit. What is supposed to happen is that you check one another out by responding to criticism, by testing each other's hypotheses, until all of you get a better picture. (But it was still my Peace!)

A few months later, composer Ellen Jane Porter and I were comparing the work of composer and author in terms of mediators. The composer's work gets expressed through the conductor's interpretation and the performer's abilities; the author's, through readers and editors. *Peace in Our Time* was filtered through four readers and two editors, so I could empathize with a composer. Ron Davidson, on WDPR, the local classical station, said that Toscanini made his reputation by getting back to the original music as the composer wrote it, brushing off the influence of a sequence of interpretations. Since, contrary to Nelle's advice, my originals had been discarded, no one would ever know how I originally wrote it. Even I wouldn't know.

By November I was becoming nervous. Events in Europe were occurring too rapidly and if I still had the manuscript, I would have made some changes. In December I had a note from Alex Holzman, editor of the Ohio State University Press, that *Publisher's Weekly* had reviewed PT favorably. So where was the book? I called Paragon and learned it was now scheduled for February. And in the previous summer all that proofreading had to be done in three seconds?

The book arrived in January, a birthday present, blue cover, white print, some uncomfortable spacing that I rather liked. It was also nice, I have to admit, to see my name on the cover in big letters, as if the author were as important as the title. This is vanity, to be sure. But since college days, when I discovered a book by Ellsworth Barnard, one of my professors, on the library bookshelf, there had been a mystique about having a book published. This was all the more wonderful if it had a handsome jacket.

I left it in the department office. It wasn't necessary to provide wine and cheese because, for insurance reasons, we were no longer allowed to serve wine before five o'clock.

So it was finally out. It had begun as "The Relational Age" in the 1970's, with the stress on the kind of period we were living in rather than the long peace, which was then not so long. Narasim Katary and then Tom Koebernick co-authored that draft, but I just couldn't sell it. Editors rejected the prospectus without looking at the manuscript, telling me that we were simply wrong, it wasn't a time of peace. Students rioting in the streets, Vietnam, what was I talking about? In the 1980's I reorganized it, making peace the main theme, the age secondary. This time I got some articles accepted and finally the book, but by the time I had coped with readers and routine publisher's delays, events in Europe that were consistent with the book's thesis had made it look obsolescent. Predicting the future looks more impressive than predicting the past. On the other hand, while the book was now less controversial, it could also be more mainstream and easier to understand.

Over the next couple months I did some of the pleasanter things that go with a book, sending copies to my children, leaving one for Nelle on the coffee table. In the past I would have sent a copy to my mother, who would have seen to it that folks back home heard about it. She had died, however, early in the previous year, and never knew that the book was dedicated to her and her great granddaughter. So I sent it to people she might have sent it to: a couple of my cousins; George Pollack, a former law partner of my father's who sometimes asked about my books; Gene Young, a friend since grade school; and Harned Isele, a Mayo Clinic doctor who, I guess, represented my high school class. As if to say, look guys, the class clown produced something serious. Childish, of course, but our ambitions were formed in those years. By the time we achieved any of them, if we should be so lucky, the people we wanted to impress had either died or left the scene.

I sent copies of the acknowledgments to the people who were acknowledged, the early co-authors, Betty Snow who typed it, outside readers, major data suppliers, reference librarians, work study students, media people like Mary Ridgway who transformed my rickety diagrams into works of art. At $25 a copy I couldn't send them copies of the book, so I sent them copies of the cover page and the acknowledgement page, with a hand scribbled note.

In April, at the International Studies Association meeting, I saw the book displayed in the publishers' room. At every major conference there is a room jointly reserved by publishers who display the latest books relevant to the fields of those at the conference. But never before had any book of mine been perceived as relevant. What a thrill! Well, a mild thrill, a warm glow of pleasure. If Joe Fahey hadn't called my attention to it, I could have missed it.

Nelle and my older children, Julie and Peter, had all read some of it, which had not been the case with my earlier books. Ellen, my youngest, hadn't mentioned it. But I could hope that she had left it carelessly in view somewhere in her college room. And Gene Young called one evening to thank me for sending the copy.

The only faculty comment I had was from David Orenstein, who noticed I didn't have an index. True. It was the first book I had published that didn't, and I always had done them myself. But the Paragon editors didn't respond to my offer to do one. Perhaps this indicated that PT was perceived to be a semi-popular book, a book for intelligent laymen rather than for scholars.

Bill Eckhardt sent me a copy of the review he would present at the ISCSC meeting in Illinois and which would later appear in the *Comparative Civilizations Review*. As I would expect, the review was fair and accurate.

And that's about all the impact the book had in its first six months out, as far as I knew. Oh, wait. I should also mention that a couple months after the book came out, I read in the program at the Dayton Philharmonic about Mahler's creative pangs, how he suffered as he worked on a symphony. Luckily I didn't have those. PT took far longer to produce than any of Mahler's huge symphonies and I was certainly discouraged, but no pangs. Maybe pangs are only for geniuses. But then, Mozart didn't have them. Only for second rank geniuses? Me and Mozart, we didn't have pangs.

There were also quite a few spin-offs from PT that were still in play. In the fall, offprints from "Peace and Deterrence" arrived. This was an article I had written for an edited collection. Now I had dozens of copies to distribute. How did you do that without being self serving? I put them on my shelf, intending to enclose them when I wrote letters to people who might be interested, but generally forgot when the opportunity arose.

Previously, in the summer, the *Midwest Quarterly* carried another spin-off piece, "The Present Age," as its lead article. It had been rejected a dozen times, until one editor took the trouble to tell me how bad it was. More like a rotary club speech, she thought, than an academic paper. Well, with the book coming out soon, I could either file it or send it out one more time. I sent it, and bingo, the next editor liked it.

Another turkey had a similar happy ending. This one, "The Great Northern Peace," had been presented as a paper at an American Sociological Association meeting, but it wound up as no more than a paragraph or two in the book. Meanwhile it was consistently rejected by journals. But it happened that *Peace Review*, edited by John Harris, was a theme journal. This article just fit the theme, though I had been unaware of it. What a wonderful game. If you lose ten and win one, you win. Just the opposite of dueling.

The article came out in December (Mathew with one "t," I noticed). Like other articles in the group, it had been outdistanced by events. I only skimmed it, not because of its obsolescence but because I had been working on this problem for so many years and, psychologically, had completed this work. For that matter, I didn't read the book either.

At the time, though, I made another interpretation. Could it be that there also lurked the idea that in the 1970's I was so far in front that no one paid any attention to me, whereas in the 1980's the world had gone past me while I was meeting the objections of six different readers? The misspelling, therefore, could have symbolized my work failing to get the attention I thought it deserved? This kind of idea is what comes of too much association with symbolic interactionists like Orenstein.

General War and General Peace

Peace in Our Time had proposed that there might be a cycle of historical events in Western history that produced a series of crises bounded by longer ages of relative stability. Decades before, Toynbee (1954) had proposed that there might be recurring periods of general war and general peace in many civilizations. And early in the one quarter sabbatical that preceded the "Professor" study, I had read Jack Levy's article on theories of general war in Western history (1985). A general war would be one in which most or all of the major political powers in a civilization were at war, as in the World Wars. A general peace would be a situation in which the major powers were not fighting each other, as was the case in Europe after the World Wars. From Levy, and earlier from Lee Snyder, I had gained the impression that general wars accounted for a great deal of the total amount of warfare in history. Might the same be said for general peace? So I had begun my sabbatical quest for cases of general war and general peace with a feeling that this was going to be an important book. Hence my initial working title was "War and Peace."

But by summer, when I presented my first findings at the ISCSC Berkeley meeting, my confidence had waned. The process of gathering was extremely primitive. I decided on the civilizations to look at, all mainstream examples that others would consider reasonable choices. And I limited my search to general wars of two decades or longer because the Napoleonic Wars—shortest of Western general wars I had used in *Peace in Our Tim*—had been about 23 years long. But for initial research purposes, each general peace would have to last at least four decades, because that was how long it took before the 20th Century Western General Peace, what Levy had called "the Long Peace," was noticed.

I had intended to use several general sources for my initial gathering of possible cases, but it turned out that Langer's *World History* provided enough data for a preliminary list. So I used very little else until I got to Western Civilization, where Langer was too long and Levy had already harvested a crop of general wars for the modern historical period. In gathering from Langer, I took the chaff with the wheat, a larger category of civilizational wars—wars that occupied an entire civilization regardless whether major powers were fighting one another—thinking that later I could discard those wars and peaces that did not meet criteria.

If the plural of peace seems odd, that is probably because we are accustomed to perceive peace as a prevailing condition that is interrupted here and there, now and then, by war. But peace can also be seen as limited in time and space. The "Long Peace," for instance, involves the second half of the 20th century in Western Civilization, but not in the world as a whole. If we want to compare this peace to the Victorian Peace that lasted from the Franco-Prussian to the First World War, we have to use the plural, the Western peaces of the 19th and 20th centuries.

This initial process of gathering data undermined my confidence for several reasons. First, the reading of Langer seemed an exceedingly superficial process. I told people I used secondary sources, but not that I used primarily one source. Then, for all the agreement I might find among civilizationists, the identification of separate civilizations still had an element of reification. Not everyone would agree with the boundaries in space and time that I chose. But most important, the delineation of the wars and peaces was even more arbitrary. I was not the first to designate the two world wars as a single event (e.g., Goodspeed, 1977), but the usage illustrated that there was an element of reification even to something that can kill you. The Thirty Years War is an event most of us agree happened, but at the time of the peace treaty of Westphalia, most Europeans would have said there had been four separate wars. The combining came later. Well, I was doing such combining, often for the first time.

I was giving names to "wars" that experts in the fields of Islamic or South Asian history had never heard of. And if that were so of wars, it was even more so with general peaces.

Then, wasn't the twentieth century on a different scale? Could you compare World War II to a conflict that occupied most of the great powers of Mesopotamia? Was that in any way meaningful?

During a sabbatical you have more time to think. By the time we met at Berkeley, with first draft tables for six of eleven civilizations gathered, I had had plenty of time to elaborate my doubts. It seemed a good time to ask whether the project should be continued. Better to stop now, with a quarter lost, then carry on a work for several years, only to find it unconvincing and, even worse, unpublishable.

At the California ISCSC meeting, two scholars thought that my doubts were sensibly grounded, and that maybe I would be wise to discontinue the work. There was also plenty of incentive at the home office. Another manuscript, "Millfield on Saturday," had become the main enterprise for fall and part of winter. And now I had begun gathering data for a book about my occupation.

Still, I rationalized. If six tables had been completed, I may as well complete the other five and bring a complete set to the next ISCSC meeting. Even if I didn't go further, they might provide a springboard for someone else. Also, a complete set of tables could provide a basis for a grant proposal. If I got a grant, that would show that someone else thought this a viable project.

So, around the edges of everything else, I plugged away at searching for general wars and general peaces in world history. The field notes were full of grumbly observations about the quest. "Today I worried about Peruvian Civilization. It's an insoluble problem." This worry, which probably most Peruvians don't have, had to do with whether to consider the Andean history of South America, the Spanish Conquest, the 19th-century revolutions and the subsequent history to the present as all part of the history of Peruvian Civilization. Most civilizationists would not. They would be more likely to say that Peruvian Civilization ended with the Spanish Conquest, in which case what we have now in South America is Western Civilization with a Spanish veneer. I talked to my wife about it, and she didn't seem persuaded that I had a serious problem. "It seems hardly necessary to add," I concluded, "that I feel an awesome sense of responsibility about having to make this decision" about the civilizational identity of an entire continent.

The work rolled on. By July the Peruvian cases were drawn and I turned my attention to Mexico. I fretted that the work seemed superficial. Anyone could do it (but who else would?). The crisis of confidence was not alleviated by Africa. What chance had I to know enough history to give a picture of general wars in Africa? When were these wars between African states and when were they wars among Western and Islamic powers fought on African territory? And then, I could see that these were not general wars in the Napoleonic sense. Individual territories were being fought for and as population expanded, sometimes these wars coincidentally occupied most of African Civilization. Would Levy consider these general wars?

In October, working in a very pleasant library corner, looking out over the quad on a sunny day, I read about a series of rebellions and Persian, Arab and barbarian invasions. As I worked, I fretted some more. Even if I could get a list of general wars and peaces that might be 80 percent acceptable, any explanation of patterns would probably de-emphasize technology. When the Ottomans swept through the Byzantine Empire, was that because of a burst of energy, a successful organizational effort, some culture pattern, or some technological breakthrough? I would not only have to study the Byzantine period but Ottoman history as well. How far should I go with that? It could be a real tar baby. At what point would such study bring diminishing returns? If I did get it published, I would have to rely on other scholars to criticize and improve. But would they? Only a few civilizationists happened to be interested in comparative war, not to mention comparative peace. The International Studies scholars, like David Singer, would regard all this as marginally interesting but essentially untestable. When I thought of people who would be interested I rounded up the usual suspects: Dave Wilkinson, Bill Eckhardt, John Hord, Bill Edwards, Lee Snyder, all civilizationists. Was I doing all this work just for them?

By January I was expanding my study into Russia, because I thought that Russia was Byzantine. Once again, as in the Latin American cases, my interpretation, though not outlandish, was not orthodox either. So I ran the risk of being criticized for having defined the boundaries of the civilizations improperly. It was a great responsibility to have so much power that I could define the boundaries of civilizations in space and time. If I could do that, why couldn't I have more influence on the General Education Program?

By February, when I finally had the Byzantine cases, I perceived that all of them, war and peace, were civilizational but not general. That is, they were wars and peaces that involved the total civilization, but they were not wars involving most of the great powers, or peaces in which great powers could have fought but did not. From the perspective of general war and peace, none of these cases would apply. I didn't like this, not only because the gathering would have been mostly wasted except for the making of the tables, but because I would lose one of my civilizations and narrow the range. I didn't want to sacrifice the work of all those days in the library and not get credit for having at least considered Byzantine Civilization. But in so far as this phase of scholarship is like fishing, you had to realize that some days (or months!) you don't catch fish, or the fish you catch are inedible.

In April and May, with another ISCSC meeting coming up in Illinois, I worked on Islamic Civilization, which at least had the virtue of being only 14 centuries long. I seemed to have been cheered by this research. There were many Islamic states, and therefore the civilizational wars and peaces turned out all to fit the general category so, compared to Byzantine, the catch was satisfactory.

I would be able to go to the Illinois meeting with ten of my eleven tables, four added since the California meeting. Perhaps the response would be more affirmative this time.

It was, or at any rate after another year's commitment I was prepared to translate whatever comment I received into the carrying on of the project which had, in my view, now gone beyond the stage wherein abortion could be considered. Francis Hsu said I needed to drop the controversial concept of civilization and work with population area relationships. Imanuel Geiss, who at the California meeting was one of the scholars who advised dropping the project, now thought I should revise the project and use civilizational families rather than individual civilizations. Taking the advice of either Hsu or Geiss would mean starting from scratch in collecting cases. Bill Edwards thought the project was doable, despite conceptual problems. Overall, I felt somewhat reinforced. I couldn't abandon civilizations: that was a matter of axiom or faith. It was the frame of reference I used and knew something about. So Hsu and Geiss were reinforcing me by discussing the project as if it were basically rational, but needed reorientation. They didn't consider it unreasonable, just poorly constructed. To Edwards, a long time member of the association, the project looked normal, the kind of thing you would expect from an ISCSC member. By contrast, when I wanted to discuss the hypothesis with political scientists Jim Jacob, Donna Schlagheck and Bob Thobaben, they put me off because they were on their way to a department meeting: necessary business before important. But when you are at your home university, there is always necessary business.

At the annual banquet, sitting next to the speaker, South Asian historian David Kopf, I remarked that I had found Indian history tough to work with. He asked me what sources I was using. How embarrassing! I didn't want to say Langer's World Encyclopedia! So I said—lied—general sources at this point while I gather the cases, from which he might infer ten or a dozen general histories. He already had the impression, I thought, that as a group ISCSC members were rather irresponsible, making assertions that he could show to be erroneous because we had used sources on Indian history that he would consider to be of dubious validity. On the other hand, now that he had been working on comparative genocide, he may have been more tolerant about the use of secondary sources. But just one source? Not that tolerant.

Millfield on Saturday

Reading Tony Watson's book for Occupations, I noted that he emarked that sociologists mostly like to study either high status professionals or people in low status situations. In that case *Millfield* violated the norm, because it was concerned with middle status people.

Millfield on Saturday was a study of a village near Dayton that had been surrounded and incorporated by suburbia. By household interviews conducted on Saturdays in October, Koebernick, Orenstein and I hoped to get a picture of how people were affected by this invasion, both on a weekend day and on a weekday, since we had asked them about what they were doing on Saturday and what they had done the day before.

In the summer and fall I made *Millfield* my primary research concern. As I worked on it, it occurred to me that I was apologizing for or trying to downplay that we interviewed only 24 households. But when the tapes of the interviews had been transcribed, we actually had a tremendous amount of data. It was an example of what Edward T. Hall calls a high context study, stronger in nuances than in numbers. Hall says Westerners are more oriented toward low context studies, hence my need to apologize.

As I proofread I noticed that there was a good deal of repetitive material. The same quotations turned up in support of different ideas in different chapters. I rationalized that this redundancy was reinforcing, that the quotations did have different applications, that this was a book of nuances. I dismissed the possibility that I was too lazy to make a choice when the same quotation was used twice, or that I was doubtful that the book was quite long enough and didn't want to give up any material. (Later, when David did the final reading, after the manuscript had been revised in response to a reader's report, he commented on the "value of redundancy.")

In November I read chapter six, "Circles of Acquaintance," in which I felt we had really broken new ground in community research. This is one in which we used maps to show neighborhoods as perceived by the Millfielders, and even verified the image that folks talk to one another on their way to and from the post office. The computerized maps, from Bruce Stivers of Media Production, were very impressive.

During this period Tom's wife, Peg, remarked to me at a party one night that the reason we would never finish the book was that Tom and I were both Myers-Briggs N's, intuitive rather than sensing, preferring mulling general ideas to specifics, therefore not sufficiently motivated to work out details. I managed to refrain from telling her it was nearly finished, because I hoped to surprise Tom with a contract in his mailbox. Thinking about it later, though, I would also bet that Tom is a Myers-Briggs P, tolerant of leaving things open, whereas I'm a J, wanting closure.

In December, reading the last chapter of *Millfield*, I became aware that a set of hypotheses had been raised in chapter one and then forgotten. So I reconsidered them according to the findings in the last chapter, it appeared that seven were supported, six not, and three were unanswerable from our data.

Hypotheses not supported can be the most interesting. For instance, we supposed that women more than men would be charmed by the community and would be its biggest boosters. This turned out not to be the case, a mild surprise to the three married male investigators.

Most surprises in *Millfield* were mild. It was not a startling piece of work, like *Peace in Our Time*, but it seemed to me a gentle, pleasant, subtle book.

By January I was checking references. Those missing came from Tom's theory chapter, and I was finding the authors by checking the card catalogue, which was hidden on the Library fourth floor. I was probably one of its last users but since the books I was looking for came mostly from the fifties through the seventies, it seemed faster to me than pressing the computer buttons, not an activity suited to an N.

While the manuscript was being polished, I had written a letter to Alex Holzman, editor of the Ohio State University Press, describing the undeniable merits of our book. Given that this was a community study of an Ohio village, this seemed to be the most logical publisher to contact. He requested three months for an exclusive consideration, which seemed reasonable given that this was my preferred publisher, though I don't think I told Tom or David that I had made the contact.

Four months passed, it was February, and I queried Holzman. We had finished the manuscript, tables, figures, references, and would be willing to send this updated manuscript if it wouldn't complicate the reviewing process. In April Holzman phoned, said they'd had delays because of marketing problems, asked me to send the revised manuscript, but released us from the exclusive. Bad news. Now we would have to try others, and the hope that Ohio State would take it without complications diminished. About like the hope that the first people to look at your house will buy it.

So, toward the end of the month, I picked out six more publishers, all midwest state university presses, and in May they were contacted and offered the opportunity to review the manuscript. In proofreading one of the tables I noted that the disguised name we had given Wright State, Brixton State University, gave us the initials BSU.

Combinations

My father once told me of a third baseman who wanted to pitch. He was a good third baseman but a terrible pitcher, so they let him pitch only in hopelessly lost games. In somewhat the same way, I was a published author of academic studies who thought he was a novelist. In the year studied I was working on a novel, mostly in longhand, in notebooks, on the bus, or at meetings. I was always somewhat embarrassed about it and didn't talk about it very much. I found it easy to write, when I did write. After all, there was no research to do. The idea was that five adults spent a few days' vacation on an island and the chapters consisted of all the possible combinations of five people interacting, the five together, all possible combinations of fours, threes and twos, and each alone. I had begun it two years before the study year, and it was getting toward completion.

Every so often there was a note about working on it, most of the notes apologetic in tone. "I can work on it next month," says one note. "I'll lose the feel for the characters if I don't. Part of me doesn't take it seriously: you're not a novelist, (that part) says."

I was also furtive because the novel required some writing about sex, either spurned or occurring between the characters or else fantasized. I was uncomfortable about the possibility that someone in my family might pick up the notebook, though none of us would be upset if we found such scenes in, say, Philip Roth. Ben, one of the characters, had made sexual approaches to two of the women on the island; now it was time to write the chapter in which both women confronted him about what he had done. After that, while jogging, I found myself thinking about other possible responses: the two women discussing Ben's behavior with Anne, Ben's wife; or Clare's husband Dick, confronting Ben; Ben's defense; Anne considering the matter alone. Ben would say they were making too much of it. But he would have different explanations for different combinations of people, and always be sincere.

One evening I was writing the section on the exchange among the three women. When Nelle asked, I told her what I was writing about and she said she didn't like my writing about imaginary women. She said it was the same as my not liking her reading Georgette Heyer because I wouldn't measure up to that author's heroes.

The Scientific Enterprise

In describing the beginning of the manuscript on general war and peace, I have referred to testing the cases at two annual meetings of the ISCSC at Berkeley and Urbana which, as it happened, marked the beginning and end of the academic year studied. The professional meetings should have played an important part in research. That was what we had them for. They were supposed to provide us with opportunities to meet colleagues with common interests and to exchange ideas with them, to get their criticisms and suggestions on work in progress. This kind of interaction is what I shall call the scientific enterprise in the sense that it is the arena in which we help one another in a collective search for, well, truth. Since the College of Liberal Arts, and ultimately the state of Ohio, paid for trips to meetings, it would be important to establish whether they performed that function.

During the year studied, I attended five meetings: the ISCSC first in Berkeley, California in early June as notetaking began, and again in Urbana, Illinois a year later as note taking ended; in the fall, meetings of the Consortium on Peace Research, Education and Development (COPRED) in Denver and of the local Peace Studies Association in Dayton; in the following spring, about six weeks before attending the second ISCSC meeting, a meeting of the International Studies Association (ISA) in Washington D.C.

The ISCSC was a small association with about 500 members who studied the natures and interactions of civilizations in world history. I was one of its founding members and in two decades had never missed an annual meeting. COPRED was a larger organization, with maybe 1,000 members, and was unusual in that it attempted to bring together scholarly researchers, high school teachers and activists. It was also about 20 years old, but I had been attending meetings only for a few years. The Peace Studies Association was a Dayton community organization which held an annual day and a half meeting and brought to the Wright State campus annually a distinguished speaker. The ISA was much larger. It had ten times more sessions than ISCSC and must have had several thousand members. The Washington meeting was the third I had attended.

Did the ISCSC have a common interest? Did we all talk to one another about civilizational matters? I don't think so. Instead several kinds of activities went on, so that I found myself listening to presentations year after year from some members while I rarely heard others. At the Berkeley meeting, however, I seemed to be mildly threatened by increased activity from world systems analysts. It began when David Wilkinson brought over Dutch historian Gunder Frank to ask whether Wilkinson's viewpoint was typical of the ISCSC. I laughingly answered that it was not, that Wilkinson was generally perceived to be a maverick. I did not then realize, because world systems were not in my paradigm, that Frank was a leading member of the world systems school. I'm stumbling a bit over these terms paradigm and school. Both refer to a group of scholars working in the same enterprise, from the same set of rules and assumptions to the extent that they read one another's articles and papers and attend one another's sessions. (My editor tells me that the paradigm is the set of rules, the school is the set of scholars.)

Anyway, the question having been asked, I became aware that at the meeting there was a great deal of discussion about the impact and spread of modernization. This seemed vaguely threatening because modernization implied a universal process that was world evolutionary, not a recurrent process in different civilizations. At one plenary meeting, after hearing the term modernization several times, I got up to ask, with more emotion than I expected, whether modernization was not a euphemism for Westernization. If it were, should we civilizationists not be cautious about assuming that what looked progressive to us was seen as progressive by members of other civilizations?

I was reassured somewhat about world systems after a discussion with Barry Gills, introduced to me by Wilkinson at the ISA meeting the following spring. Gills was presenting a paper co-authored with Frank. He was interested in the world system in history, particularly trade and information exchanges between civilizations. This is what, in the seventies, our first American ISC-SC president, Benjamin Nelson, would have called the study of intercivilizational encounters. But it is ironic that I would legitimize the world systems paradigm by referring to Nelson, because in the 1970's he represented, to me, the dominant paradigm of the ISCSC, which I tolerated because we comparativists needed the Nelsonians in order to have an association large enough to function. Now that the comparativists were dominant, did I fear that the world systems analysts were about to engineer a takeover, leaving the comparativists once again in the minority?

One aspect of the general scientific enterprise I was involved in was the peace research network of COPRED. My job was to provide a linkage among members of the association who were particularly interested in peace research. Toward improving this scholarly linkage, we sent a questionnaire to members of both the Research and the Peace Movement sections. From this we would learn what our range of interests were and who was doing similar work. Thus, those who were doing similar work would be able to contact one another for information and confirmation.

Another way in which paradigms manifest themselves is in the identification of heroes. Most readers will not have heard of Martin Wight, who directed my Ph.D. dissertation. But at a COPRED breakfast a student, Ian Rowland, was visibly impressed when I told him I had worked under Wight. Martin Wight? The author of *Power Politics*? At the ISA meeting Barry Gills was even more impressed. He had gone to the London School of Economics looking for the legacy of Martin Wight and not finding it. Imagine that, three decades ago, I should have been supervised by the Man Himself! So you could say that name dropping is an art form. The right name has to be dropped in the right situation.

Gills, however, would be much more successful than I was, because he was working in a growing paradigm and co-authoring with Gunder Frank, an established scholar. He was getting an earlier hearing than I did. I don't mean to suggest that success is a matter of luck, though that is a factor in everything. My paradigm, the study of civilizations, was in decline, or at least normalization, when I entered it, and the founders of the ISCSC did not have the widespread respectability that world systems had attained. Besides that, I taught in a small junior college for a dozen years and attended very few professional meetings. Gills was also a superior scholar, reading a book a day, so that he already had more information than I ever had. So it would appear that level of professional success has something to do with the success of one's paradigm combined with ambition and ability. I should also say that while Barry was not unaware of the current power of the world systems paradigm, he didn't choose it for that reason. He was attracted to it because it was providing answers to questions that interested him.

Bringing Scholars Together

Riding on the bus one day, I asked Jim Runkle of the Biology Department whether it was true that at natural science meetings people sat on the edges of their chairs taking in the new developments of their colleagues' research, knowing already what had been done and what the current presentation added to knowledge within the field. He thought this a flattering description, but only the case when the field was narrowly defined. As it happened, I was engaged in trying to broaden a field, to bring the work of scholars in separate but seemingly related areas to the attention of one another. Let's see whether this had any effect on chair edges.

Since I had begun writing a book on general war and general peace, for the upcoming meetings I had organized sessions and round tables on war, peace and civilization, to see what input I could get from others on the research I was doing. In the ISCSC the focus would be more on the relation between war and civilization, while in COPRED and the ISA it would be on what we knew about war and what we would need to know in order to develop a conceptual framework. If the round tables were good enough to continue, I hoped to slip peace in as a topic at a later stage. What would be unique about the round tables was that I would develop a mailing list, take minutes and send them to participants whose names were on the list. Since members from all three associations would be on the mailing list, they might become familiar with perceptions others had. The ISCSC members, for instance, might be subject to the more rigorous and focused work of ISA members and the ISA members might be introduced to the comparativist perspectives of the civilizationists.

The conceptual framework part came about because two noted war scholars, David Singer and Jack Levy, had written that there was no overall framework for the study of war. This amazed me, because I had thought the study of war involved a large number of scholars communicating with and reading one another. But when I attended an ISA meeting in London the previous spring, there was only one session in 400 on war.

So I was trying to see if any scientific enterprise existed on the study of war but for selfish reasons I wanted to expand the parameters topically to include peace and historically and geographically to include other civilizations.

At the California meeting of the ISCSC, our sessions were devoted to the development of an idea that had been agreed upon the previous year: namely that civilizational war was the most important kind in history, in that it accounted for more casualties than all other kinds. A civilizational war was one that involved most of a civilization for a significant period of time. A general war was a civilizational war involving most of the major nations or states within that civilization. After these sessions had been held, a group of participants met to frame an agenda for the meeting scheduled for the following spring in Illinois. We hoped to follow that idea at the Illinois meeting by exploring the causes, recurrence, evolution and meaning of civilizational wars.

Before that conference there would be the COPRED gathering,

in which I hoped to set an agenda. Then came the ISA meeting with two round tables on what we knew about the cause of war and what would be needed to form a conceptual framework. The same topics would also be used for round tables at the ISCSC meeting in Illinois. I was using the term "conceptual framework" rather than paradigm because the latter term, made famous by Thomas Kuhn (1962), carried some emotional baggage. People often had definite but different conceptions of what did or did not constitute a paradigm. I hoped they would be more tolerant of "conceptual framework."

At the California ISCSC meeting I began to collect a mailing list for the project. During the summer I wrote a general letter to those on the list on what I was planning. Jack Levy was concerned that the subject was too broad, could easily degenerate into "useless generalities." I responded confidently that this could be prevented by bringing the discussions back to the point, by taking good notes, by telling participants in the minutes what had been achieved, and by setting up relevant follow up sessions. I seemed pompously confident that all of this would happen. Even if it did, given that there was only one meeting a year, this could take a long time.

I had good luck on the ISA roundtable. David Singer, Kenneth Boulding and John Vasquez agreed to participate. Singer and Boulding in the same session guaranteed a good attendance. Levy had already agreed to participate in two other sessions, wasn't eligible for this one but he agreed to be there as an informal discussant.

I wrote also to the ISCSC members who attended the California sessions about the proposed sessions for Illinois. I hoped to get some focus on factors leading to war and on general war. But these sessions were partly to get the people to the meeting who would be useful to the round table. Their formal papers would be on whatever they were doing and might fit only loosely into the framework I was trying to establish.

At the COPRED meeting I discussed the round tables with Bill Eckhardt, Kenneth Boulding and Michael Andregg, but I didn't plan any round tables for COPRED itself. Even within the research network there didn't seem to be enough interest and Eckhardt, Andregg and Boulding would all be at the ISA meeting.

I arrived in Washington for the April meeting of ISA feeling pretty tight. Would I be able to keep the questions on the subject and still take notes? I should have delegated the chair perhaps, but I wanted to control the meeting. My fortune cookie at dinner said the current year would bring me much happiness. Did that mean the academic year? In that case there'd be only two more months for this happiness to occur. Well, I thought, let's have some tomorrow.

As it turned out, it was a good day. Our official round table, in a room with 40 seats, was packed to overflowing. It could have been unproductive, because both Singer and Boulding argued that there was little that we know, with Boulding discounting even predictability. Fortunately John Vasquez presented 14 points of what we did know and Boulding, in his quaint way, provided a great deal more. Another round table, organized by Stuart Bremer, and an informal evening discussion provided a great deal of information about what people thought was needed for a conceptual framework. I thought this framework would be enriched by considering civilizational and world systems contributions, and I inferred that Levy thought so too. But Singer felt there was a tradeoff in that the wider and deeper your geohistorical framework, the less reliable your data.

On one hand, the range of study demonstrated by participants in the three sessions appeared to be wide if you consider subject and method. Within the Bremer session, for instance, Charles Gochman was simulating flow models while Russel Leng was studying diplomatic interactions. But they were looking for cause and recurrence within a similar framework and clearly they read one another, argued with one another, were familiar with one another's references. What they disagreed about seemed to me to be details within the framework.

I tried to convey this in writing the minutes. It was rare, perhaps unique, to take minutes of sessions. Usually scholars went to sessions, made their presentations, listened to comments, and never heard anything else. They might remember this or that idea, but had no session record. Or if they were compulsive note takers, they might have a record that would fade, as notes do. But minutes would be shared, could be corrected and discussed. Naturally they would be skewed toward my perception, and stressed a conceptual framework that probably wouldn't be there if Singer or Levy had taken the notes. But every secretary has the power to shape the minutes. And every participant has the power to ignore them.

The minutes were sent out quickly because I corrected them before I got home and Lynn Morgan typed them up. The only comment I got back was from Ross Maxwell of the ISCSC, who had read the minutes but not attended the sessions. He noted the narrow focus, mostly Western, mostly since 1815, and a lack of psychological considerations, an area of interest for him. Psychological considerations would require some attention to what might be universal as compared to what applied in particular situations. Such a question would be more likely to interest ISCSC members than those from the ISA.

In late May the ISCSC meeting at the University of Illinois provided both sessions and a round table on war and peace. The sessions didn't produce much to help the round table because they were not at that level of generalization. The round tables produced a set of generalizations about war, but they scarcely touched the generalizations from the ISA. There was a difference in basic data, of course, the ISCSC members drawing from a broader but less statistically specific body of material. The ISCSC style was also different, taking on the form of a meeting, with proposals being discussed and approved or rejected as too debatable. Jack Levy had felt the conclusions at the ISA were at a pretty basic level and Imanuel Geiss felt the ISCSC conclusions tended to be tautological. Whatever we could agree on was either obvious or self fulfilling.

Were these round tables worth the method? Would they promote conceptual frameworks and expand consciousness, or would they soon be forgotten as scholars returned to their day to day work? It remained to be seen whether there would be a collective will to persevere, and it would take more time before one could ascertain whether the round tables were having an impact on scholarship.

Sometime around graduation I received an invitation from Tom Gregor, an anthropologist at Vanderbilt, to attend a five day Guggenheim invitational conference on the study of peace. The conference was to be held in October in Charleston, South Carolina, a city I love. I didn't get an invitation like this very often, and it fit with my current research and the War and Peace Project. In any event, it would be an opportunity to meet other scholars who might be interested in the broader aspects of studying peace.

Orenstein dropped by one morning to discuss his approach to contemporary theories, and what he said seemed quite relevant to the scientific enterprise. He felt you could classify some scholars as positivists, those who think a good theory is testable and the testing will verify or refute the theory. In this sense Singer, Vasquez and Levy were positivists, except they weren't able to agree entirely on the theory being tested.

But Orenstein felt there were others who thought that what is most important about a theory is what it explains. What mattered was not how testable it was, but that it encompassed the widest possible number of variables, that it included what was most important. This was closer to Evan Luard (1987), whom I happened to be reading at the time, and better described most of the civilization-ists. It wasn't that they didn't test, but that they looked more at how the theory as a whole explained the data available. From a sociological viewpoint, the ISA scholars were more positivist in approach. They believed that if only standards were rigorous enough, truth would be found. This difference in outlook may have been a factor in the lack of overlap between the ISA and ISCSC roundtables.

I had also been reading an article by Tzvetan Todorov advocating that scholars write so that they can be read by interested specialists from other fields. I agreed with that. But thinking it over later, I wondered if the existence of paradigms or conceptual frameworks doesn't preclude understanding. Perhaps you have to be at the boundary of one scientific enterprise to see into another.

Regarding the Question

Scientific Estate or Boondoggle? Certainly there was enough coherence in this year to justify the trips to the ISCSC and ISA meetings. About COPRED I was less sure. It appeared that the research connections were weak and the connections with high school teachers and activists were not being made.

Connections, however, were necessary but not sufficient. If there were obvious connections within the discussions at the ISA and ISCSC, that did not mean the collective work was progressing. The focus in the War and Peace project was still concerned with identifying a conceptual framework and therefore probably not yet ready to address agreement on a body of accepted knowledge.

So the body of accepted knowledge was perceived to be either obvious, so basic that you wouldn't need a conference to confirm it, or tautological, embedded in its own logic. It was also being perceived as invalid, as the feedback slowly filtered through, with ISA members seeing ISCSC members as woolgathering and ISCSC members seeing ISA conclusions as provincial.

Still, that was the first year of the project. It would take more than one year before results could be assessed.

As for the broader enterprises, they were even harder to assess. I would see David Singer as the founder of a paradigm and Levy as a field foreman and successor, but they didn't see themselves that way. And it was probably significant that in the year preceding the roundtables, the ISA had devoted only one session to the study of war.

I had a two decade perspective in the ISCSC, and was for the first time perceiving the rise of world systems study as a challenge to the comparative study of civilizations. This led me to reconsider the decline of the Nelsonian paradigm. It had not necessarily failed, but the scholars who followed it either were led to other work or else, after the death of Nelson, no longer saw the ISCSC as a promising venue for discussion of their ideas and theories.

As for the comparative study of civilizations, which ought to be the main area of concern in the ISCSC, it had grown in the seventies and been dominant in the eighties. I had myself co-edited a book (Melko and Scott, 1987) that showed how the society pursued this study. But the book showed process better than progress. I really couldn't say what we have learned, what we were sure about in the 1990's that we were doubtful about in the 1970's.

But, perhaps, that is the nature of the enterprise. It may be that there are long periods of refinement, when less and less is studied with greater sophistication. Pockets are explored and mined. The essential breakthroughs are made. The apparent decline of the Nelsonian paradigm could have been a repositioning of the Nelsonians. The threat to the comparativist paradigm could be the movement to an area perceived to be more rewarding, where greater growth is possible. But, except for David Wilkinson, the movers were different people. They seemed to be taking over a convenient host. They may have been viruses from my perspective, but I suppose the host looks different if you happen to be a virus.

So the ISCSC, a major center of activity in my professional life, might turn into something else. Wilkinson or Chase-Dunn might become presidents and the name might change to the Society for Systems and Civilizational Studies, the SSCS. And by 2010, members would wonder why Civilizational was in the name, destroying the symmetry of those S's. And the enterprise to which I gave so much of my time and energy would be remembered, if at all, as the curious pre-systems period, before the association found its purpose and focus.

The Jews as Mesopotamians

Not everything I did related to my own conceptual framework. In November I had given a presentation at Temple Israel in Dayton on the Jews as Mesopotamians. In some discussion with David Orenstein I had said that I regarded the Jews as the last carriers of Mesopotamian Civilization. He was a member of the program committee at Temple Israel and thought the members would be interested. The night before the presentation I began to worry a bit. I was no expert on Judaism and some people attending would be. Nor would it be easy to explain in a short time what I mean by civilization.

It turned out to be a well organized and well attended program. People arrived around ten for a breakfast of bagels, coffee cake, tea and coffee. Then I spoke for about 40 minutes and there was a whole hour for questions. Perhaps 50 to 60 people attended.

The questions could have been tough. I was asked to assess the European genocide from a civilizational perspective, and really couldn't. I was asked to elaborate on Mesopotamian style, couldn't beyond humor and this-world orientation. Asked why Jews do so well in science, I said it was a combination of marginality (which I got from Orenstein) plus present world and empirical orientation. How come the Diaspora had been preserved for two millennia? I thought it was some combination of Talmudic scholarship and innovation provided by the reformed Jews I was talking to, enough of the former to keep the Faith, enough of the latter to prevent the fossilization Toynbee thought he saw in the Diaspora. None of this was in my presentation. But the questions weren't as tough as they sound, partly because the audience was politer to a guest than, say, a professional association audience would have been but even more because the audience took to the idea, topped my examples with better examples.

Once I had presented the talk, I thought I might as well give it to the ISCSC as a paper. The questions from the Jewish audience had augmented my vague idea. But this wouldn't augment any work in progress, wouldn't develop into an article or book. It was just an interesting sidelight.

The following spring, when I was writing the ISCSC paper, Tom Koebernick poked his head in the door and asked what I was doing. He wondered if it might not be a burden to be the last carrier of Mesopotamian Civilization. It might, you know. Awareness of being Mesopotamian, if it were to spread, might tilt the balance in favor of the conservatives and terminate the civilization. Oh, the power we scholars might unleash!

Presenting a paper on the Jews as Mesopotamians might come in the category of boondoggle, since I knew very little about what I was presenting and it had little to do with my present research or the research of anyone else. I have deleted a first draft chapter that I thought would show that although scholarly meetings do include as much boondoggle as scientific enterprise, that isn't necessarily bad. On reconsideration, a whole chapter of boondoggle seemed a bit much, but there is one sentence I think must be retained.

Overheard at lunch, during the ISCSC Urbana meeting, Francis Hsu's remark to Sted Noble: "My Theory of Everything is better than Your Theory of Everything."

A Call From the East

In February I received an invitation from the Japan Society for the Comparative Study of Civilizations to give a "Commemorative" address at Kokugakuin University in Tokyo. The subject requested was "The State and Civilization." The JSCSC was the only other civilizations association in the world. One of their members had attended a couple of our meetings, but we had never attended theirs. So it was something of an honor to be asked. On the other hand, I got homesick even at American conferences and this one would mean a week away from home in a country in which I didn't understand the language. But I felt ashamed of not wanting to go, considering I was supposed to be interested in other civilizations. Nelle thought I should go so she could tell the children. It was not to be until December, a long way off, but then also a long time for apprehension to build up.

It took me a month to answer the letter and after expressing hesitancy, which I supposed they would take as appropriate politeness, I accepted.

In April I received a call from the University of Illinois telling me that Shuntaro Ito, the president of the JSCSC, had been visiting the ISCSC president, Michael Palencia-Roth, and would be coming the next night to Dayton. I was to have breakfast with him the following morning at Stouffer's Hotel.

At breakfast Ito asked whether the ISCSC was really international, and I explained to him how it had been transferred from

Europe to the United States in the early seventies, how we had called ourselves the ISCSC-US for several years, hoping there would be ISCSC's developed in other countries, and how I was one of those who favored deleting the dashes as redundant when no other societies appeared in other countries.

The following month I received a letter from Keisuke Kawakubo, Director of the JSCSC, making arrangements for the trip. In responding, I suggested delicately that it wouldn't be necessary for me to fly executive class (egalitarian Americans!), and wondered if things might be so arranged that I could stop and visit my daughter and granddaughter in Hawaii on the way home.

The last time I had been to Japan was in the fifties, when I was in the Army. Coming out of a restaurant, I found a few Japanese exclaiming over my size-13 boots, parked outside the door. Possibly they were waiting to see what would come out to put on such monstrosities. Now, writing to Kawakubo, I felt again like a big American in great boots clumping around in a Japanese garden.

Was this a boondoggle? I was qualified to present such a paper, though the ISCSC's David Wilkinson would have been a better choice. But this may have had more to do with strengthening relations between the two societies, and I may have been chosen as the only former president of the ISCSC who had been concerned with international relations. At least the Japanese, not Ohio, would be paying for the trip.

Afterword

The idea of "afterwords" for this book was suggested by David Orenstein, probably so that there would be one on *Millfield*. I sent it to about 15 publishers before our own university press agreed to send it to a reader. The reader recommended a number of changes, and I must admit that David took over the task of rewriting, final editing and otherwise responding to the reader. Carl Becker, editor of the Wright State University Press, accepted the revised manuscript and it finally came out a decade after the data had been gathered.

Despite the lack of first year support from ISCSC members, the War and Peace project rolled on, with periodic criticism and encouragement from Wilkinson, a political scientist from UCLA who had long been a member of the ISCSC but was also comfortable in the

ISA and among world systems analysts. Along the way I presented findings at ISCSC and ISA meetings as well as at a meeting of the American Sociological Association. Peace, alas, was reluctantly abandoned, 38 cases of general war were found and studied, and a manuscript was completed.

Whether anyone would publish it remained to be seen.

And despite Nelle's reservations, the "Combinations" novel was also finished, and I sought an agent. Repeatedly I would send an agent the first 30 or 50 pages, and repeatedly she or he would send it back. It was too slow. Partly I fumed that novels like *The Sound and the Fury*, say, or *Sophie's Choice* would never have been published on the basis of their first 30 pages. Or might they have been better novels? Nah. But partly I did feel knocked out of the box. Go back to third base.

The world systems analysts didn't take over the ISCSC. Instead, one of them, Steve Sanderson, edited first a journal issue (1994), then a book (1996) in which civilizationists and world systems analysts duked it out. A good time was had by all. Possibly the world systems analysts saw us as provincial, but they attended our meetings less, and held their sessions under the umbrellas of the ISA and the World History Association. If they left us, we'd probably miss them. And then I discovered they had a subsection within the ISA, so I joined them. I'll try to refrain from taking it over.

The results of the COPRED survey of peace researchers showed me that only Bill Eckhardt and Michael Andregg shared my interests, and I could talk to them at ISCSC and ISA meetings. COPRED was a charming organization, but it could do little for me or I for it. After serving as local arrangements chair for the following annual meeting, I remained a member but no longer attended its meetings.

In July, after the academic year studied had ended, John Vasquez proposed an ISA session on what we knew about peace for the next year's meeting in Vancouver. It turned out to be a lively session, with seven participants and Vasquez once again produced a very concrete list. This was followed, after a hiatus, by a round table on general war, with many who had written on the subject either participating or in the audience. But no coherent war and peace study group appeared in the ISA, and I wasn't insider enough to organize it. There were such groups in the American Sociological Association and, of course, COPRED, but they were more concerned with war prevention than cause. At the ISCSC, Wilkinson and Eckhardt were the only members consistently interested in the macroscopic study of war. Both were extremely helpful to me. But it really didn't appear that the round tables had contributed significantly to the study of war and peace. No flurry of scholarly interaction followed, or if it has, it is on the Internet and I'm missing it.

I did attend the Charleston meeting, enjoyed the city, rubbed elbows with Boulding and Johan Galtung. But Boulding and I already knew about each other's work and Galtung's approach came from a very different perspective. Others attending were anthropologists doing microwork. My presentation on general peace looked ungainly among the others. There was clearly no conceptual framework to which I could contribute or relate.

I also made the JSCSC trip to Tokyo. I had the impression that my presentation of the Western debate about state systems did not fit well with the questions that engaged the JSCSC. It is hard to be sure when crossing cultures and languages. But Ito remained involved with the ISCSC, continued to attend its meetings, and at a meeting held at Wright State, was elected its president, making it truly an international association.

8

A Professor's Work

How the Professor Gathered His Notes. How Colleagues Responded to the Project. How He Failed to Protect Everyone from Defamation Suits or Obscene Phone Calls

I have explained (Ch. 1) how I decided to gather notes for this book without preparation, rationalized that a sociologist was better equipped than most professionals to play the role of participant observer, argued that Wright State was a particularly good choice for such a study and that a number of attacks on the profession in the late 80's and early 90's gave further impetus for such a study. But could a sociologist maintain his observer perspective without tilting his account in favor of the professor? While I was doing the study, Peter Bracher, chair of Wright State's English Department, asked me how I was coming out. It took a moment to realize he was asking how well I appeared to an outside observer. Not all that well, I thought.

Work in Progress

Orenstein had suggested I take an anthropological approach to the book, look at the professor as an anthropologist would. I don't think I went nearly that far, but the idea was helpful to the observer trying to wrest equal time from the participant. When at a monthly pizza seminar on research, I told the department faculty what I was doing, Bob Riordan and Amin Islam saw this as anthropological fieldwork in which I was documenting what I saw within the subculture. Once I had the notion that I was doing a field study, my style and choice of material may have undergone some modification.

This perception of myself as anthropologist coincided with using Georges and Jones' *People Studying People*, a study of anthropologists in the field, in my Social Life class. It was some comfort to learn that famous studies in the past sometimes involved as little preparation as I had made. I had thought, if I thought at all, that I'd just take a few notes every day, sort of a journal, because after all I wouldn't have to write before the following summer. But already in July, the first month of the study, I was commenting: "My supposition that I could just take notes in the interstices isn't going to work out. There are no . . . interstices." Note taking was soon cutting into research time and causing me to miss points at committees I was supposed to be covering as observer for the book, not to mention attending as participant.

At the pizza lunch, three of the sociologists--Jerry Savells, Jeanne Ballantine and Len Cargan—thought more ought to be done. There ought to be confirming surveys on questions like whether professors care about costs of books. A hallway survey of the first ten people you met wasn't really adequate. I was asked if I didn't have some topical categories, so my paragraphs could be placed in the proper folders. I said I was trying to stay open, because if I designated topics, I might tend to note only what seemed at the time to fit those topics.

Reading Tony Watson's *Sociology: Work and Industry*, I noted his observation that when a worker moves from one shift to another, he notices differences that those always on the same shift can't see. It occurred to me that the same was true of the anthropologist studying another culture, but not of a participant-observer studying his own subculture. I might well take for granted what a businessman or a professional in a different field would immediately see as striking or unusual.

Reading *People Studying People*, I became indignant that researchers had been secretive when they could have been open. I thought it was time for honesty in research. I tried to be overt, writing a letter to *The University Times*, which was sort of a company paper, announcing that I was doing the study. Few read the announcement, and those who did seemed to forget. I also gave the research presentation at the pizza lunch and was careful to tell classroom students about the study. But I could see little evidence that anyone cared or remembered. Eventually I took to wearing a tag on my jacket or sweater that said: "Caution: Data Gathering in Process."

Two who had seen the announcement were my squash partner, Business Law Professor Charles Hartmann, and Bill Irvine of the Philosophy Department. After the announcement had appeared, Hartmann told me he wouldn't be able to play squash with me during the coming year. It turned out he did, of course, and pictures were taken of one of our matches. That was covert because I had told the photographers not to let me know when they were coming. On several occasions, before or after a match, Charles would say, "I shouldn't be telling you this" after he had.

And when I asked Irvine about his ideas on cost of books per course, he responded that of course he would give false information since it might go into the book. He would pass by my door and tell me, though it was four p.m., that he wasn't going home but to the library to do some extra research, probably wouldn't get home until quite late, and even then he'd be thinking about it while driving. Coming in one morning, he poked his head in the door to say that he hadn't slept well the night before, he was worrying so much about his students.

One day I talked about the book in the hallway with Bob Thobaben of Political Science. From his perspective, the work of a professor was continuous. Bob said that when he went bike riding he carried a 3 x 5 card to make notes on (hazardous, I'd think). When he had an introductory class, even, he wouldn't spend less than two hours preparing it. Writing books, he thought, was rewarding, but hard work. The only book he enjoyed writing was one with Carl Becker on their experiences in World War II (1992). He hoped my writing this book would be similarly enjoyable for me. In all my notes, I think this is the only time anyone was moved to stop and reflect how he would view his own work.

Protecting Everyone

As notetaking got under way for *A Professor's Work*, it became evident that there would be two kinds of protection to be concerned about. To what extent did I have to worry about protecting the people I was studying, and to what extent did I need to protect myself?

Like other universities, Wright State had a Faculty Committee that reviewed all studies of human subjects, so that people who were studied were protected against harassment by the researcher. As I became aware that I was doing a field study, I realized I ought to run this study by the committee. In doing so, I explained the absence of middle level occupational studies, and that as far as possible I would make my study overt. I had written the letter to *The University Times* and had tried to inform groups and classes that I was doing the study. But, I added, "there are many people with whom I come in contact who would be unaware that what they say or do could become part of my notes."

There were other aspects of the Human Subjects form that seemed to risk confrontation. Did the nature of the research require deception? Well, each subject wouldn't be constantly informed. Did my project involve risk to the subject? Possibly: who knows? Indicate how benefits outweigh risks. You couldn't do any sociological study without such risks. Provision for informed consent? None. What if the subject withdrew? He couldn't. How are you protecting confidentiality? The question had not been addressed.

Over lunch I was interrupted by flashes of fantasy: Nelle leaving me because I thought more of the book than of protecting our family; the Human Subjects Committee telling me I couldn't write the book unless I got the permission of all the "subjects"; the Committee on Removal of Tenure calling me in for interview; the Department angry at me for bringing it notoriety and ruining chances of getting another faculty line; Psychologist Dennis O'Grady telling me I've lost my sense of proportion or that I see myself embattled against childhood forces of evil.

At the end of the fall quarter the Human Subjects Committee responded that my book was exempt from its consideration. I was described as using a personal diary as a basis for a textbook. Even though the study was exempt, it did suggest "that any names used therein which are based on real individuals need to be change(d) automatically."

So what did I do? Did I file the report and go on with the research, ignoring the unofficial advice? Oh no. I wrote a memo to Jack Gruber, chair of the committee, arguing that what the committee saw as a personal diary for a textbook I saw as research notes for a study. Did that affect the exemption? Then I went on to point out other studies that did not protect identities (Balzer 1976, Berendzen 1986). Were we in danger of being overprotective, of interfering with research, of creating confusion and implicating people where clarity would have protected them? Was the Human

Subjects Committee, in this response, protecting itself as well as everyone else? Did they really want *all* the names changed, or only selective protection? Was this the memo of a consummate professional, wanting to be certain that he was behaving ethically, or of a closet journalist who hoped to stimulate an amusing bureaucratic response or at least to be able to write the paragraph I have just written?

Eventually I had a conversation with Gruber in which we agreed the protection needs to be contextual, that I would protect a person where it seemed appropriate.

The other concern was protection against suit, against me or possibly against the University. On Jeanne Ballantine's advice, I called Gwen Mattison, University Attorney, to see what she would say about insurance. Unexpectedly we got into a warm discussion, most of the warmth being on my side. Her job, of course, was to avoid suit. So from her perspective, I ought to inform each of the hundreds of people mentioned in the book (including Gwen Mattison) about what I had written and get permission to print it. So, presumably, everyone who ignored me would be deleted. No journalist, I exclaimed, could possibly work under such restrictions.

Also, Mattison said, if I were sued, it would be up to whoever happened to be state attorney general at the time to determine whether I was operating within the requirements of my profession, or whether I had defamed someone.

Could this be another reason for the scarcity of participant observer professional studies? Is it okay for Dick Balzer to study Western Electric workers, since they aren't likely to sue, or weren't in the seventies, but not for me to study my colleagues, because they may be litigious? If our society becomes more litigious, will we litigate ourselves out of social studies altogether? Perhaps studies of Americans will have to be done by Kenyans, just as our anthropological studies are done by cultural outsiders.

Well, Mattison's job was to advise me how to be reasonably sure of avoiding a suit. My problem was to carry out a study that couldn't be done if I were to take her advice. I concluded that you do the study, take what reasonable precautions you can, but not precautions that would seriously affect the integrity of the study.

Whatever view the University may have taken on protecting subjects, the Liberal Arts College Faculty Development Committee granted me $500 for pictures. Was I supposed to give people in the pictures different names, call President Mulhollan "President Roosevelt?"

The photographers, Jack Davis and Roberta Monnin, were usually instructed to turn up unannounced for classes or meetings, take pictures without identifying themselves, and leave. When they came to a class, I was not to know they were coming. They took pictures of our Department and General Education retreats and of the emergency meeting of the Peace Studies Committee on the disastrous flier (Ch. 4). They took my research presentation at the pizza lunch (Ch. 8); the first meeting of the ad hoc General Education Committee to which no one else came (Ch. 3); a squash match with Charles Hartmann and a session of the NEH symposium (Ch. 4). They also took pictures of the breakfast with President Mulhollan and Vice President Hathaway (Ch. 4), and of my Occupations, Honors and Careers classes (Chs. 5–6). So that the pictures wouldn't be all of meetings and classes, Jack Davis followed me around for an hour one day and photographed my errands and hallway encounters. Jack thought my work looked boring.

The members of the Department didn't seem to be worried about notoriety. It happened to be my turn to chair the annual Merit Review Committee, the one that made recommendations on raises for the following year. I tried to shirk my responsibility for the year by pointing out that I should be excluded from their meetings altogether, since these were confidential meetings at which I would nevertheless be taking notes for possible publication.

The consensus was that I should chair. Orenstein pointed out that my avowed methodological approach was to do whatever I would normally do. He and Gordon Welty cheerfully informed me that they would just sue me if they didn't like what I wrote (Gordon on principle, David for the money). No one seemed to be worried about the revelation of Department Secrets.

One other comment on protection. Leaving the local Oakwood Library one December evening, I spotted a book entitled *Is My Armor Straight?*, which turned out to be a catchy title over the sub (real) title *A Year in the Life of a University President*. It proved to be a journal of one year in the life of Richard Berendzen, president of American University in Washington D.C. What for me would be research notes to process were for Berendzen an already completed book.

He didn't seem to have the protection problems I did. "If I told people I was keeping a journal, they might act differently. But if I did not tell them, would I violate a confidence? Finally, I convinced myself that I would not, for I did not intend to harm anyone or to disclose privileged information." Life must be so simple for presidents.

Afterword

When the year was completed I found I had taken more than 1,000 pages of notes. These field notes had to be topically organized so that both detail and overview were obtained on the year's teaching, research and service. This took a long time and I knew of no way to use the services of a computer. Amin Islam remarked that I was experiencing a problem familiar to cultural anthropologists.

Topical organization, for all the work it takes, has one disadvantage when compared to a journal. Topical organization gives a false impression of coherence. We see the search for a new department member uninterrupted by preparing classes, grading papers, sessions of the Monster Committee, trips to meetings, worries over the kitchen contractor (Ch. 10). We try to achieve a retrospective clarity that was not evident when events were occurring.

But retrospective clarity is at the core of a professor's work. He comes out of the daze of daily impressions and asks, "What Happened?" In one sense, topical organization helps answer that question.

My first draft ran over 600 pages and might serve as a historical document to describe what it was like to teach in an urban university at the end of the 20th century. But editors of university presses, to whom I talked at association meetings, shook their heads at the prospect.

So I revised the manuscript, cutting it to something under 500 pages, probably deleting the secrets of the Merit Evaluation Committee the Department made me chair. But the editors said, look, do you really claim to be a good enough teacher to write a manual on how to teach? And do you think your readers will really care about your arcane discussions with editors? So I revised again, giving just a chapter to teaching supplemented by a chapter on the students, and asking the reader to tolerate just one chapter on scholarship. That is, besides this one.

Oh. Yes. Remember Richard Berendzen, whose one-year journal of his college presidency would not disclose privileged information? Well, it appears he disclosed some privileged information somewhere, because he lost his job after having been arrested for making obscene phone calls. Even Gwen Mattison had not forseen this danger in the participant study of university work.

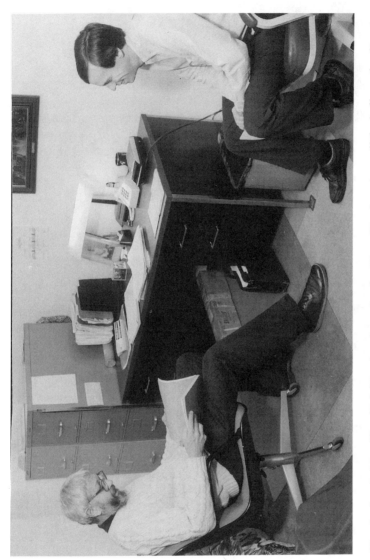

The Author in his office, Bob Riordan dropping by. The office location, off the hallway leading to the Department office, as Len Caran had warned, was convenient for people to pop into, and made Melko the secretary's receptionist.

Paula Herzog, Sociology/Anthropology Department work study student, looks a bit wary of the summer exhibit at the BevRon Gallery in the hallway outside Melko's office (Ch. 4). What she is trying to decipher is a set of charts prepared by Media Services Graphic Artist Mary Ridgway, greatly improving some rough charts by the author, which were soon to appear in Peace in Our Time (Ch. 7). Each square shows a five year period in which warfare for a particular area was violent (black), mild, or absent (white). The Gallery claimed 10,000 visitors a year, because that is how many are estimated to pass by on their way to and from the parking lot.

On the wall, inside office door, is a pantheon of great civilizationists (Ch. 7). Clockwise from upper left: Jacob Burckhardt, two pictures of Arnold Toynbee, Oswald Spengler, A. L. Kroeber front and side, Pitirim A. Sorokin, Carroll Quigley, and two pictures of Rushton Coulborn. The bottom photo of Toynbee and the Quigley were sent to me by their wives. Spengler and an ideational Sorokin were drawn from encyclopedia pictures by Julie Melko. Kroeber came off the cover of a biography by his wife, Theodora. The large drawing of Coulborn was given to me by his wife, Imogen Seger Coulborn, after his death; and finding the large black backing required pictures of other civilizationists to fill in. The smaller picture of Coulborn was taken at Bradford Junior College during the last year of his life.

The office becomes a meeting room for the powerful Sociology Curriculum Committee, with Chair Jeanne Ballantine sitting in. That's David Orenstein to the left, Dennis Rome to the left of Jeanne. The cartoons, on the door over Dennis's head, were rotated daily (Ch. 4). This was a busy, productive, explosive committee (Ch. 2).

The cockpit of the department, from which secretaries Glena Buchholtz and Lynn Morgan dispensed information, soothed students and explained reality to faculty.

The first meeting of the Ad Hoc Committee on General Education was
not well attended (Ch. 3). Absent (clockwise) were Herb Neve, Charlie
Funderburk, and John Blair. Brian Kruger was not present.

Melko tries out a great idea on Bill Rickert, Dean of Monsters (Ch. 3), and gets the usual response.

Melko explains his perception of the problem with the new brochure on the Peace Studies Concentration to members of the Peace Studies Association: Tim Wood of Environmental Studies, Jerome Clemons of Geography and PSA Steering Committee Chair Reed Smith of Political Science (Ch. 4).

The NEH seminar with Bill King leading a discussion of *Moby Dick* (Ch.4). Around the table are Chuck Taylor and Ron Hough of philosophy, King, Cynthia King and Jan Gabbert of Classics. This is the conference room in the Administrative Wing and that's an aerial photograph of Wright State in the background.

Academic life isn't all fun. Twice a week there is squash, in this case with Charles Hartmann doing nothing in particular and Melko chasing a ball he isn't going to get. Before and after the games, Hartmann provided the author with crucial information and unique analysis (Ch. 4).

The college chess table (Ch. 4) at which faculty gave advice, exchanged information. Here Martin Arbagi of History, who always played black, makes one of his regrettable late afternoon moves.

Vice-President Hathaway telling Melko how it really is during a breakfast with the president (Ch. 4). Around the table from lower right: Carolyn Stephens of History, Phil Messner of Education, President Paige Mulhollan, Jim Daily of Management, Tom Whissen of English, Ann Farrell of Math, Ivan Goldfarb of Chemistry, Edna Harper of Education, Charles Hathaway, Melko, Denise Potosky of Communication and Chien-In Chen of Engineering. President Mulhollan and Vice-President Hathaway tried to meet periodically with randomly selected faculty for an 8:15 continental breakfast.

The uninvited photographer visits the Occupations class (Ch. 5), where she catches the author making what appears to be a point after touchdown. From the chart on the board I guess he is discussing the work of Charles Sabel. The author went to first grade during a period when cursive writing was taught without printing as a prerequisite.

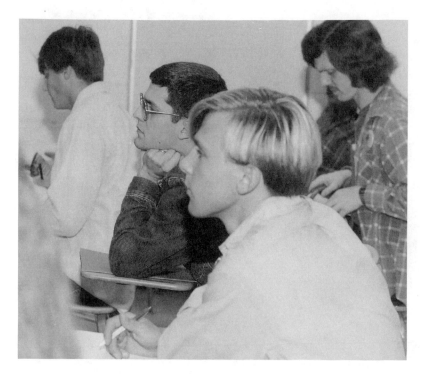

Out of a number of pictures of class reaction it is likely you will find one in which the students appear at least unbored. This is the Occupations class. That looks like Ted Schaefer on the left, though that isn't where he usually sat, then Rod Bear, Beau Wagner and Martin Moore.

Tom Koebernick was a guest speaker at one of the sessions of the Careers class (Ch. 6). He was discussing urban careers which, as you can see, have their lighter moments.

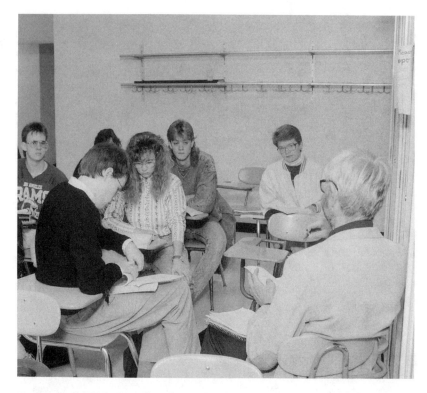

This is the honors class that the author thought was so wonderful, though these students had very mixed opinions about him (Ch. 6). They look dubious at the moment, don't they? Let's see, from left to right, Karen Sachs, Matt Dewald hiding from camera or question, Scott Siebert, Tony Arnett, Jennifer Ramsey, Tony Ackerman and April Berger. The coming of the photographer was unannounced to students or professor.

The last researcher to use the card catalogues. Replaced by computers and hidden on the fourth floor, their location was known only to the author (Ch. 7).

A Department pizza lunch in the Anthropology Lab. But to get the pizza you have to listen to a presentation. In this case it is on "A Professor's Work" (Ch. 8). Clockwise from the presenter are Bob Riordan, Len Cargan, Amy Karnehm, Jeanne Ballantine, Pam Trimble, Norma Shepelak, Susan Makowski, Bonnie Adduccio, Suzanne Francis and Jerry Savells. You can see this is pretty grim stuff.

Photographs by Jack Davis and Roberta Monnin

9

Serving the Community

The Professor Seeks to Provide
Shelter, Peace, and Culture

A professor in an urban university does not have to worry about being perceived as lost in an ivory tower. In my case I bused to work every day through the center of the city, along with lawyers, school teachers and janitors. Still, most of what has been discussed here occurred either within the halls or classrooms of Wright State or in the confines of other universities or, for the ISA meeting, a downtown hotel.

Two episodes in my notes, almost a year apart, particularly illustrate the ways in which an academic can get separated from reality. The summer I started taking notes, Mark Smutney of Westminster Church was telling me that Sinclair Community College was opposed to increasing temporary housing for the homeless downtown. It would increase the visibility of homeless people during the day and could cause problems or dangers for the students attending the downtown college. As a business, Sinclair was concerned about its middle class clients even though its sociologists might be actively concerned about the ability of the college to meet the needs of the working class and their children.

The other episode occurred the following spring when I was driving Keith Hudson (Ch. 4) home from an evening class. I started to let him off at a different corner, one closer to his house, but he asked to be let off at a more distant but safer place. I had been unconsciously harboring a white stereotype: that a black man would be more comfortable downtown at night than a white man.

Like other academics, other professionals for that matter, I had some ambivalence about this perceived detachment from reality. The professor, like the doctor, should not be oblivious to his community. On the other hand, he should give primary attention to his job. *The Dayton Daily News* saw it that way too. In a fall editorial, it praised Wright State for its community involvement, but warned against carrying this so far that its primary mission was stunted. In our suspicion that the Nutter Center could be draining resources from general education, we were responding to the same idea.

In any event, within the community my activities were limited, as they probably were for most other full time professionals. During the year in question I played supporting roles in three different kinds of activities: the Community Life Committee of a downtown church, the annual conference of the Peace Studies Association and, most amazingly and incongruously, the Board of Directors of the Early Music Center.

Community Life

I hope other people were better citizens than I. During the year studied, I read the daily paper superficially if at all, giving more attention to the sports page than to community or national news. On the two occasions we had to vote, I put in fewer pins than I left out.

On election night, Nelle and I were having wine when we remembered we hadn't voted. I argued that we shouldn't bother because the Sinclair levy would pass anyway, since the suburban voters would outnumber the city voters. In the end, what decided Nelle on our voting was that she didn't want my notes to say we middle class citizens hadn't voted. So I voted for the levy, for a provision on the appointment of a lieutenant governor that I didn't understand, and for two Oakwood schoolboard officials, only one of whom I knew. Nelle voted the same, but for a different schoolboard official, and for a judge. How do you vote for a judge?

But still, I was a member of the Community Life Committee of Westminster Presbyterian Church. The committee had a budget of nearly $50,000, which it tried to use to help alleviate community problems. I was a member of the committee because I belonged to the church, but of course I chose that committee because its activities coincided with my professional interests and helped me keep in touch with the real world. If, possibly, I could help the committee because of my professional knowledge, in return the committee helped me keep in touch with the city in ways that impacted directly with areas about which I taught.

The committee consisted of about 30 members of the church, with typically 15-20 showing up for a meeting. The previous year, after discussing the matter with Fred Bartenstein of the Dayton Foundation, we switched from something he called an exposure approach, giving something to a number of organizations who apply for funds, to an impact approach, concentrating our giving to a certain area, in our case, homelessness. In the current calendar year we were giving 40 percent of our budget to two organizations: the Religious Coalition for Low Income Housing, which was trying to deal with long term systemic problems, and Habitat for Humanity, which was building housing units.

But in August, as the new applications came in, two issues claimed more attention: crack and AIDS. In the applications for the coming year, there were three AIDS-related requests. How did these issues compare to those with which we were already trying to cope? What obligation did we have to organizations we were already supporting? Should a switch require a burden of evidence from the newer applicants?

Also, I wondered, looking at applications, how were we doing? Was the city any better off because of our activity? Were we having any impact on homelessness? After serving almost three years on the committee, I didn't know. I was revved up for the meeting. I wanted to get some subcommittees going and somehow follow up on our previous appropriations, see what effect they were having.

Regarding AIDS, Herb Shroeder asked if we gave money to any of these applications, would we be endorsing immoral behavior? Our staff minister, Mark Smutney, argued that Jesus ministered to people who had made wrong decisions.

I found myself arguing against appropriating $1,500 to a Task Force Against Racism. Can you imagine? I felt, with our limited budget, money given for more direct help to the poor and distressed would automatically help a disproportionate percentage of minority people. But it sure was uncomfortable.

When I had time to consider the meeting, I felt that I had been too precipitous, too blunt. My New Jersey style caused me to interrupt, jump in, not listen. I was successful in arguing that AIDS should be considered separately from other terminal illnesses, so that we would not appear to be an all white, middle class committee dismissing the question on what would be interpreted as moral grounds. Herb argued that we should have the courage to do precisely that, and not worry about how we would appear.

But it was not the time to seek more information. No subcommittees got appointed. Were our two main approaches to homelessness effective? Habitat did get houses built, but only a few a year; and they would go to people who were already housed but not already owners. If we used vouchers with $20,000, we might get about eight truly homeless families housed. Would that be a better approach?

Many of our decisions meant accepting the plug-in figures of our chair, Pat Porter. She made rough estimates based on past experience, so the committee would have targets to vote on. But we had only one evening, a two-and-a-half hour meeting. We could debate only so many applications, accepting the others without discussion. We didn't even consider coming back for a second meeting.

A couple weeks later, at the beginning of September, I had a chance to talk to Pat about Community Life concerns. She agreed that we should have a question in our application form about the social effectiveness of an organization. What had been achieved? As for crack, she was not persuaded that we could do much more about it than we were presently doing. She agreed we ought to have some minority members on our committee, if not from our church, then from another church. There was another Presbyterian church, not a mile away, that had a much larger black membership than we had. Could we ask them to contribute a couple of members to our committee?

In October I attended a subcommittee meeting on goals and objectives with Pat Porter, Pat Shroeder and David Leach, who taught art at Wright State. Pat Shroeder defined the difference: goals are general and unobtainable, objectives are specific and reachable. We produced a list of objectives, including a long term planning objective that said we ought to review the objectives annually to see if we still agreed with them. In other words, as these objectives were reviewed annually by a committee whose members change, they could also change. So there would be short term stability, long term flexibility. Could a list of objectives be internalized by the larger committee? As Pat Shroeder said, the members of the Community Life

Committee would have to have ownership of the objectives. Otherwise it would just be a sterile list.

A few weeks after this meeting, Social Work Professor Bela Bognar told me how the Romanian Government had bulldozed 8,000 villages in order to force people to move to the cities, a modern enclosure movement! It boggled the imagination when we were discussing whether we could build one Habitat house or two, that the Romanians could have destroyed 8,000 villages. It was as if all our work had been negated at a blow.

In early November, Nelle returned energized from a conference in Chicago, thinking about what she could do to improve the Dayton system of adult protection, not from abuse but from neglect through ignorance of care and services. It occurred to me that in her job as Community Geriatric Nurse, by helping people get the services they need to continue living at home, she was probably doing more for preventing homelessness than our whole committee could hope to accomplish.

By the time of our January meeting, we knew that we would not get what we asked for. If our cut was proportional to the shortfall in pledges, we would receive about $3,700 less than we had anticipated. We had $5,000 in reserve, either as contingency money or because it hadn't been spent, so Mark advised Pat Porter to offer $3,700 but keep the $5,000 in mind as a backup figure. In other words, even in a cause that ought to assume honest, straightforward interaction, we took negotiating strategies as a given.

As it turned out, though, when Pat reported back in February, she had given up $6,000 the Church had received as an anonymous gift for housing, plus $1,100 in our contingency fund. The $6,000 had been given to Habitat, and then our budget was cut by that amount. I was irate. It seemed to me that the spirit of the gift had been violated, that we wouldn't have lost the $6,000 if we hadn't had it as a gift; and what had really happened was that the gift had been used to cover the deficit. Moreover, grabbing surviving contingency funds would encourage committees to make sure in future years that they spent them instead of keeping them for future emergencies.

At the same meeting we heard a presentation by Barbara Friendly, Director of "Places," a home for the mentally retarded. It had about eight adjacent apartments and people lived together, supporting one another. I found myself wondering if we wouldn't do better giving heavy support to an organization like this rather than to

Habitat. This would be difficult to sell, because Scott Porter was heavily involved in Habitat and his mother was chair of the committee. Habitat, moreover, drew large numbers of church members as volunteer labor, so it served the important function of getting many more church members involved in service activities. Well, maybe we should switch our religious coalition money to Places or something that does the equivalent? I mean, Places was housing individuals who would otherwise be street people, putting them in a community situation, and even finding work for them. Didn't that come closer to our objective?

At our March meeting we had reports from liaison members of various agencies to which we contributed. Beth Neher reported on Artemis House, "a domestic violence resource center." Two women started it, working with both the battered and the batterers. They had a crisis line, went to emergency rooms of hospitals to talk to battered women. She compared the batterers' support group to Alcoholics Anonymous. Artemis House consulted with 6,000 families a year. That was an average of more than 20 per working day, and that was just one agency. There is a lot of trouble in the world.

Scott Porter reported that Habitat had completed four housing units the previous year, maybe one or two more this year. Moving into those four units would be two single-parent families and a single grandparent family, with the residents of the fourth undecided. It cost about $30,000 to build a unit. It had turned out to be cheaper to build from scratch than to repair old houses.

Obviously there was much to be done on the Community Life Committee. We didn't have a good handle on our objectives and we had virtually no measure of our effectiveness. For whatever reason, our church was much more effective at getting volunteers out to work on building houses than it was at getting people to think about priorities or measure effectiveness. Maybe it was because Scott Porter was so enthusiastic and well organized, or maybe because middle class people would rather work around a house on Saturday than plan, prioritize or measure, something they do every day in their regular work.

Thinking about this I was reminded that on television I once saw and heard Harold Macmillan respond to the question of what his favorite cabinet position had been. His lugubrious face almost brightened when he responded "Minister of Housing." Minister of Housing? When you are Foreign Minister, he explained, things get a little better or a little worse, but you can't tell what effect you had.

But when you are Minister of Housing, you say let's build 5,000 houses here. Six months later you visit the site and there they are, being built!

The Annual Peace Conference

The driving force behind the Peace Studies Association was Reed Smith, a mostly retired professor of political science, an old liberal and veteran of many causes. The PSA, which has been described experiencing disaster (Ch. 4), also had a community function, the running of an annual Community Peace Conference. This year the conference was being held at the University of Dayton, and the two universities were joint sponsors.

One of the presentations at the conference particularly related to community participation in a broader sense. Louis Laux of nearby Wittenberg College did a workshop on resource management in Costa Rica. He came in his tourist shirt and hat, the latter with a cool flap, the former sporting a glorious bird.

Laux told us about Dan Jansen, whose work in Costa Rica was an interesting example of a situation in which research related closely to social action. Jansen took his students yearly to Costa Rica, where they both studied forest ecology and worked on forest replenishment. What an ideal situation: you did your research, taught your students, and had the feeling of service accomplishment all at once.

If that didn't make me feel jealous, Jansen, through Laux, laid a bit of guilt on the rest of us. We should cut down on the number of (forest consuming) academic papers we write and spend more time saving the environment. Between trips to Costa Rica, Jansen raised both money and consciousness. It certainly seemed more satisfying to study forests, where you knew what to do, than work on peace, where you didn't. Well, Reed did. I resisted him because I thought I could do more with paper than I could by marching, petitioning and advocating. But since I also didn't like doing those things, there was more than a slight feeling of shirking.

It happened that the COPRED meeting in Denver occurred right after the Dayton Peace Conference. COPRED members had an above average sense of social responsibility. For instance Pat Mische gave a paper in which she advocated giving "Nature" a seat in the United Nations, in order to defend ecological interests. She or somebody else was managing the circulation of a petition needing three million signatures supporting this advocacy. I would probably sign such a petition if it were passed to me, but meanwhile limit myself to participating in the Oakwood recycling program, shutting off unused lights at home and at Wright State, and Not Littering. (I noticed, by the way, that three speakers among the activists had five styrofoam cups.)

Of course, activists suffered from guilt too. At the COPRED meeting somebody from Sane/Freeze in Syracuse said that activists often claimed only a limited, finite role. They did their part, not everything. I suspected they often needed to remind one another of that.

Liberals can find endless guilt. We had Armistice Day off, and Vietnam veteran Ron Flint (Ch. 5) reminded us what it was for. So besides being thankful for the day off, I tried to be thankful that others had been killed in wars instead of me. Not quite the right spirit. A week later I was apologizing in my notes for not attending the unity meeting against racism out on the quad and not responding to Reed Smith's giving us telephone numbers to call to urge that we stop sending armaments to El Salvador.

The rest of the year, I am afraid, was for me a peripheral effort to keep the Peace Studies Association, well, peripheral. Reed kept me informed about his efforts to raise more money, while I suggested ineffectually that perhaps money wasn't an important problem. One of the reasons for needing money was the annual Peace Lecture, for which, along with keynote addresses and distinguished speeches, I had little enthusiasm. And then, not six weeks after the conference at U.D., the PSA met to begin planning next year's conference, this one to be focused on Eastern Europe. I was glad that it was to be held at the Union Theological Seminary, not only involving another local institution, but also greatly reducing our workload.

And I continued to shirk my world responsibilities, failing to make any calls to Congress about Nicaragua's elections, not even opening a message to the Peoples of the World from the Universal House of Justice, failing to appear on the quad to participate in shouting "Good Morning America" (Ch. 4), neglecting to join my colleagues in a Washington March over El Salvador, even refusing to wear one of the ribbons Reed was passing out in memory of Kent State. Didn't fit my image.

One day in May, Reed came by to discuss a grant proposal to start a Peace Studies Center. I reminded him that he was in his last quarter of teaching and that he ought to be looking for a successor, who would have to face the problem of whether to establish a center.

In my notes I wrote that I would be surprised if the Peace Studies Association lasted a year beyond Reed's real retirement. The membership was substantial, but its commitment was limited. People were willing to carry out specific tasks, being treasurer for a conference for instance, but not to take over the chronic problems of unpaid and not very prestigious leadership.

How did that Syracuse maxim go again? We have a limited, finite role. Let Reed take care of El Salvador while I turn my attention to the preservation of Early Music.

The World of Early Music

We use the term "world" to describe subcultures, groups who, among themselves, are so contained that we say they are in "another world." I could have referred to the ISCSC in this sense, but when I was in it I didn't see it that way, because it was *my* world. Only when I write about it can I see that others might have perceived it as somewhat odd.

In the case of the Early Music Center, however, I often had the sense of being a visiting alien. During the year studied I was well into a three year term as member of the Board of the Early Music Center. It was an activity that had little to do with any other in which I was engaged. I was the only member of the board who did not play a musical instrument and, as a matter of fact, I wasn't a great listener. I saw early music as background music, pleasant if there weren't too many shawms. But if I hadn't been a board member, I doubt we would have gone to concerts. When I did go, I was as much interested in the variety of weird instruments as I was in how they sounded. In fact, I had the heretical idea that our Early Musicians would make an excellent warmup group for one of the area string quartets.

The reason I was on the board was that Pat Olds, the Early Music Center Director, had known me from AAUP activities when she taught in the Music Department at Wright State. When she established the Early Music Center as a retirement project, Nelle and I made a contribution, in part, perhaps, because I was gearing up to teach general education history courses and was interested in the preservation of historical art forms. Pat reasoned that I was interested in music and that my AAUP experience and administrative abilities would be useful in a board member. When she invited me to join the board, I talked it over with Nelle. We agreed that it would be good to have a different kind of experience. My work always had been concerned with the study of society and social service. I had never done anything for the arts, unless you count giving up the clarinet.

I considered the board a learning experience, but peripheral to my other activities. When I listed all my service activities in order of importance for merit evaluation, I listed membership on the Early Music Board last. But I had not allowed sufficiently for Pat Olds, who was totally dedicated and committed, and most of all, focused. Even though she was a victim of MS, Pat, by her drive and enthusiasm, attracted people into the group; but the same characteristics, in the long run, also wore them out. Well, enough background. Please let me introduce you to the World of Early Music.

On a Saturday night in June, the Early Music Board had an unsuccessful pot luck in Pat Olds' delightful colonial house outside Yellow Springs, about half an hour from Wright State. Only two board members came. We were coming off a spring performance of the Early Music Group that had not been well attended; our fund drive wasn't going well; our coming summer workshop barely had enough participants.

But the following Tuesday the Early Music Group would be performing for the first time at the Dayton Art Institute, where an audience of more than 100 was pretty well guaranteed for a weekly series of music performances. This would give us some exposure, help our drive, attract new people to future performances. To be sure, Pat had reservations about professionals' giving free performances. Once that started to happen, would the community come to expect it?

Well, we got exposure all right, but not the kind we expected. The DAI concerts were given in a small classical amphitheater under the stars. Card chairs were set out, or people brought their lawn chairs or spread blankets on the grass. I counted the crowd at around 150, a very large audience for early music. Jazz pianist Matt Cooper played the first half of the performance. I thought his part a bit long, but I may have been overly anxious that our group would have enough time.

As it turned out, it didn't. Countertenor Kurt Zeller had sung one Spanish song to gamba accompaniment and was introducing the second when rain came from nowhere. No warning drops, no "Is it raining?" Just ploop! People grabbed the instruments and ran for cover. Among the things they grabbed were Pat Olds' canes, so she got drenched along with the harpsichord. What a catastrophe! Publicity lost, rehearsal time wasted, and fat chance of getting Pat ever to try it again.

Our July meeting gave primary attention to our coming Renaissance Fair. I was out of my element as the members planned children's games, the cooking of Renaissance period food, and the arrangement of toilet facilities. In the end, "portajohns" won out over Renaissance realism, which would have meant the bushes. As secretary of the board, I took minutes. As chair of the Marketing committee, I would write the news release and the public service announcements for local classical radio stations.

I didn't like writing these releases. Partly it took me back to my journalism days of the 1950's. Worse, it was the kind of writing that a beginner did, or even a stringer. So I felt relegated to my preprofessional days. It seemed a comedown from trying to unravel the causes of war. But, as an old journalist, I could write them fast and to the point. The Public Service Announcements were kind of fun because you did 30-, 20- and 10-second versions. The 10-second version, running about three-and-a-half lines, was virtually a haiku.

Pat Olds had also mentioned to me that the Marketing committee, which I chaired, was supposed to have some members who were not board members and to hold its own meetings. Well, I thought, I'll put a committee together but my hunch was Pat would be uncomfortable about its getting out of control.

I realized that perhaps I was also uncomfortable perhaps because I did not like selling. Even though the product was worthwhile, there seemed to be a conflict between the ethics of the professional and those of the merchant. On the Renaissance Faire, for instance, I wanted to make tickets easy to come by without bullying friends to buy them. I reminded myself that one of my grandfathers had been a merchant, the other an artisan. Their labors made it possible for my father and me to be professionals.

At the August EMC meeting, Pat worried because we had no idea how many people would come to the Faire. How many would descend upon her house and grounds? Would there be only a few, or two hundred? This was the kind of problem an entrepreneur has to contend with, but not the professional. That may be one reason why many of us regarded local arrangements for a conference as the worst thing we ever had to do.

Also, we each agreed to try to sell four season tickets to Early Music Group performances. But I didn't want to approach people in the hallways, or even worse, try to sell tickets by phone. I could put a sign on my bulletin board, but that wouldn't reach many people. Or I could stuff selected mailboxes, the least unpalatable alternative. I decided on the latter and addressed the problem, feeling fellow professionals would understand:

> What a dilemma. What it is, I think, is that a professional can't stand to be a merchant. Enmity goes back several centuries. Can't call people. Can't approach them in the hall. Could stuff mailboxes and then make believe I didn't. I've got season tickets for the Early Music Group. Fritz Magg, Cello, 3 Bach Suites, Oct. 22. Introduction to the Dance, Feb. 4. Chaucer and Music with Henry Limouze April 22. All at 3 p.m., Sundays, Yellow Springs Presbyterian Church. $20. Your Significant Other may be surprised to receive tickets as a gift. May be appalled. For tickets send checks to room 480 Millett. Make out to Early Music Center. Or stop by Rm 476 on other business and, as if by accident, leave check behind.

The Renaissance Faire was to be the capstone of an Early Music Workshop that was held at Wright State after the summer quarter, when housing was available. One of the features of the workshop was a concert by the Early Music Faculty, really a tremendous performance. It was wonderful to see an audience so enthusiastic for esoteric music. But knowing even as little as I did, some of it was quite wonderful, including the affective interaction among the performers: Judith Davidoff, Shelley Gruskin, Scott Rice and Ben Bechtel.

I spent four hours the following Saturday selling tickets and even confronting a gate crasher at the Faire. There were strange food and strange games, dancing in the garage, and music from the workshop leaders in the music room (ominous rising early music).

ARS Abandons EMC

I arrived at Pat's house for the EMC meeting on a beautiful Saturday afternoon, fourth quarter of the playoff game with the Giants leading the Rams 13–10. But the Rams were on the Giants' 39 when I had to go in for the meeting. What a sacrifice. Not one of the board members would understand.

The big news of the meeting was that the EMC had lost its American Recorder Society sponsorship for workshops. A complaint had been made by Scott Rice, one of the performers who, I remarked above, had performed with such empathy at the summer workshop concert. Pat talked to Allen Moore, Executive Secretary of the ARS; and it turned out he had not contacted Shelley Gruskin or Judith Davidoff, who had been members of the Workshop Committee. I shared the group indignation and volunteered to talk to Moore. But, I'm afraid, I also thought "National versus Local: good material for the book!" Pat later called to tell me that Scott Rice ran a workshop of his own. Could his complaint about the EMC workshop involve Corporate Greed?

In January I followed a letter to Alan Moore with a phone call. He said the ARS Workshop Committee Chair had received a complaint from Scott Rice about the workshop and contacted two people who supported Rice and two who supported Olds. On the basis of information received, he had recommended withdrawal of the ARS endorsement of EMC workshops.

He said letters for EMC were received from all over the world, but the tone of some of the supporting letters suggested there were underlying problems. There had been complaints about the previous workshop that had not been relayed to Pat until Rice's complaint had been made. Also, supporting materials from the EMC had arrived that had not been considered by the committee because they were too bulky for the ARS mailbox. The matter was apparently reviewed by the committee under a new chair and the previous decision was sustained. But, partly as a result of this case, review procedures were being formalized.

In April, as board member and author, I called Neil Seeley, chair of the ARS Workshop Advisory Committee. He said he knew there had been previous problems in the Early Music Workshops that had not gotten resolved, but he wasn't a member of the committee at the time. He said he would send me a checklist on the running of a workshop and gave me the name of the chair who presided over the withdrawal of the ARS endorsement. It was evident that emotions had run high.

But I hadn't budged the ARS. The Early Music Center would have to run its workshop without national endorsement.

The Great Marketing Controversy

What were for me strange experiences continued through the fall. There was the Fritz Magg concert on solo cello, not to my taste, though I love the cello with other instruments. But it was well attended by other cello players. There was a jazz concert as a fundraiser. And an early music dinner in the 1910 house of Diane and Andy Doss in Urbana to which we wore 1910 costumes (Nelle, her Hawaiian Mumu), ate a medieval dinner, and listened to the Early Music Group play and sing early music and jazz while the Doss kids played with our 1910 skittles board.

But while we were enjoying these pleasantries, Pat and I were also in conflict over the Marketing committee. When it met in September, I felt Pat took it away from me, wanting it to sell season tickets before it did long term planning. I persuaded her to stay away from the next meeting, which Beth Gage and I attended at Micki Adams' house over mulled cider and Stella D'oro biscuits. This time the committee did brainstorm, proposing to develop a system of volunteers to make phone calls and to participate in making phone calls for the local Public Broadcasting System fund drive. Telling Pat about the meeting, I had the feeling that she felt excluded. It wasn't easy to let your child grow up.

I followed up on our brainstorming idea about volunteering for the Public Television fund drive. Were we ever naive! It turned out that the host who supplied the volunteers paid the television station $2,500 a night for the privilege. That was why the volunteers came from the National Cash Register Company rather than the Early Music Center. So much for that idea.

At the next meeting of the Marketing committee we decided to help sell tickets for the spring concert—Micki Adams and Beth Gage would—and put off our plans for setting up a system of callers for next year's series, an example of the short term once again upsetting the long term. But we would also recommend to the board that the EMC try one more DAI concert and ask for help in finding names of callers. It was a compromise between Pat's objectives and mine. A couple weeks later, however, Pat called to tell me she was pulling Micki and Beth from the committee. Micki would join the board, Beth would engage in fundraising. I felt relieved that the marketing task was over, confirmed in my guess that Pat really was uncomfortable about an autonomous committee, but still curious whether a planned telephone campaign would improve ticket sales next year.

You would think that after I was able to make only two of my 13 points at the Marketing committee report to the board, and Pat referred to the committee as not quite a fiasco, that I might let long term planning quietly die. But no, in April Pat and I were back at it, with me arguing that if I could get a pyramid of callers set up, she wouldn't have these worries about sales for each particular concert. Part of me said I'll do what I can, but I'm not deeply involved. Part of me got dragged into involvement because I felt I was being dismissed as wrong, not only by Pat but by the whole board. What was amazing was how deeply you could get involved even in what you thought to be a peripheral activity. And here I was, a person who hated to make telephone calls and hated to be called by anyone selling anything, arguing for a program what would inflict a million phone calls on our unsuspecting community.

Finally, with Pat's help, I got together a list of 30 names of people I would call, asking each to call five others to buy tickets for next year's series at the Salem Street Unitarian Church in Dayton. The plan was to do a pair of concerts each quarter on the same weekend, one in Yellow Springs, one in Dayton. So if pyramiding didn't work, at least it would be wasted only on the pilot Dayton programs. And note that somehow, instead of my calling five to call five to call five, I was now calling 30 to call five, a one-tier pyramid with calls from the man who hated both sales and phone calls.

Between squabbles about the Marketing committee, Pat and I visited Arts Dayton on the 15th floor of Kettering Tower to discuss funding EMC. If power is measured by elevation of office floors, this was as high in the power structure as I had ever been. Listening to Pat, the Center sounded pretty good. Taught classes. Performed. Ran workshops, special events, fairs. Not affiliated with any university. I was impressed.

There were wailing entries in my notebook through June, past the allotted time of note taking, about making the phone calls. When I made my first two calls and both were incomplete, I realized it was going to take a lot more than 30. My final note in June concluded that the calls would go on through much of the summer because it took about five calls to reach one person, and I was making two a day. I didn't say that the shorter the time period people had for making their five calls, the more likely they were to decline this marvelous opportunity.

So ended my year of service on the board of the Early Music Center, what could be euphemistically described as a learning experience. What, do you suppose, would it be like to serve on the board of the Dayton Philharmonic?

What Pat Olds and Reed Smith had in common was a clear focus on their mission. Each was convinced of the Importance and Justice of The Cause. To them the rest of us must have seemed weak, flabby, selfish, uncommitted.

Afterword

The goals and objectives of the Community Life Committee were incorporated within the year's agenda by Pat Porter and her successor, Barbara Marshall. So the long run goal of paying recurrent attention to long run goals was achieved—at least in the short run.

And my prediction that the Peace Studies Association would not long survive Reed Smith's departure proved to be overly pessimistic. Under the leadership of Barbara Eakins-Reed, the PSA continued for a few more years to hold annual cooperative conferences and to sponsor a yearly speaker. Reed continued to serve in the ranks and sometimes grumbled with rueful cheerfulness that the group wasn't doing all that it might, particularly in the area of fund raising for a permanent center. As for the 1995 Dayton Peace Accords, as far as I know, the Peace Studies Association did nothing to prevent them.

My phone calls had no effect on the withdrawal of ARS support. We were not able to get the ARS to reverse its decision. A workshop was tried without ARS support, and was poorly attended. There was power out there in the world of Early Music!

And I am afraid the local phone campaign also had little impact. Perhaps my sell was too soft, perhaps it came too late, perhaps the Dayton neighborhood in which it was to be held—there had been quite a bit of publicity about drug sales and drive-by shootings—was not conducive to Purcell even on a Sunday afternoon. In any event all those calls that I hated to make, which produced five times as many more calls bothering people weekends or evenings, did little or nothing for concert attendance. Now Pat Olds would never be converted either to soft sell marketing or to long term planning.

For all my efforts, the city was no richer in shelter, peace or culture.

10

Even Professors
Have Families

From Hawaii to the Grand Canyon to the Kitchen Sink

September 8 was the anniversary of my father's birthday and on
that day I reached the age he was on the day of his death. Curious,
when that happens. From then on, any memory I had of him was of
a man younger than I was at the time of the memory. He was a
second generation Slovak American, a high school dropout who
became a lawyer, a politician and a professional with very high ethical standards combined with a robust, somewhat bawdy sense of
humor.

I had learned only recently that my mother also never completed high school, but dropped out to go to business college. So I was
the first member of our nuclear family to graduate from college,
though I was preceded by my cousin Jack, the son of my father's
oldest brother. My mother was virtually a second generation Dan-
ish American, a housewife who was very active in community affairs. My parents lived in Perth Amboy, New Jersey and I carry their
Eastern accent and what may be perceived in Ohio as a kind of brash-
ness or rudeness of style.

My wife, Nelle, was also the daughter of a lawyer, but both her
parents were college graduates. Her father went to Harvard Law
School, mine to night school in Newark. So you could say that so-

197

cially I married up, though I wouldn't have realized that at the time. We met at Alfred University in the early fifties, separated, reconnected, and married. We first lived in London, where I got my Ph.D. while working on the North American desk of Reuters, the British news agency. I taught for a dozen years at Bradford Junior College in Massachusetts, then for a few years in the State University of New York, returned for a couple years as associate dean when Bradford converted to a four year college, then came to Wright State as department (in those days) chairman. We had three children, Julie and Peter born in the London years and Ellen, born 12 years after Peter.

Since coming to Dayton we had lived in a suburb a few miles from the center of the city. My wife was Dayton's Community Geriatric Nurse, a health professional who made house calls. Of our children, only Ellen still lived at home, and she only summers, when not attending college.

Our house was an unpretentious two story, six room, wood framed structure. We were blessed with a front porch. We never had a great deal of money, were rather inclined toward low technology, bought small cars, ran them over 100,000 miles. A college teacher and a nurse who stayed home until her children went to school, we did not expect to get rich. In this we were not disappointed.

Nelle and I

Nelle and I were sitting on our front porch on a Sunday afternoon in August, both working. I was writing notes for what turned out to be this paragraph; she was preparing for a workshop in which she was to participate during the following month. She rarely had time for that kind of work during her regular day, which involved either visiting and helping clients or documenting what she had been doing. Next I was going to work on my Monday history class, rationalizing that the last week of a summer class was especially hectic so this would be an exception. Ordinarily, between Friday evening and Sunday evening I would try not to do any work directly related to the university except for reading books or journals. That made a clear break in my time and prevented me from being a dawn to bedtime workaholic. I also made an exception for the notes for this book, because they needed to be done as near the precipitating events as possible. Plus, they were sort of fun.

If the practice was violated, this was usually noted and explained. On a Friday night in October Nelle asked me if I were doing reading I *had* to do. I said yes because I had assigned the class so much reading that I couldn't keep up with it myself. In other words, ideally, it was okay to read on a Friday night if the material were for a future course, but not if it were material for the current quarter. It sounds silly put that way, but I did think that in a profession like mine, it would be possible for work to take over. In the same sense it was okay for Nelle to be reading material she would use in next month's workshop, but not to be documenting her cases. It was okay to write, but not to type, because typing involved physical removal from our normal centers of evening activity. In fact most of the notes for this book were handwritten in the house, on the bus, or in a plane, because when I had a typewriter at hand I needed to do other things. And it was important for us to ask each other what we were doing so that we would be aware that we might be slipping into a weekday work mode too often.

In the past couple of years we had been experiencing what the occupations textbooks call a dual-career marriage (Ch. 5). She had worked before, when the children were in school, as a pediatrics nurse or nursing instructor. But after Ellen was well established in the local school, Nelle had gone back to graduate school in both sociology and nursing to retrain in gerontology. Her studies had been rewarded when, after a period working in a nursing home, she had obtained the Community Geriatric Nurse position, working from Grandview, a downtown hospital. She was the only person in the city holding that position; and it was her job to visit elderly people, to assess their health problems, and to get them connected with available services. It was a demanding and interesting job, each day different from the last, with a story or two to bring home each evening.

One beautiful evening as spring was in the air, we were having wine and Nelle expressed concern that we were getting dull, working all the time, tired at night. So we went out, bought a fast food supper, and ate it at Cox Arboretum south of the city, watched the birds, walked around looking for early flowers. But that was hardly a regular evening activity.

The one other evening variation was more like a Dagwood Sunday cartoon. I came home from a night class and found that Nelle had bolted and locked our new kitchen door before going to bed, so I couldn't get in. I couldn't get the front door open either, because

I'd fixed it over the weekend. I tried throwing pebbles at the bedroom window. No luck. I got the hose out of the garage and hosed the window, but even that didn't wake her. While I was trying to decide what to do next, a car drove in the driveway. Oakwood police answering a call about prowlers? Nope. Nelle coming home from a late church session meeting.

Of course her key wouldn't open the side door either. She had locked it from the inside, gone out the front door with Virginia Preston. So we got the workmen's ladder from beside the garage, I climbed on to the front porch roof, tore the screen and entered the bedroom window.

My perpetual difficulties with teaching evaluations created a low level anxiety. These evaluations ought to have been high on my list of things to do something about, yet I rationalized that evaluations had to be kept in perspective. I shared some of this with Nelle, but tended to hold back because it added to her anxiety. Though holding back probably increased my anxiety, which she would quickly sense. Presbyterian Angst. On one occasion during winter quarter, Nelle bullied me into staying home from church, suggesting I cared more about returning borrowed books to the church library than I did about my students and my reputation as a teacher. She also asserted that I continued to take on too many peripheral activities and wasn't getting the basic one (teaching) done. (The state legislators would agree.) So I stayed home and graded papers— first making the notes for this paragraph, which proved her point.

On a couple of occasions she expressed concern that my work might affect our family life. Once was when the general education controversy grew warm. "You won't get into trouble, will you?" she asked. She was concerned that somehow I would get myself fired and, most immediately, how would that affect Ellen at Northwestern?

She often shared her professional concerns with me, often over wine we drank before dinner. She had come home energized, for instance, after a trip to a conference in Chicago, thinking about what she could do to improve the system of adult protection against neglect through ignorance of care and services. There appeared to be only one doctor in Dayton who still made house calls. *Newsweek* had an article on partner work in the home, a study showing that women who work do about 15 hours a week more work than men, if you count household chores. I would guess that would be less true if the male is a professor, who has a flexible schedule. When I was on sabbatical in the spring, I did much of the cooking, and continued to do so afterward. Weekends, Nelle was needed to do the ironing and washing, and with the fall she needed to give more of her attention to the reconstruction of our kitchen. As for parenting, for us it was a matter of phoning and letters, plus checkbook, plus Nelle worrying.

We both read novels, though I would allow myself such an indulgence only after 11 p.m. One novel we both read was Paule Marshall's *Praisesong for the Widow*. It was about a 62-year-old Black woman who left a cruise ship to stay on a French-speaking West Indian island to recover her heritage. We liked it because we were also thinking about our heritage as the result of the recent deaths of our mothers, and because there weren't so many novels about older people. Novels also took you out of specific professional concerns, or such house concerns as wallpapering, planning, backyard foliage or cleaning the garage.

Just before going to sleep one night, Nelle was rereading a biography of John Adams by Catherine Drinker Bowen. I then dreamt that I was considering asking George Washington to coauthor a paper with me. If he would, should he be senior or junior author? One evening we heard about the death of Robert Penn Warren. It caused us to ask what had happened to poetry. We used to read poetry when we lived in England. Where had it gone? How had we lost it? But the sadness shared did not lead to a reintroduction of poetry in our lives.

No poetry at the bus stop.
No poetry in the bathroom.

One night in August Nelle considered when she would retire. I worried a little about that, though it would mean she would have more time for things she wanted to do at home. Would the loss of professional satisfactions be compensated by home activities and volunteer work? Some evenings later, after I had expressed vexation about summer teaching, she asked me if I had given any thought to retirement. I brushed her question off quickly, but later admitted I had felt the idea threatening. Reagan and Bush were older than I when they took office. They never considered retiring!

But without a mandatory retirement age, when would I retire? When I could no longer teach effectively. But how would I know when that would happen? Who would tell me? Imagine asking Orenstein or Jeanne or Bill Rickert to tell me. "Look, Matt, there's something I've been observing lately . . ." It appeared that I might be entering a new stage of socialization.

Oh, and one other note tangentially related to this subject. When my father died three decades earlier, I inherited his black overcoat. But during the Christmas break, Ellen had appropriated it, and wanted to take it with her back to Evanston. Nelle supported that, saying it was time I bought a coat of my own. We looked at one in Elder-Beerman, but I was put off by the $150 price tag. Nelle, however, pointed out that it would be my last overcoat.

Somehow I did not find that reassuring.

The Professor's Children

Professors, like anyone else, may have children. You might suppose these children would have some advantages. A professor has, perhaps, more time to spend with them than do business fathers. They may be exposed to somewhat more reading and less television. Having a professional mother as well, and a pediatrics nurse at that, they may have had some advantages in terms of inculcated values and health care.

There may also have been disadvantages. Parents thought about that a lot. Lower income may have meant fewer opportunities, such as, oddly enough, a more limited choice of college. They may have an exaggerated idea of their father's attainments, perhaps not realizing that he was a very ordinary student in high school and college. Every profession had such advantages and disadvantages. And all this ignored the individual personalities of the children. It struck me that we blamed ourselves for the problems our children have, but didn't credit ourselves for their achievements. Yet, we didn't blame our parents for our problems.

Our older daughter, Julie, lived in Hawaii. She had a BFA from Alfred University, a Masters in Art Therapy from Wright State. She had taught in a Montessori school in Hawaii for three years, was currently running a summer and day care school for children, painting and sculpting, and operating an art gallery. Peter was a paver, living in Dayton. He had been to college but had no degree. Ellen was in her second year at Northwestern, majoring in English.

Julie was experiencing the process of divorce from Kevin Gray, who taught high school. They had one eight-year-old daughter, Gwen. Neither Peter nor Ellen had married.

One advantage of having a daughter living in Hawaii was that it gave you incentive to vacation there, as we did directly after the ISCSC conference in California. Julie and Gwen lived in a little house in the town of Paauilo, with her friend, Cathy Breth, a fellow artist and business partner. The town was located on the north coast of the "Big Island," Hawaii, which gave its name to the state.

While we were there Julie was considering a Montessori vacancy in the town of Hawi, about 45 miles from where she lived. From my perspective, she was casual about applying. I hoped, if it were a good position at a respectable salary, she would go after it vigorously. Then do the best she could for her daughter in terms of schooling and environment.

Her priorities were a bit different. First she was thinking about schooling. She felt Gwen was in a fairly good one at Paauilo, but was not confident of other schools in the area. Also, being in the process of divorce, she did not want to add to the stress by widening the distance her daughter had to go between households. If she continued to live in Paauilo, she would have to commute 90 miles a day.

I would do it. In fact I had done so for three years in upstate New York, precisely because I wanted the best schools for my children. But Julie was also considering whether a combination of substitute teaching, tutoring, day care management and, if necessary, unemployment compensation might not be better in terms of reduced stress, time for painting and environment. Her career commitment was one of several variables. For me it was crucial. The stress for me would be much greater if I didn't have a secure position and regular pay. Julie took pride in her teaching, was concerned about her students. But she did not seem to have a great need for security or position.

Art for Julie was what research was for me. She and I both felt uncomfortable when we were not painting or writing regularly. Many others who would agree with me about the primacy of position would not about the importance of writing or painting. For me, the research expectation was a tremendous asset for the position. For others it was a burden. So, however I may have differed with Julie on her priorities, we understood each other on the necessity for a creative outlet.

In the end she stayed with her multifaceted situation in Paauilo. We were distressed, however, to learn the following spring that she was thinking about pulling Gwen out of school the following year and home educating her, because she wasn't doing well within the school. We felt with the stress of divorce, it would not be a good time to separate Gwen from other children. In Hawaii, being a Haole (Caucasian), Gwen was experiencing some of the problems minority children do experience in school. Perhaps it would be a valuable experience in the long run, but you didn't want to have that laid on your grandchild while her parents were divorcing.

Though Peter lived nearby, we did not see him often. He worked long hours during the warm weather, had his own friends. I got a holiday in December after the fall quarter and before Christmas. About that time, as the weather got cold, his work slowed down. So I proposed that he and I make a December trip to the Grand Canyon.

We enjoyed our trip. We stopped in St. Louis to ride to the top of Saarinen's Arch in a little spacemobile, creaking all the way past a series of criss-cross stairs described in Jonathan Franzen's novel *The Twenty-Seventh City*. The Arch seemed a marvelous concept. It was impressive to see it encompassing a second day moon sliver or with the set sun still reflecting off the top as we came up to it through the park in icy weather.

The museum below the Arch was also worth a visit for travelers going west. The pictures reminded me of Expo '67. There were some wonderful quotations, including one from an explorer named Long who said the land could never be inhabited by people dependent on agriculture. Having just published a book on the future (Ch. 7), I felt empathy for Long.

We arrived in New Mexico after dark, stayed overnight in Tucumcari, and awoke the next morning in a very different setting. Tucumcari looked like a garish frontier town on a bright sunny day, beneath the first mountain we had seen. As we left a Tucumcari restaurant after breakfast, the cashier called: "Have a Nice Day!"

"Is that a New Mexican expression?" I asked.

"Oh no," she said, "I've heard it as far away as Kansas!"

We did have a nice day. The landscape was austere and beautiful, pale scrub grass interspersed with cedar-like shrubs and some sword plants. The mountains were red. Everything looked stranger in the late fall sunlight. I told Peter that on a previous trip we had seen antelope, but only in Wyoming, and you had to look for them. So we looked and in less than two minutes saw our first and only herd, maybe 20, near the road.

It took us until the middle of the afternoon to get to Chaco Canyon, after a very satisfying ride through the Nacimiento Mountains, a mixture of reds and grays. Then came a harrowing 25 mile trip over washboard roads to Chaco, hoping our old Omni would survive.

Chaco, which had been recommended at a pizza lunch (Ch. 8) by Ann Bellisari, was worth the drive. It was late afternoon with an early sunset, but we were able to visit four sets of pueblos, each distinctive, with many rooms. We were even able to go into a religious kiva, which had an echo inside and a half moon overhead. What remarkable structures, built by North Americans 900 years ago, when Europeans were first building their Gothic cathedrals. The valley itself was gorgeous in the late afternoon sun, with golden cliffs and blue sky. We were lucky enough to see a gray fox who sauntered in front of our car and took his time picking his way into the brush.

The next morning we visited Canyon de Chelly, another golden chasm. The beautiful "white house" was lodged in a cliff several hundred feet high, though the house was up no more than 30 feet. It was a pretty canyon in the morning sun, but we agreed that if you had time to visit only one, Chaco was the one to see. The variety of structures was incredible.

The trip to the Grand Canyon was through Navajo and Hopi country you might not see from the interstates. Under the low sun it was often beautiful, but bleak and depressing. We continued to encounter varieties of fauna. We encountered a mule doe and fawn near the Canyon, seemingly unconcerned about us, and marveled at sheep dogs maneuvering Navajo sheep. Do the owners say, "Harry, just take them over to the south pasture"?

Peter had his first look at the Grand Canyon at dusk, when it was purple and blue. The next morning we went down. It was splendid, of course, so every so often I would try for a picture, but without much hope. Maybe I could catch the blue sky, the Coconino cream against Redwall, the amazing green of the Colorado River at the bottom. Going down you met many people, mostly Europeans. But when we got into the Vishnu Schist at the bottom, we encountered hardly anyone except a solitary singer who passed us by in earphones. He had been singing to his music.

The bottom was cold and there wasn't much to do. We had to eat before it got dark at five. Coming in we crossed the Silver Bridge, which mules won't cross because they can see the water below. Again we encountered fauna, a wild turkey and a velvet antlered mule deer; at one of the rest stops, a perky, chubby ground squirrel. And during the night we were visited by civet cats. We weren't cold, but it was a long night for me watching Cassiopeia, Orion and the Big Dipper pass over the canyon while I turned left, back, right trying to stay on the mat and out of the dust, envying Nelle who that night was attending a Dayton Philharmonic concert.

Of course pain is part of the canyon. First the knees, the good knee before the bad one, then boots eroding the ankles, causing me finally to take the laces out. This helped wonderfully, except they no longer served as boots. Coming up my knees and ankles were better, but my legs were gone by Angel Shale, the eighth level. You counted them coming up like the tiers of Hell: Vishnu Schist and Zoroastrian Granite, Tapeat Sandstone, Angel Shale, Mauv Limestone, Redwall Limestone, Subai Conglomerate, Hermit Shale, Coconino Sandstone, Toroheap Conglomerate, Kaibab Sandstone. I was so sore and stiff that when I got into the car I had no intention of getting out again before supper. If the geologists were right, the Colorado had cut one twenty-fifth of an inch deeper since I had last descended seven years earlier. I noticed the difference.

Even on a trip like this, Peter remained an enigma. We talked a great deal, and shared what we perceive to be wit. But he didn't let me in, perhaps no one else either. For the rest of the year he was a peripheral figure in my notes, present at Christmas, declining dinner at Easter.

The only other note about him concerned a night he did come to dinner and *USA Today* called to ask about the Nobel Peace Prize. I said, "Oh, have I won it?" They said no, but it was to be announced the next day, and they were asking people who they thought should win it. Overcoming the temptation to say I should, I nominated David Singer, had to explain who he was and why he should get the prize.

Peter asked what the conversation was about. When I had told him what I have written above, the phone rang again. "Maybe they've changed their minds," Peter said.

A sermon from Bob Lowry at Westminster, "Surprises From God," (e.g., Sarah's pregnancy, the burning bush) brought to mind our surprise from God: Ellen. She was 12 years younger than Peter, really grew up as an only child except that she had the advantage that her parents did not have everything invested in her. Unlike her older siblings, she had gone through a single school system in the small Ohio city of Oakwood. Wanting to get away from small schools, she had chosen a large, cosmopolitan university, Northwestern. We were able to afford it with considerable financial help from her grandmother.

Having worked the previous summer selling men's clothing, she thought that she would work the summer before her sophomore year on call for temporary service, figuring she would get a variety of experience and some days off. As it turned out, she got too many days off. On some of those, she worked for me, helping me prune my files. She went about this with gusto, undoubtedly throwing out some things I would later miss, but also turning up some that had been lost. One we did keep was the record of my application for the chairmanship (as it then was) of the Sociology, Anthropology and Social Work Department (as it then was). I was kind of pleased that she had a chance to read this document and that, as she said, she was getting an idea of what I do. It sometimes seemed as though my children had little idea beyond Peter's first grade description: "he carries a suitcase to work and marks blue books."

Finally, well into August, Ellen got work with the United Way that promised to last the rest of the summer and to be interesting besides. Then, the very evening she had told us so enthusiastically about this job, she met with a strange accident. As she and a friend were leaving a downtown movie, someone from a passing truck threw a raw egg and hit her in the eye. We first heard from the hospital emergency room. There was possible damage to the iris that could have a permanent effect on her vision, which hadn't been all that good since she was quite young.

Nelle's boss, Louise Morrow, covered for her at an important meeting so she could stay with Ellen through the medical process that followed. I saw some of it too, and couldn't help seeing it also from the perspectives of the professionals in action. Nelle was impressed with Dr. Tom Files, the ophthalmologist on call, a teaching doctor who explained very carefully to her each aspect of Ellen's optical problem. I was impressed with the bedside manner of her regular ophthalmologist, Dan Juergens, so much better than mine, in laying her worries to rest without minimizing the seriousness of the injury.

When it came time for Ellen to return to school, I realized we had not discussed the coming academic year. It seemed to me that I gave freely of my talents to others I didn't know, but rarely provided guidance for my own daughter. Had we not talked because of the chemistry of our personalities? I didn't know but I had to acknowledge after reading Jessie Bernard that I didn't worry about the children nearly as much as Nelle did. We may have been reasonably egalitarian about housework, but not about worrying.

There was an article in *Newsweek* on members of the younger generation being so hooked on a higher standard of living that they were not able to adjust to the real world. College graduates were living home rent-free, or running up hundreds of dollars worth of parking tickets. Ellen, I thought, recognized the problem, but wasn't addicted to a higher standard, though she did need to work on her budgeting. Julie and Peter, meanwhile, half a generation older, lived nearly at the poverty level. In this sense, then, we had been successful parents.

It was in the spring quarter that I decided to reread *The Brothers Karamazov* because Ellen was reading it and it would be something we could discuss. The following weekend we called her and I asked how far she had gotten. She said she had finished it in four nights. Oh. Say, what did you think of the first two chapters?

In the spring, Ellen wanted to work for the summer in the Chicago area. I struck a bargain with her. If she would do an internship this summer, the following summer she could stay in Chicago. She agreed and we considered several internships. For once I was able to be helpful; I talked to my other squash partner, Dan DeStephen, about an internship with his Center for Labor Management Cooperation, work I thought she might like since she seemed to devote a great deal of energy to resolving conflicts among her friends. I felt that a summer of really meaningful work without pay would be more valuable than earning her own money in a more limited kind of job. It might open a career for her, at least get her thinking about alternative possibilities. If not earning her own money cost her something in self esteem, she had a good supply of that (self esteem, not money). And perhaps it added something to mine to do something parental for a change.

Plus, she would be home for one more summer.

The Extended Family

Both Nelle's mother and mine had died within a couple of days of one another the winter preceding this study. We went from one funeral to the other. That experience had sensitized us to our extended family. Several years earlier my mother had gathered information about both her side of the family and my father's, and now I sent her charts to my cousins. I wanted as many people as would be concerned to have them, so there would be a better chance that memory, somewhere, would survive a little longer. For the same reason, I put the books I had written together on one shelf in the den, hoping that some day, when the children were getting ready to sell the house, that one of them would say, "Hey, look! Here are all Dad's books!"

Both our extended families were scattered. Nelle's niece and nephew were still in Rochester, where she came from. Her surviving cousin lived in California. My cousins lived in Washington State, New York State and Florida, with three cousins still in New Jersey. America is a big country, and dispersal is one of the prices you pay for being middle class. Even if I had joined my father's law firm in New Jersey, most of my kin would have moved.

As I mentioned, we were reading the Paule Marshall book. The heroine decided she was going to rebuild her grandmother's shore house, have the grandchildren come summers, and tell them about their roots. My mother had such a summer house, and we encouraged her to give it up because we were not committed to regular summer visits. Now Nelle had visions of a summer cottage somewhere to which children and grandchildren would periodically return.

The Bad Provider

In the fall, just when Ellen was returning to school, I read for Occupations an article by Jesse Bernard on what she described as "The Good Provider Role," an image she dates from 1830 to 1980. The Good Provider keeps his family well fed, clothed and housed, is a good contributor to church, and educates his children. His work might be demanding, but it was expected to be. If he were also kind, gentle, generous and not a heavy drinker or gambler, that was frosting on the cake. Loving attention and emotional involvement were not part of a woman's implicit bargain with the Good Provider.

I grew up with an ideal something like that. And even with my children all out of the house, I was haunted by still having to budget, as if that were not appropriate at my stage of life. Perhaps I was also not comfortable that my wife was expanding her kitchen from her own funds, suggesting that I couldn't provide her with something she really wanted. And I was feeling guilty that I still had to teach summer school, taking money from younger faculty who needed it for their homes and children. There would be inheritances from the deaths of our mothers, but if the inheritances were to mean freedom from budget and summer teaching, that would be unearned, not the result of the efforts of the Good Provider.

The Good Provider, the Professional Disdainful of Commerce, the Child of the Depression, the Father Who Preached Against Avarice: I had too much history, too many roles.

Do Professors have Fun?

I'm sure many do. But perhaps Nelle and I had less than average, partly because of our work, though our choice of work, in turn, reflected the kind of people we were. Not exactly fun loving. Often what we chose to do shaded into our professional lives, or in any event it was more likely to be "serious."

Our music was serious: church music, early music, classical. When it was early music, it would be mixed with a service component. I sold tickets. On symphonies I have only three entries. There was the one I didn't go to because I was at the bottom of a canyon. There was a whole evening of Berlioz, "Symphonie Fantastique" followed by "Lelio," a rare combination though they were designed to go together. But my only comment was that because of the concert, I couldn't finish reading the reports submitted by the 201 class. Another evening, Zafskofsky playing Berg—as if I would always know who Zafskofsky was—with Bach's Third Brandenberg and Beethoven's Seventh. It could be that when I was taking notes I saw Philharmonic nights as nights off, therefore not to be recorded in notes on my work.

We saw eight or nine movies, of which only "Pretty Woman" and "Parenthood" could be considered fun. In "Parenthood," Steve Martin didn't get a partnership in the firm because he wouldn't sacrifice his family to his job, wouldn't wine and dine clients, get them laid. He quit the job but was asked to come back at a raise. He accepted, we supposed, because he needed to support his family and had made it clear that he had ethics. In retrospect, it doesn't seem that even Steve Martin was much fun.

"Pretty Woman" was fun though. Corporate raider Richard Gere spends $100,000 on hooker Julia Roberts, and then marries her. We presume they lived happily until the following Tuesday.

Among the others were "Cinema Paradiso," "Henry V," "Do the Right Thing," and "Enemies." All of these were films *The New Republic* critic Stanley Kauffmann liked, which makes them suspect. I was somewhat bored and impatient with Hermann's problems with three wives in "Enemies." He needed an interesting career to balance his life.

It would have been great to see Branagh's version of Henry V on successive nights with Olivier's. It sure made war wet and unpleasant, and you felt the dirt of Mrs. Quickly's tavern. And there was an incredible scene in which Henry V, reciting lines from the play, walked over the gory battlefield. It was as much an anti-war play as Olivier's had been a war play. Neon Movies, our one serious theatre, was sold out on opening night. This was certainly gratifying, because we were always concerned about whether it would survive. That this was the only film we saw there for the year didn't indicate we were providing much help.

"Do the Right Thing" we saw for a second time on video at church, which we discussed it after a pot luck. Two viewings of this film should have created some profound observations from a teacher of urban social problems. But what struck me after the second viewing was that maybe Mookie, the black assistant, had saved his Italian boss, Sal, from a mob by throwing a trash can through the window of his pizza parlor. The mob trashed the parlor instead of Sal, but in the aftermath the police killed one of the trashers.

By the time I wrote my notes, I had already forgotten the name of the director of "Cinema Paradiso," and it was crucial because it was a biographical film reviewing his childhood as a movie projectionist in a Sicilian village. The child was particularly endearing. I was left with longings for a village life I never had. I loved living in small towns in England and New England, but we didn't have the films, the Philharmonic or even Early Music.

We saw just one play, Tom Stoppard's "The Real Thing." It was a play about reality. What was real life? What is really good writing? Is fidelity good or constrictive? The couple that opts for fidelity was unfaithful. One of the characters says there isn't commitment, just a series of bargains. From the perspective of my *Peace in Our Time*, it was about the relational outlook and the difficulties it brings. From another perspective, it was an exploration of sociological interactionism.

Did we enjoy the play? My notes don't say.

Only once, besides the picnic out on Route 741, do my notes refer to getting out in nature. I would have thought we did that more often, Greater Dayton providing a surprising selection of wooded parks and trails. Nelle and I spent the Fourth of July exploring the gardens, fields and forests of the Allwood Nature Preserve. You might hope the notes would reflect the beauty of the gardens, the serenity of the trails, how good it was to walk with your Lady on the cool and pleasant trails. But no, they comment instead on my abysmal ignorance of flowers. I didn't know either their names or their family relationships, which Nelle seemed to be able to tell from the leaves.

Since I have been a professional, novel reading seems to be all the recreational reading that I allow myself (only "Good" novels, approved by *The New Republic* or some other qualified reviewer). Otherwise I read what I needed for teaching and research, and not nearly enough, either. No time for flowers.

Friends

This had become something of a worry. Our professional work kept us busy. What with the kitchen adventure, to be described next, we didn't entertain at home, but rarely had in the past. We knew very little about the domestic lives of our fellow workers. One morning, at the end of spring quarter, David dropped by the office and mentioned that his mother's pacemaker was in. Jeanne, passing in the hallway, stepped in to inquire, mentioned her daughter Kate being 12 going on 13, wanting to stay out late. That is the only family conversation I find in the notes.

We belonged to a church group, the Presbyweds, about 15 couples within which we were median aged. This met monthly, though my notes refer to only two. Each month we met in a different house, all of them more spacious than ours. Because of our renovations, we combined with Carl and Ruth Mirre, they providing the house and we providing the food. But Nelle felt that if most of the group came, even our expanded house would be too small. I was afraid she felt our house was a little mundane, a little bourgeois for the Presbyweds.

When I went to these gatherings, I was somewhat guarded, trying to turn the conversation to the interests of the other person so that I wouldn't sound weird. The other people were certainly interesting. One evening, for example, Hugh Stevenson was telling me about trying to use the California Personality Test for NCR employees in Turkey. And Dan Elliott told about challenging a group of medical doctors to provide evidence that theirs was really an exceptionally stressful profession.

At the April meeting I provided the entertainment, showing the slide projection "We Will Not Be Moved" that we use for Social Problems. It was about the consequences of gentrification in Cincinnati. Now watch the train of the notes.

> Anne Herr responded by recalling the history of Dayton, the deconstruction or urban renewal of the core, apparently long before historical districts had been conceived. Dan Elliott suggested that without historical districts, not only would there be no gentrification but there would be deterioration, because landlords would not improve housing, might abandon it. I really didn't know. I thought I knew why cities sometimes unslum, but not what conditions would bring that about. Could Community Life use our $50,000 more effectively by providing small loans than we do in funding Habitat or agencies? I wish I knew. Certainly the best idea is finding a way to get people to help themselves.

So that was having fun at a Sunday social with Presbyweds.

I had contact with two friends from earlier days, Gene Young, whom I knew when I was growing up in New Jersey, and Bill Brison, my college roommate.

Gene, who had for years been involved in the growth of computer programming at Rutgers University, called in November to discuss a situation in which his Computer Science section was being combined with Library Science, giving him an opportunity to move to a less demanding, more long term planning position as a prelude to retirement. Unlike me, he had felt an increasing burden from problems externally imposed. Since I had known him for a long time, and since in my own case the internal factor was so obvious (city schools, Ad Hoc General Education Committee, this book), I asked him to consider to what extent they were externally imposed and to what extent the manner he carried out the tasks was a factor. Would it continue to be a factor in the new position, or in retirement? I was speaking to myself as well, of course.

He considered that and followed with a letter. The job change would be good, he thought, in terms of health. He had had angioplasty. But the cost would be power, authority, status, control. At 4 a.m. he asked himself if he should have pushed for a vice-president's position, but he felt the struggle was not worth the effort. If he had, he would be a vice-president, perhaps (or dead, perhaps?).

I responded that when commitment is scattered, power diminishes, something I hadn't said or written before. I would like prestige and fame. But lacking those, I did like power, e.g. trying to influence the general education program through the Ad Hoc Committee. You learn about yourself in trying to advise your friends.

Bill Brison, engineer turned clergyman, Archdeacon of Bolton, England, wrote around the time of my 60th birthday to explain why he would live only nine more years, his estimate based on genetics, ecology and lifestyle. I wrote back, arguing that his calculations had some shortcomings. By a system Nelle picked up in a gerontology class, he had at least two more decades. Plus was he forgetting the Eternal Life that came with his profession?

This caused me to consider my own mortality. Maybe twenty years? Twenty years ago we were still in Massachusetts. Ellen had just been born. That wasn't very long ago. Better make some good choices over the time left. With friends like Gene and Bill, I couldn't afford too many more. Too depressing.

Including the Kitchen Sink

It happened that in the year studied, we were enlarging our kitchen. It was the first time we had ever engaged in a project of this magnitude. In a way it was odd to be expanding our house—after all, the children had moved out—but we had about decided that we were going to stay where we were, near the library and bus service. Bob and Henrietta Light, across the street, were respectively in their early 90's and late 80's, so perhaps staying in your house was healthier than retiring to a new environment. And besides wanting a bigger, brighter kitchen that looked into the yard, Nelle also wanted to put all the necessary facilities on the first floor so that, if necessary, we could live without using stairs.

I always opposed home improvements, at least to the extent of saying I didn't see that they were needed. The dining room didn't need to be repapered; we didn't need technological replacements; and so forth. Nelle went ahead and did them, and they always looked good or were used after she did. So I regarded the kitchen expansion as unnecessary, but she was doing it with her own money, the power of the independent career woman. In September, on the day we were taking Ellen back to college, the bulldozers arrived. And for the next couple months things went as planned, the yard being torn up, the back of the house smashed, and me taking pictures of the destruction.

But when it became apparent that Christmas would follow Thanksgiving with a cold, dusty, almost useless kitchen, we began to fray. We had a typical Myers-Briggs F vs. T conflict (or was it Venus vs. Mars?), with Nelle feeling that it was my duty as a husband to support her and lean on contractor Doug Readenauer to get this project finished. But I continued to look at the matter "objectively," considering what the work of a contractor must be like, the temptation to promise what you hope will happen, the tendency to underestimate the time a project will take even after you have the experience of other projects, as I think this book has shown. When you are feeling angry and ill-used, however, it is not particularly helpful to have your best friend playing participant-observer.

Our anxiety was not reduced when Nelle was told by a maintenance man working on the kitchen that Readenauer was going out of business. So it could be that the work was being strung out not because Doug had too many projects going, but because he didn't have the cash to pay for the next steps. And since we had already paid most of our bill, we couldn't help him.

Because we were both home from work for Christmas, and because the inconvenience was heightened by Peter and Ellen's being around for the holidays, our differences intensified. Nelle wanted to keep the pressure on Readenauer, since pressure brought response. But I was part of the pressure she wanted to assert and her image of that pressure was strong and angry, no nonsense. My argument was that this wasn't my style, but that I could be effective in the style I do have. This was. as anthropologist John Thatcher once described it, relentless. But gentle.

For instance, Nelle wanted to call our lawyer, Bob Jefferis, to see what legal steps could be taken. I preferred to use the unpaid money we had left, more than $2,000, to pay the people who needed to be paid to do the next things for us. Carrot before stick. In which case our question to Bob should be how we could make such payments and be sure it is counted as contract payment.

While we were discussing that, we learned there was a mechanic's lien against us for bills not paid if Doug didn't pay them. So we reviewed what needed to be done and discussed with Bob the best way of achieving our objectives. But we were trying to do this against Nelle's image, certainly justified, that we had been naive about the whole project, and at a time when our professions were making heavy demands. For her it had been a cold winter, and clients needed more than the usual amount of help. I was gearing up to teach a heavier winter load of three courses.

The day after we talked to Bob and learned about the lien, Doug visited. It was a tough session for all, because Doug must have had his own heavy load of other problems if he were going out of business. Nelle lit into him from the perspective of a woman wronged, or a woman whose kitchen has been violated. I was upset because I didn't want to seem to be siding with him, but I didn't want her to cross the bounds of acceptable professional insult. I wanted to be an acceptable husband in her eyes, but a professional in his.

By January, the kitchen was shaping up. Nelle was waiting for Dan Stump, the kitchen assembler, to finish a last cabinet so the counter tops could be put in. Once they were, the plumber could put in the sink and we would be able to use our kitchen. But Dan told Nelle that Doug owed him $1,300. I wanted to help Doug with this part of his cash flow problem by paying Dan, and told Dan I would pay him if it was okay with my lawyer and Doug. It reminded me of our general education problem, where we had to get several people together to negotiate before doing anything. But this was cleaner, because you got a kitchen, whereas with general education you got maybe smaller classes in five years, with incalculable side effects.

By mid-February we were over the hump. The kitchen was nearly completed and it looked wonderful. That inspired team of Nelle Melko and Doug Readenauer had produced a truly remarkable result, light and beautiful, with an old world charm that came from a combination of angles produced by the supporting of a stairway closet and the inspired inclusion of a skylight. So it was with pleasurable anticipation that I walked from the bus to the house on Friday, February 16.

To be greeted by detectives.

It turned out that someone had been arrested for using one of our credit cards. It was connected with a home loan line that was to be used, if needed, for the kitchen and because it had a larger limit—$20,000—I kept it in my desk drawer. One of the persons reported arrested was Dan Stump, the builder employed by Doug

Readenauer. The builders had been working in our house for months, and needed to go to the hall landing to work on reinforcing the closet. The card should have been placed in our safe deposit box, but I hadn't taken that precaution, perhaps because I was a professor with an underlying ideology that worldly goods were not important. I did have guilt feelings because I knew that Dan wasn't being paid and that he had an adorable little daughter with serious medical problems. It is probable that one of his men poked through my drawer, and the temptation to use the card was too much for Dan. The stuff they were buying suggested they intended to sell it for the cash.

Dan was charged with forgery. I appeared as a witness at a hearing, but he didn't show up, probably had left for Utah, from whence he had come. Since the card and goods had been recovered, the police did not seem overly concerned.

Discussing the episode one evening, Nelle said it made her angry because it capped the whole thing: the failure to complete the job, the lien, and finally the credit card, as if we were just stupid. I felt we had been trusting, had expected the contractor and builder would have ethics similar to ours. But each of them was dealing with problems that we really never had to deal with, bills to be paid and no money to pay them.

Afterword

Kevin Gray returned to Ohio and Gwen began a practice of spending alternate years with her parents, some 6,000 miles apart. She seemed to be thriving. And we had been concerned about her having to travel 45 miles!

Ellen surprised us by entering a Ph.D. program in literature at the University of Denver. I was pleased by her choice, but both Nelle and I worried about whether she would be able to find a position after all those years of preparation.

How Nelle and I approached retirement and the arrival of the next grandchild are stories that might be more fascinating to us than to the reader. But sometimes we looked at people with young children with pity: how did they manage it? Sometimes with envy: their problems seemed simpler.

11

Is the Professor a Professional?

Is He Really Honest, Ethical, Serving, Committed, Autonomous, Humanitarian, and Cool?

The original reason for undertaking this study was that I wanted a book for my Occupations class about the work of a professional. Since I couldn't find one about a doctor or a lawyer I decided to write one about my own work.

The course I taught was called the Sociology of Occupations and Professions, but on my motion the department shortened it to Sociology of Occupations on the ground that a profession is a sub-set or a characteristic of an occupation. Most occupations, even that of a professional criminal, have these qualities to a greater or lesser extent, or in any event strive for them.

So here I want to consider to what extent, in the year studied, my colleagues and I behaved like professionals. The term has a range of meanings, often only implicitly understood. Nelle is not pleased when a student calls and asks for Mr. Melko. She sees this as a failure to respect the profession, possibly a symbol of What's Wrong With America. What is in the titles "Professor" or "Doctor" that carries this aura?

In Chapter One I mentioned that the textbooks say that professionals usually are members of some sort of associational body that sets standards, that they are expected to be scrupulously honest and

219

ethical, have a strong desire to serve their clients, are intrinsically committed to their work, maintain autonomy from external controls, conduct themselves in a style that commands respect while reflecting humanitarian values, avoid any suggestion of commercial motivation, maintain a perspective beyond everyday emotionalism and irrationality, and make the most of their talents. Most of these qualities come from what is called the attributes model, which tends to emphasize the ideal over the practice.

The process model, on the other hand, looks at practice as related to ideal. It singles out some less lofty characteristics, e.g. a tendency for professions to upgrade themselves in order to command higher salaries, to expand their control of wider varieties of work, to increase standards to make it harder to enter the profession, and to continually steal work from each other, all of which tend to help the professional obtain higher status and income.

What does this study say about these contrasting views?

The Professional Association

In August, when Jeanne returned from the American Sociological Association meeting, it occurred to me that she may have been the only member of the department who went. In other years Jerry, Norma, Dennis or I might have gone. I had not been to a meeting in four years because I was getting more return from the International Studies Association in terms of War and Peace research. I was thinking of returning to the War and Peace Section of the ASA instead of COPRED, not because it was my professional association, but because I might find more people there who were nearer my paradigm. Norma was the only member of the Department who has ever had an article published in the *American Sociological Review*, the premier journal of the association and I didn't know anyone who regularly read it. So even though several of us were members, only Jeanne was consistently active as officer and participant.

There was one encounter with the ASA, however, that showed the association in an interesting perspective. Apparently the previous year I had sent the ASA my membership form without a check, and didn't discover this until the following year. When I called to ask what I owed, I was advised just to make my payment for the following year and I would get my back journals anyway. Well, it was probably a student on the phone, a business major she said. But here was the voice of my professional association, which is supposed to be monitoring our profession, telling me to just forget my debt. When I paid it anyway, I got a letter back from Carla Howery of the ASA staff thanking me for my persistence and integrity. It seemed as if making a routine back payment called for special commendation. It was a unique episode and bad luck for the ASA that I happened to be collecting data for a sociological study.

Honesty

I organized the notes for this chapter on the dining room table in a whole lot of piles making little sub-head notes for each pile: honesty, money, power, etc. Then I numbered them in what seemed like a logical order of presentation. What I wanted to present first looks to be the positive face of professionalism: honesty, responsibility, service and courage. When I was done I used big paper clips for the thick piles, little paper clips for the thin piles. Honesty and service have big paper clips, responsibility a little paper clip. Courage and truth had no paper clip because there was only one note for each. (It's possible that I was generally cowardly and untruthful, but let's assume that courage and truthfulness were such constants that they went unnoticed.)

As for honesty, my father was a lawyer and a politician, but also a professional with very high ethical standards. This had left me with a keen ethical sense, sometimes too keen, bordering on Goody Two Shoes. It was surely no coincidence that my wife also had a very high ethical sense.

I have a handful of examples of ethical questions that came up during the year, and they tend to illustrate the margins of what is acceptable. I was asked, for instance, to write a letter of recommendation for Roger Wescott of Drew University, who was being considered for a distinguished visiting professor position at Auburn. Since the request came during the summer and I was to be off campus for a few weeks, I requested a copy of Roger's curriculum vitae, the academic equivalent of a resume. (In the singular we refer to one of these, incorrectly, as a "vita.") It was, as I knew, indeed distinguished, but it contained a cover letter that described Wescott as the president-elect of the ISCSC. In fact he had been a candidate for the position, probably would have had it without contest, but he withdrew. So it seemed very careless of him to be presenting himself as president.

In discussing the matter with Nelle, I told her I thought I would call Roger and tell him I didn't feel I could write the letter. She thought this would be pompous and annoying. So I wrote the supporting letter, getting around the problem by mentioning that he had declined to be considered for the presidency. But now I was withholding information.

The next day I did call Roger, though I very much didn't want to. He said he had written the letter when he thought he would be president. When later he revised the letter, he failed to catch the misstatement. I understood how this could happen and, with his agreement, I wrote a P.S. explaining how the paragraph had been inadvertently left.

And because a professional did not lie, we did not lightly question someone else, as I had Roger. But you can see how cautious one had to be, and why professionals might cover for one another rather than risk the embarrassment of even appearing to question a colleague's honesty.

Letters of recommendation are a problem because you could not lie, but any reservation might be seen as a warning of serious flaws. I wrote a letter for Bob Pruett, who was applying for a dean's position, presenting his strong qualities, but not disguising that every virtue has its own defects. I saw Pruett as an outrageous but effective mover and shaker, a sort of friendly Billy Martin (I didn't put it that way). I figured that if that's what the prospective employers wanted, they would like Pruett. If not, they wouldn't.

As it happened, neither Wescott nor Pruett took the positions for which I wrote recommendations (I don't know whether they were offered), so I didn't know if my honest letters could have weighed against them. I had to figure they knew me well enough to guess the kind of letter I would write.

Another story, more trivial, like the kitchen conflict in the previous chapter, involves the crossing of the ethic of the professional with that of the merchant. Leaving the ISCSC meeting at Berkeley, David Kopf was waiting for a van he had reserved and talking with Win Wenger and me. A cab came up and Win and I took it. David wanted to continue the conversation, but his van was due. He asked the driver to wait two minutes and if the van hadn't come, he would go with us. It didn't, we loaded the cab, and just then the van appeared. David had a professional dilemma. Should he get his bags back out of the cab and shift to the van, perhaps looking a trifle neurotic to us? Certainly it would annoy the South Asian cab driver who had exclaimed, "I made my hit."

Well, David chose to go with us, continuing the discussion of Krishnamurti, insisting that it was 1:16 and the van had been due at 1:15. Clearly he was uncomfortable about failing to meet his obligation to the van driver. But he was evidently a little more uncomfortable about inconveniencing us and losing a chance to expound on a favorite topic and perhaps experiencing the disdain of our taxi driver, who came from a people he had studied much of his life. But I suspect that David was aware of a dilemma that would not have occurred to others who were not in a professional position.

These stories are extremely uncomfortable to write because they concern honorable people and the infringements are borderline, . You could hardly get a scandal headline out of any of them. The next involves a note from Bill Edwards, including a vita and a review. He thanked me for helping him circulate the vita as he explored the possibility of moving from private industry to academia, and enclosed a review he did of an early book of mine, which would appear in the *Comparative Civilizations Review*.

It may be a fine point, but the juxtaposition of the vita and the review might be considered unprofessional, though probably not to a businessman, which was the role that most absorbed Bill's time. In the first place, was it a courtesy or an infringement to send a copy of the review to the author of the book reviewed? I knew it was often done, but it really could be done only if the review were favorable. Therefore the question arose, did a decision to send a review influence what was said? Best not send the review, and then you didn't have the problem.

In the second place, you probably don't want to juxtapose a vita, which requires a professional favor, with the favorable review, which sort of looks like payment for the favor. To a businessman, a quid pro quo may be only fair and certainly human. While I'm asking you to do something for me, I'm reminding you that I'm doing something for you.

As I review these paragraphs, I'm thinking my colleagues are not going to be pleased about what I have written. But if so, consider how minor the transgressions are. That I am concerned that my colleagues might be annoyed or angered at these trivial anecdotes suggests the degree to which scrupulous honesty is important to the professional.

Now, lest you think I am perfect and it is only ISCSC colleagues who backslide, let me tell one on myself. Charles Berry had been very hard on Peg Regan's thesis paper (Ch. 6), and it was my job to summarize her committee's comments. But I never told Charles that I disagreed with his comments, I just softened them in the re-write to her (copy to him). He probably expected that I would do that, which gave him license to be fully candid with me. But my wife might say on this one that I had been dishonest with him, be-cause withholding information is dishonest. I'm not sure whether it was dishonesty, cowardice, or diplomacy. Total honesty could get in the way.

This came up in a discussion with Bill Hanks, whose persuasion course emphasized avoiding deceit. I mentioned my withholding from Berry and he mentioned failing to oppose a statement at a meeting. I felt you weren't obligated to oppose every statement you disagreed with. That level of integrity would be dysfunctional. This was particularly so in groups trained in critical thinking. They had to discriminate on what was crucial and what could be allowed to pass even if not satisfactory.

Our secretary, Glena Buchholtz, was always tactful, but I'm afraid she regarded it as an idiosyncrasy that I wouldn't col-lect receipts from restaurants or cab drivers when I traveled. It seemed unprofessional to me to do so. It implied that the professor was not believed by his own institution. (Wright State always paid me anyway.)

Outside my professional work there were a few notes on the topic. Henry Fairlie wrote an article on Adlai Stevenson in *The New Republic* arguing that the very things about Stevenson that were admirable to me—sticking to his principles and his apparent reluc-tance to run—hurt the Democratic Party and narrowed its base. A politician needed to have allies, to find what he could say to sup-port farmers and labor, and had to want to run. It wasn't that a politician couldn't be honest but certainly he had to be selective in what he shared. My very honest father was a politician. But he al-ways lost.

There was a sermon by Dr. Lowry on inner light, showing your light, being on the outside what you were on the inside. It was a commendable idea, and probably Stevenson came close. But our inner lights are multiple and complicated and give confusing and contradictory messages. "What you see is what you get" can be a pejorative comment, implying excessive simplicity.

Yet honesty, it would seem, is at the base of a professional ethical system. You expect the professional to be honest. You are disconcerted on the rare occasions when he even appears to stray.

Service

An article by Ellen Stark in *Psychology Today* said that psychiatrists and psychologists generally approved of and recommended self help books, though you might think they would perceive them as rivals. I wouldn't. I would expect a professional to use whatever she could to help her client. If she didn't, she wouldn't be a professional.

I expected a professional to be personally concerned about his clients, though sometimes this conflicted with the need to remain objective, to appear professional. When my Ellen sustained her eye injury, I was impressed with Dan Juergens' approach, (so much better than mine as a parent), showing concern for her worries yet acknowledging the damage to her eyesight.

It wasn't always easy to be empathic. Nelle was telling me about attending a lecture for health professionals on loving the elderly. The elderly priest sitting next to her fell asleep frequently; and when he did, he leaned on her. He was also incontinent. At the end of the lecture he asked her for a ride back to the University of Dayton. Here she was, the Community Geriatric Nurse, trying to love the elderly.

We also tried to be free of class bias. I suggested to Phyllis Risner of Nursing, chatting before a graduate committee meeting, that sometimes the Visiting Nurses pulled out of a situation because professionalization had set standards that were too high for poor people to meet. This had been Nelle's experience. Phyllis wouldn't buy that, since public health nurses were taught not to make judgments based on middle class standards. We were experiencing conflicts between education and socialization, with socialization perhaps the more powerful.

Because social concerns were part of the fabric of our work, it was disconcerting to realize that among students or in church, many people lacked such a concern, didn't feel guilty about what they were not doing. When I asked students in the Careers class to look back on their lives from the perspectives of their 70th birthdays, the majority did not consider whether they had performed any social service. They were much more concerned about how their families turned out and where they lived.

Peter Drucker (1986) says the wonderful thing about our country is our persecution mania. Doctors talk about how nobody appreciates how they bleed for humanity. It's unbelievable how terrible the lot of university professors is. Well, I don't think it is quite as bad as all that, but we did play games of "Ain't It Awful" and we did feel unappreciated.

One area where I was sensitive to this was the message I got from the church. When I was working at home on Thursdays, at 9:15 I switched from one classical music station to another, and on the way always stopped at the Cedarville station to get a one minute message from the preacher, Dr. McGee. One day his message was that it was no good promising God we're going to do something, because we weren't. We had to rely on His mercy. I thought, "Dammit, McGee, you write notes for your sermons every day. God may inspire you, but you do it."

Even worse were the Presbyterian Confessions of Faith we recited in unison each Sunday at Westminster. "We have been quick to claim our own rights and careless of the rights of others. We have taken much and given little." Come on! Where did this collective masochism come from? Who wrote these things? I didn't mind that others are not aware that I am scrupulous of the rights of others or that I give much, but it wasn't fair to be asked to join others in lying about it on my day off. And it was unprofessional to lie.

Here's another. "We are often silent when we should speak and useless when we could be useful. We are lazy servants, timid and heartless, who turn neighbors away from your love." And do you know what the title of Lowry's sermon was? "Maybe It's Tough to Love Yourself." I wonder why?

On the other hand, another of Lowry's sermons was on Jesus returning in the sense that people with his spirit pass through and affect others. "Father, who was that Professor?" "That, daughter, was Jesus, passing through." I'm afraid there was little evidence in this study (not even Karen Gary in Ch. 6) that I had that kind of impact on anyone. But the great thing about a professor's work, particularly teaching, is that you never knew what influence you may have had.

The Unused Sperm Cell

The next set of aspects having to do with being professional have a less altruistic connotation, because they bring personal rewards. One is commitment to the work, which is an intrinsic reward. Another, greater for some than others, is the exercise of power. And related to capacity for service and honesty is a perceived need for autonomy.

When my daughter Julie was less anxious than I was that she apply for the Montessori position (Ch. 10) in the distant town of Hawi, I noted that the stress for me would have been much greater if I didn't have a professional position. So was she less professional than I? She worked hard as a substitute teacher, was genuinely concerned about her students. But she did not have to have a position. She would not pay the price I would to have it.

The intrusion of professional on personal life was a mark of this commitment. The defenses we created to protect part of our personal life reflected this commitment. When Nelle and I were sitting on the front porch on a Sunday, both doing our work, we were doing what we wanted to do. But we did worry whether sometimes commitment shaded into addiction. For one thing, there were no artificial limits. You could always read another article for your class or your paper. You could never have enough knowledge or experience.

A different aspect of commitment may be illustrated by Jim Runkle's decision to teach an upper level summer class for free. The class didn't have enough students enrolled, so he had to teach a lower level class instead. The upper level would have been canceled, but Jim elected to teach it without pay. It was a professional decision, because the needs of the students were more important than money. But from a trade union perspective, would it not encourage the administration to raise the number of students necessary for a class, knowing that if the number weren't reached, the professor might teach it anyway? And what about Pat Olds' view (Ch. 9) that a professional must be paid in order to maintain his status as a professional?

Power was not easy to separate from commitment. It involved your capacity to have effect. You took for granted that what you were committed to was good, and that to the degree that you could implement your ideas, you were performing a service. My conversations with Gene Young (Ch. 10) were partly about power. When he moved into planning, would he be trading immediate impact for long-term power, the chance to have a greater long-term effect?

When I went to the trouble of creating an ad hoc General Education Committee, my hope was that the committee would have a positive impact on the General Education Program. I was fair in inviting committee members because I wanted the committee to be truly representative. I knew that Charlie Funderburk would not always see the problem as I did but also that his membership on the committee gave it greater credibility and therefore greater power.

During the year studied I read Jonathan Franzen's *Twenty-Seventh City*. In that novel professionals played very little role in running the city. There were engineers and bankers who had a professional component in their work, but there were no doctors, lawyers or professors. It was the political leaders, a police chief and businessmen who were the leaders. Again, recalling the change in the title of the Occupations course, all occupations have professional aspects but for some the professional aspect is more consciously asserted, whether or not practiced.

That was true in Dayton, too, except that lawyers do become political leaders. One of our faculty members, Jim Uphoff of the College of Education, was a member of a local school board. When one of my students, Carleton Harris, wanted to do something to reform the prison system (Ch. 6), I asked myself what I would advise him to become: a legislator, a prison official, a journalist, a judge? Surely not a criminologist. Then I wondered, if I could have another career, would I become more involved in civic or world affairs, instead of observing them or teaching others who would become involved?

Well, the general education conflict, the fight over the quarter system, everything that affected the kind of place Wright State would be, those were not detached from the world. But I would have to admit that the choices made in teaching classes, whether I was successful in helping students write more effectively, were pretty far removed from power. In fact, if the majority of them did not have service values, I may well have helped them become more effective in achieving selfish ends. And in my wildest dreams I could not conceive that my research was going to change the world. But it was likely that the freedom to carry out this kind of research, which went back at least to Galileo's struggle in the seventeenth century, has surely had an impact on the growth of Western Civilization. It was also probable that it required many people working in an atmosphere of scientific and academic freedom to allow a few to burst through with contributions that were significant.

It was sort of like being a sperm cell that didn't get used.

Autonomy

This is one of the more controversial aspects of professionalism. The professional needs to make contextual judgments, to work in a framework that provides considerable autonomy. When he is working within a state institution, this sometimes leads to suspicion that he is not doing anything. And that could well be the case.

As my study year began, I was finishing up 16 weeks of sabbatical, 13 of which were spent at home storing up introvert energy. And I could let myself be jealous that other faculty members had gotten two or three quarter sabbaticals. But few in other kinds of work get this kind of opportunity, not even other professionals. Throughout the rest of the year I usually worked one day each week at home, thereby avoiding the telephone, students, filing, chess, Orenstein and other interruptions, piling up a solid day of class preparation and memo writing. But also napping and having lunch, which I didn't get when I went to the office.

Attempts to make professionals accountable, while understandable, were usually ineffective. Nelle was telling me one day about a conference with her boss over the counting of health treatments. The grant that supported her position called for a certain number of treatments and she was making too many! When she checked with the agency that recorded this information, however, she discovered that the number they had recorded was double the number she had given. No problem, however, because they just made a downward "administrative adjustment." In which case, why bother counting at all? The less tied down Nelle was by accounting and hours, the more professional she could be.

In the same sense, the more we tied raises to performance, the less professional we were. We quantified our student evaluations, the number and types of articles and papers we got published, the number of committees we served on. We thought this should be done in the sense that we, as professionals, were monitoring ourselves. On the other hand, we were always unhappy with the process because we could only judge the quantity. We didn't want others to judge the quality of our papers or our teaching because we didn't want to be limited by others. Autonomy was unquestionably necessary and unquestionably abused.

Tenure insured our autonomy. I could fight the battle over general education without worrying whether the university or college approved of what I was doing. I didn't have to worry about losing my job or even being penalized by a reduced raise. If anything, it would protect my raise because the dean, if he thought about it at all, would want to be a little more than fair so there would not even be an appearance of harassment from the administration.

But if I became disenchanted or angry and said that from now on all I was going to do was teach my classes and go home, tenure still protected me. My colleagues might chastise me; I might find early retirement literature in my mailbox; but there would be no way of getting rid of me so long as I met my minimum duties.

One day I was filling out a form to send to Employee Benefits along with a check that would allow us to use Dayton's Old River Park during the summer. It was a park for National Cash Register Company employees, with a big pool, a river for boating, and lots of trees and grass for picnicking. Since NCR had decentralized there were fewer employees working in Dayton. So the company had opened the park to employees of other institutions.

I was uncomfortable, almost irritable, filling out the form. Because I was taking notes for this book, I stopped to consider why. I think it was because while filling out the form, I felt like an employee, not a professional. Beneath that was the knowledge that in the early part of the century, NCR was a particularly paternalistic firm, and one could argue—Gordon Welty might—that the company was spreading its imperialism around the community.

The organizational limits of autonomy were made clear in the late spring by the resignation from our church of our senior minister, Robert Lowry, whose sermons I have quoted. His departure was rather sudden, after only two years in the position, a surprise to many in the congregation. The reasons were complex. Elmer Hesse, who served on the search committee that brought Lowry, saw it as an unfortunate mismatch. Lowry had compassion, but apparently his administrative style brought conflict in our large, committee dominated, downtown church.

Bob was gracious, said he thought he had come for a ten-year ministry, but God had other plans. His closing sermon, "Some Things

Don't Last." Grace, for instance. Don't store it up. Accept it when it comes to you.

Grace? No position. A house to sell. Your wife better placed to find a position than you are. Any professional had to think: it could have been I. How would I have handled it? And maybe: Am I pushing my autonomy too far?

The Professional Style

Bill Stoesz gave a paper at the California ISCSC meeting in which he described the pre-Mauryan lay Buddhist as one who treated his friends as one's self, with a sensitivity toward inner feelings while at the same time maintaining a good reputation, living an orderly life with a steady, self-possessed demeanor, enjoying physical life including sex and alcohol, so long as he maintained control. How professional, I thought. Stoesz's portrayal demonstrated a resolution of caring and control, exactly the balance a professional tries to maintain.

Lillie Howard sent me a graceful note of praise for a column on Eric Davis in the *Pine Tar Review*. It was scrawled on her desk notepaper, which showed a stiff snake on a round stone with the caption "RELAX" underneath. She wrote of my casual brilliance in moments of leisure. My column had made her feel proud and enlightened, also made her smile. Just the right touch. An administrator, but also a colleague, takes time from a busy schedule to notice. You may be cynical, because the column reflected well on Wright State and was quoted in the local newspaper (though that could also be seen as a professional wasting his time at public expense). But it was also a classy thing to do.

Nelle, I mentioned, was not pleased when on a couple of occasions students called and asked for Mister or Matthew Melko rather than Dr. Melko. She felt they should be taught to show a little more respect. I said that the syllabus gave my name, not my title; and while I didn't want to be called "Matt" by a student, neither did I want to be so stodgy as to write "Dr. Melko" on a syllabus. Once again it was a matter of being accessible while maintaining a professional distinction. I was a friendly fellow even though a Professor.

I remember feeling, on the day I ran to catch up with a looping bus to recover my briefcase, that it wasn't dignified for a professor to be running across town to catch the bus, to be laughed at by the bus driver. It is fine to chat with bus drivers, but you ought not look silly.

Or there was the day I made Rishi Kumar furious when I occupied his 24-hour parking space in order to return some video equipment, making him late for a meeting. As he put it, I occupied his "property," appropriate terminology for an economist, I suppose. I, in turn, equally angry, pulled $10 out of my wallet to pay for the time (idiotic, but testing his cupidity?). All this in the rain.

The next day, in a more rational mood and both embarrassed, we discussed the episode. I was the most recent of a series of people who had taken his parking place. Moreover, he said, his presentation at the meeting was terrible because he had lost his cool. I was equally embarrassed, of course, about offering the $10, too sensitive an item even to mention. But both of us were really embarrassed because we had lost control. For a moment we were not professional.

On another occasion, Charles Derry of the Theatre Department was angry because during graduation ceremonies students bounced around an inflated naked doll. I got equally furious hearing about it and fantasized, as had Derry, that I had challenged the students. Yet it was their day, and they surely had a right to whatever symbolism they wanted. I think we were really angry because they were so unprofessional, so lacking in dignity as they were about to enter the professional world. They demeaned our professional work, embarrassed us in front of their parents.

Dr. Lowry had commented in a sermon on how thin our veneer of civilization may be. People become degraded when they lose it. But the sociology books say something else. Tony Watson notes that we professionals maintain a monopoly on specialized knowledge through "esoteric language" and "special mystique" in order to maintain our position as "prestigious elite." So, were Derry and I maintaining civilization or just protecting ourselves?

Were we in danger of deprofessionalization if we permitted student evaluations or taught critical thinking so that students learned to criticize us? If we were forced by our administration to use the merit system, would it become evident that our merit was limited? If students called me "Mister" would they challenge my expertise or dismiss it as worthless? Would the Monster Classes literally produce Monsters?

The M Word

Tony Watson sees professions as coming out of the tradition of gentlemen. A profession is an occupation in which you are paid so you can work rather than one in which you work for pay. It comes of gentlemen's redefining themselves in a world of industrialization, commerce and avarice (a professional pejorative for making money). The professional began as an amateur in the 17th century with the scientific revolution. In learned societies the stress would be on gentlemen seeking truth through hypothesis and empirical experimentation with no commercial influence. So it is today, hence our hostility to the idea of lawyers' and dentists' advertising.

During the year studied I noted in the mail a flier from a group of dentists headed "We Cater to Cowards" and offering a $100 gift certificate for general dentistry. The accompanying letter said "your comfort is our priority, listen to beautiful music on stereo earphones, contemplate our colorful yet soothing aquarium . . ."

Obscene, I thought. What if I advertised in the *Guardian*?

Take the *Pain* out of *History*! Take HST 102 from Matt Melko. Enjoy the magic worksheets that practically fill themselves in. Take your significant other to the Dayton Art Exhibit for the Spectacular Scavenger Hunt! Satisfied student Leila Grogbarger says: "Matt's class was just fabulous!

But didn't I sell sociology? I hoped not. I told students what careers I knew sociology majors had attained, told them what alternative majors they ought to consider, never urged, never said sociology was best, because for them it might not be. We were overloaded with majors and our classes were filled, and I liked to think my soft-sell, virtually non-sell, had contributed to that. So I tended to be mildly condescending about people who hard-sell their majors.

Another day Charles Hartmann challenged me about selling textbooks, originally received as complimentary copies, to buyers who in turn sold them second-hand to students. He argued that doing so put more books in the market, lowered the price for students. Feeling I had not defended myself adequately for not selling books, I asked Jim Runkle's opinion. He responded that the practice actually raised the price, because it was an inelastic market and the sellers would increase the price to reach expected revenues. Besides, he added, if we sold the books, it would discourage the publishers from sending us free books, thus cutting down on the range of books we could consider for a course.

None of the above! Jim's last point showed me the "real" answer. We didn't sell the books because they were given to us and it would be unprofessional to make a profit where there had been no input. I say we didn't, but there were book buyers, and that meant they must find books to buy. But whoever sold them was not proud of it, probably mildly guilty. Charles aggressively defended the practice, but didn't say *he* sold books.

It was probably the mercantile factor that made Charles angry about changing the name of his department from Management to Human Resources Management. What he didn't like was the implicit commercialism in the warmer, more commercially satisfying name. Actually, "human resources" sounded to me like people stacked in a storeroom.

The professional vs. merchant conflict was also involved in merit raises. We didn't like writing about our achievements in order to persuade our colleagues to give us higher ratings and a few hundred more dollars. But such raises could amount to thousands of dollars over the years, and we did not feel well paid in terms of where we live and what it cost to send our children to college. So we were likely to be particularly crabby and sarcastic about our merit system.

While the merit evaluation was going on, Dave Petreman asked me what I thought about Will Clark's $15 million contract. Didn't bother me, I said, as much as it would to learn that Dave was making $500 more a year than I was.

You may recall that I mentioned American University President Richard Berendzen being arrested for making obscene phone calls (Ch. 8). Some weeks later, according to *Newsweek*, he appeared on television with a Johns Hopkins psychiatrist and the recipient of the calls. She took the view that he should have controlled himself; the psychiatrist, that he had been a model patient. But appearing on popular television? Either he had a very strong commitment to public education or, being a college president, was addicted to publicity. But even worse, was he *paid* for that television appearance?

The tension between professional and merchant, I think, was at the bottom of our conflicts at the Early Music Center. Remember, I had referred to that conflict in the notice I used in an attempt to sell season tickets for the EMC (Ch. 9). Possibly it amused, but it didn't sell. And when Pat and I were arguing about the focus of the Marketing committee, she was focusing more on her responsibility for raising support for the organization while I, not having this concern, could afford to focus entirely on taking a professional approach.

This was also a source of conflict about phone calls, which possibly could have sold more tickets than radio public service announcements but disrupted people's lives. Did we enrich the culture of our community if we undercut it with commercial phone calls?

One day I even took the trouble to write a letter to Marilyn Borchardt, market director of Food First, which I think is a very effective organization, to contrast the form letter I got from her with a personal letter. When she wrote the personal letter, she addressed me as "Dear Mr. Melko." When she wrote the form letter, it was "Dear Matthew" and accompanied by a pitch for a new electronic gift worthy of Wal-Mart.

So what? Well, the enterprise was cheapened by the form letter. Food First is concerned with feeding the hungry of the world. Electronic gifts seem obscene in relation to that cause. Only doctor's secretaries and siding solicitors called me " Matthew." But I knew I was in a minority, that Food First would probably find "dear first name" letters, accompanied by special offers, bringing in more money to feed the hungry and teach them to feed themselves. In such circumstances, could they afford to worry about the niceties of professional conscience?

For the merchant there was a different set of values, values that arguably had contributed to the development of democratic institutions. There was no way, for instance, that David Kopf could have explained his dilemma to the cab driver. He was trying to get the right nuance in an area that to the cab driver was clearly legitimate for capitalist competition. It must have seemed as if he didn't understand his own country!

Something of the same kind was involved in our conflicts with the contractor and builder. We were incensed at what seemed to be dishonesty on their part. Doug was exasperated by Nelle's exasperation. She was just an unhappy customer who needed to be mollified, a response that, of course, made her all the angrier. Toward the end of the project, Nelle said she got angry because we were made to look stupid and naive. We may have looked that way. But we were trusting because we assumed the contractor and builder were professionals who would have ethics similar to ours. If we had discussed it with Doug, not as customers but as friends, he may well have argued that no contractor could survive attempting to use the level of ethics we advocated.

The Cool Professional

The professional is cool. He doesn't get excited, lose his head, become involved in personalities. This ideal is not only beyond the capacity of most of us, but it also comes into conflict with the expectation that we should be warm and caring about our clients, the students.

A professional, for instance, is supposed to take the long view. One of the controversies between Pat Olds and me was on the long range function of the marketing committee, my professional willingness to wait conflicting with her commercial need to achieve a certain level of ticket sales.

The afterwords that appear at the end of many of the chapters are there because even a year was not long enough, in many cases, to get a true sense of outcome. In a year projects were pushed along, like the general education memos, but merely reached another level. Or they sat there not moving at all, like city schools, while information was being gathered. When my former graduate mentee, Francis Padinjarekara, called from Milwaukee and asked what I was learning from gathering data for this book, I said I had an increased awareness of the slowness with which accomplishment takes place. A year simply wasn't long enough a period to assess many of our projects.

One of Bob Lowry's sermons was on Type A and B personalities. I was an A, Orenstein a B. God, Lowry thought, was a B. (God and Orenstein, an amazing juxtaposition.) God takes a long view, doesn't worry about how many times you blasphemed yesterday. It made me think that one of my objectives was to be less of an A. More professional to be a B. But then, thinking about my type A behavior at work, and how much I had to do the next week and how much I wasn't getting done, I became anxious and lost track of the sermon.

Preserving confidence comes in the category of being cool. We didn't give way to our desire to spread the news about people. When I was complaining to Jeanne about Mark Olsen's not calling a committee meeting, she thought she might know why. She asked whether enough time had elapsed for her to tell me what happened at his tenure meeting. I stopped her from telling me, not without feelings of regret on both our parts. If she had told me I might relate it here, because a cool professional relates his findings regardless of consequences.

Another day Charles Hartmann (of course) challenged me when I declined to reveal the source of something said at a department meeting (though I may have revealed it elsewhere in this book). He said a department meeting was an open meeting. The discussions weren't confidential; they were in the minutes. But minutes were edited to deliver the instrumental, not the emotional.

An extreme example of confidence was the University Library's policy of not revealing who had taken out a book. If I needed a book, I could request it; and the person holding it could return it, even if it turned out to be Ron Fetzer across the hall. But it was not my business to know whether Ron was reading Marx.

Nelle told me that Sara Sayer, local head of the Visiting Nurses Association, refused to send her a model report the Visiting Nurses had developed, because she had heard that Nelle's boss, Louise Morrow, had put down the VNA. Totally unprofessional! I was unprofessionally outraged to think that clients might be denied possible benefits because of a personal disagreement between supervisors. Even if Sayer were denying Nelle the model for that reason, you wouldn't think she would want to say so. (Of course, honesty is an even more crucial characteristic of the professional.)

I have mentioned that in one warm conversation Nelle and I had with Doug Readenauer about the kitchen (Ch. 10), I had a tough time because I was trying to play the conflicting roles of outraged husband of a woman wronged and of cool professional in control of the situation. And even while it was occurring, the sociologist was thinking, ah, a role conflict! No, without the exclamation point. Ah, a role conflict.

The Exploitative Professor

It may be that it doesn't show over such a short period of time as a year, or at such a low level as a single university, especially focused on a college of liberal arts. But the exploitative professional of the model proposed by Andrew Abbott and his predecessors was hard to find in the 1,000 pages of notes I had taken. There was a sense of upgrading in the perception that there were higher and lower universities, but since ours was not among the higher, you would expect that idea, if anything, to be opposed. It never was.

The idea of improving our status in order to obtain higher salaries was not, in the year studied, supported by the faculty, who showed little interest in collective bargaining by AAUP or anyone else (though see Afterword, Ch. 4). There was considerable discomfort, moreover, about the idea of making merit judgments to determine distribution of raises.

In other colleges, apparently, and in our Communication Department, some professors were interested in increasing their income through consulting. But it never was an issue that came to my attention, even though the Communication offices were adjacent to ours. It was not a subject of jealousy or even hallway conversation during the year studied.

There was considerable concern about standards, but these applied to our grading practices, with an underlying assumption that our colleagues, though not we ourselves, were more lenient in grading students than they used to be. In some other year, not this one, I had seen a chart showing student mean grades for our department that indicated stability since the beginning of the university in 1964.

It was probably true that standards for tenure had been raised. This related partly to wanting to increase the status of our Department and University, partly to a decline in the total number of faculty positions available in the country. Having fewer positions available probably did raise the level of competition. We failed to fill our Department vacancy, however, not because we could not find a promising scholar but because we were not agreed about whether our applicants could handle a new kind of teaching situation for which we had not advertised. In other words, on this occasion, scholarship that might have raised our collective status was not the issue. Teaching, which is supposed to be secondary according to the process model, turned out to be crucial.

As for stealing from others, there were no conflicts concerning our right, as criminologists say, to impinge on the corrections profession. In this particular year there weren't even any interdepartmental conflicts over control of subject matter.

This is not to say that the process model is poorly conceived.

But it certainly was not visible in a one-year study occurring within a single university.

Using What You've Got

Nelle and I had recurrent discussions about talent. Discussions isn't quite the word. Rituals maybe. Basically, Nelle envied people who had specific talent: they communicated well, they could run a computer, they had administrative gifts, they were quick responders. Her abilities were subtle, holistic, generalized, therefore not easily visible to other people. My view, at least in this ritual, was that talent was not as important as character, integrity, compassion, responsibility, a capacity to see a task or problem through.

Driving in to work one spring morning we discussed mediocrity and aging. Each of us felt we were not outstanding as individuals or professionals. She felt her professional work didn't have impact; she was just a trouble shooter; and usually she didn't know the longer term outcome of her intervention. I had been taking notes for several months about my ordinary work, and the ordinariness was beginning to get to me. But most work was routine, even if interesting to the person doing it and perhaps we got some mileage, some stimulation, from exaggeration. We saw our conflicts as more crucial, our successes as more momentous, our failures as more disastrous than others would. Considering retirement, or becoming an observer rather than a participant, had the effect of putting the work in perspective. That, perhaps, tended to be diminishing.

We had a sermon a couple months later from Methodist Bishop Emerson Cahow on making a miracle by using what you had in hand. Try to do something worth doing, take a chance, know the joy of victory, the sorrow of defeat. The joy of victory turned out to be getting the vice president to agree to class sizes in the calendar; the sorrow of defeat, a peace studies brochure that was unusable. We have to use some creative imagination to make these joys and sorrows.

In a *New Republic* article, Jed Perl cautioned us that we are in danger of forgetting that many great developments in art had taken place away from the public eye. Even artists who did have a public, like Picasso or Matisse, often kept whole bodies of work out of the public eye. Other artists couldn't show because no one wanted to see them. Perl thought this painful or even devastating in an era that celebrates celebrity.

I'd call it normal. Who, for instance, was Jed Perl? How was he getting on without world fame? Most people do. We manage, most of us, we unsung heroes.

Overview

It seems to be the norm, in studies like this, that there be some sort of summary saying concisely what you have already said at length. It is sort of a professional responsibility.

Organizing work topically has the effect of clarifying it on one hand, but looking at the complex development of classes, research and committee work also leaves an impression of layered complexity. Many faculty members, Type A's like me, have a struggle to organize sufficiently to keep a perspective on what they are doing. Others, Type B's like Orenstein, worry less about it, presume they do more good than harm along the way.

If one had the advantages of hindsight, better choices could be made. It is often hard to see what a commitment will lead to. When you look back, you can see that one or another student project, research venture, or committee was a waste of time; another should have been pursued with more focus and vigor. But the afterwords also show that even hindsight can be wrong, that a longer view shows success to be failure, failure to be success. That is the nature of professional work.

My view is just one. Orenstein's year, or Ballantine's, or Hartmann's, would look very different. But I suspect all would have layers of confusion, interest and frustration with only dashes of excitement. However different we were in personality and sociological perception, I suspect we would be in agreement about that. I suspect other professionals would, too.

To prove this, we would have to see replications by other professionals, replications in the sense that they study their own work over an extended period of time, whatever they perceive to be a cycle. That is what the scientific enterprise is supposed to do, and I hope it will. Meanwhile, I'll have to take comfort from one of my less modest sociological predecessors. Pitirim Sorokin:

"Let anyone who can do better, do better. Unfortunately, so far, no one has."

What an arrogant conclusion! How fortunate that I can blame it on someone else.

Afterword

Three years later, Roger Wescott was elected president of the ISCSC.

To be fair to Presbyterians, Westminster's Glenn Leupold has pointed out to me that the Confession of Faith is collective, we are responding to the sins of the congregation, not just our own.

The Sorokin quotation looks more arrogant after reading James Phelan's book on the work of an English professor. All right, a book at least cousin to this one has been done; and even though it isn't topically organized, isn't a study, was probably easier to do, it may well be better. In any event, Phelan's book does convey confusion, interest, frustration and only occasionally, excitement.

Those, perhaps, are the normal qualities of good work.

Cast

Acronyms are organizations in connection with which a person is mentioned. Number indicates chapters in which person appears. C indicates mention in photo caption. Faculty members are identified by their areas of specialization, e.g., sociologist, unless that seems too awkward, in which case the identification is by Dept., e.g., English Dept. Most identifications were made for the year studied, unless the person appears only in an Afterword (e.g., future President Flack) or remembered (e.g., former President Kegerreis). Members of the ISCSC, ISA or COPRED are connected to the associations, not their universities, since that is where they were encountered. The name of the Dept. of Handicapped Services was subsequently changed to Disability Services.

Abdelrahman Abdelrahman	candidate for sociology position	2
Tony Ackerman	student	C
Bonnie Adduccio	student	C
Mickey Adams	EMC Marketing Committee	9
Beth Adler	student	5
Melanie Aper	student	6
Michael Andregg	biologist, COPRED, ISCSC, ISA	7
Martin Arbagi	historian	4,6,C
Tony Arnett	student	C
Paul Baker	visiting workshop conductor	5
Jeanne Ballantine	Chair, Sociology Dept.	2,4,5,8, 10,11,C
Richard Balzer	participant-observer	1,8
Alan Barclay	School of Professional Psych.; President, WSU AAUP	4

Ellsworth Barnard	revered college professor	7
David Barr	Religion Dept.	4
Paul Barrett	student	6
Fred Bartenstein	Director, Dayton Foundation	9
Eric Barton	student	6
Rod Bear	student	C
Ben Bechtel	early music performer	9
Carl Becker	emeritus professor, editor	7,8
Joan Beddes	student	6
Ann Bellisari	anthropologist	2,10
Richard Berendzen	President, American University	8,11
April Berger	student	C
Charles Berry	historian	6,11
John Blair	economist	3,C
Bela Bognar	Social Work Dept.	9
Marilyn Borchardt	market director, Food First	11
Kenneth Boulding	economist, COPRED, ISA	7
Peter Bracher	Chair, English Dept.	3,8
Stuart Bremer	political scientist, ISA	7
Cathy Breth	artist and tax preparer	10
Bill Brison	Archdeacon of Bolton	10
Robert Brun	student	6
Paul Burgess	host, Hot Stove League	4
Don Burnette	student	6
Glena Buchholtz	secretary	11,C
Jacob Burckhardt	paradigm forerunner	C
Bunny Byrum	organizational communicationist	4
Len Cargan	emeritus sociologist	1,4,8,C
Emerson Cahow	Methodist bishop	11
Cindi Carlson	student	6
Brad Carpenter	student	5
Ceil Cary	English Dept.	4
Norm Cary	English Dept.	4,5
Christopher Chase-Dunn	world systems analyst, ISCSC	7
Chien-In Chen	engineer	C
Jason Christenson	student	6
Leanne Clare	student	6
Will Clark	ball player	11
Jerome Clemens	geographer	4,C
Matt Cooper	jazz pianist	9
Imogen Seger Coulborn	ISCSC sociologist	C
Rushton Coulborn	pioneer civilizationist	C
Brian Coy	student	6
Larry Crum	Chair, Computer Science Dept.	4
Jim Daily	Chair, Management Dept.	C
Judith Davidoff	early music performer	9
Ron Davidson	classical radio host	7

Eric Davis	ball player	11
Jack Davis	University photographer	8,C
Larry Dalzine	Chair, Central State Soc. Dept.	4
Ken Davenport	Director of Admissions	4
Charles Derry	Theatre Dept.	11
Dan DeStephen	Director, Center for Labor Management Cooperation	4,10
Matt Dewald	student	C
Frank Dobson	Director, Bolinga Center	4
Linda Dorsten	candidate for sociology position	2
Andy Doss	host to EMC 1910 Dinner	9
Diane Doss	EMC Board Member	9
Carole Durcynski	student	6
Katie Dvorak	Religion Dept.	3
Barbara Eakins-Reed	Communication Dept.	4,9
Bill Eckhardt	peace stds., ISCSC, COPRED, ISA	7
Bill Edwards	anthropologist, ISCSC	7,11
James Edwards	student	6
Dan Elliott	surgeon, Presbywed	10
Phil Engle	Chair, Social Work Dept.	4,5
Aprell Evans	student	6
Joe Fahey	peace studies, COPRED	7
Lou Falkner	registrar	3
Ann Farrell	mathematician	C
Ron Fetzer	organizational communicationist	4,11
Tom Files	opthalmologist	10
Donna Fletcher	sociologist, Sinclair Comm. Col.	4
Ron Flint	student	6,9
Suzanne Francis	student	C
Mary Frost-Pierson	adjunct, sociology	3
Rudi Fichtenbaum	economist and Faculty Vice President Elect	4
Harley Flack	future President of Wright State	4
Ron Fox	Dean, School of Professional Psychology	4
Gunder Frank	Dutch world systems analyst, ISCSC, ISA	7
Barbara Friendly	Director, "Places"	8
Charlie Funderburk	political scientist	3,4,11,C
Jan Gabbert	Chair of Classics Dept.	2,4,5,6,C
Beth Gage	EMC Marketing Committee	9
Johan Galtung	Norwegian peace studies	7
Jewell Garrison	social worker	4
Karen Gary	student	6
Imanuel Geiss	German historian, ISCSC	7
John Gibbs	student	6
Fred Gies	Dean of Education	4

Barry Gills	world systems analyst, ISA	7
Jim Gleason	English Dept.	4
Charles Gochman	political scientist, ISA	7
Ivan Goldfarb	chemist	C
Mel Goldfinger	biophysicist; future President WSU AAUP	4
Gwen Gray	dedicatee, secondary school student	7,10
Kevin Gray	high school teacher	10
Tom Gregor	anthropologist, Vanderbilt	7
Leila Grogbarger	mythical student	11
Jack Gruber	obstetrician	8
Janet Hall	student	6
Bill Hanks	Communication Dept.	11
Edna Harper	College of Education	C
Carleton Harris	student	6,11
John Harris	editor, *Peace Review*	7
Charles Hartmann	Management Dept.	1,4,5,6, 8,11,C
Charles Hathaway	Vice President for Academic Affairs	2,3,4,C
Melissa Hedden	student	6
Ann Herr	brokerage associate, Presbywed	10
Carolivia Herron	Author, visiting speaker	4
Paula Herzog	work-study student	C
Elmer Hesse	University Planner	4,11
Lisa Holliday	student	5
Courtney Holmes	student	6
Alex Holzman	editor, Ohio State University Press	7
John Hord	civilizationist, ISCSC	7
Ron Hough	Chair, Philosophy Dept.	4
Lillie Howard	Associate Vice President for Academic Affairs	3,4,11
Carla Howery	staff member, American Sociological Association	11
Francis Hsu	civilizationist, ISCSC	7
Keith Hudson	student	4,6,9
Jim Hughes	English Dept.	4
Allen Hye	Modern Languages Dept.	4
Art Iberall	physicist, ISCSC	6
Bill Irvine	philosopher	1,6,8
Harned Isele	physician, Mayo Clinic	7
Amin Islam	anthropologist	5,8
Shuntaro Ito	President, JSCSC	7
Jim Jacob	Chair, Political Science Dept.	3,4,7

Bob Jefferis	attorney	10
Dan Jansen	ecologist	9
Tim Jerome	student	6
Diane Jennings	manager, Dayton company	5
Patrick Jones	work-study student	6
Dan Juergens	opthalmologist	10,11
Peg Kane	production coordinator	4
Amy Karnehm	graduate student	C
Narasim Katary	geographer, urban planner	7
Keisuke Kawakubo	director, JSCSC	7
Robert Kegerreis	previous President of Wright State	4
Ping Pong Keller	mythical ball player	4
Bill King	classicist	4,C
Cynthia King	classicist	4,6,C
Helen Klein	psychologist	3
Tom Koebernick	sociologist	2,4,6,C
David Kopf	historian, ISCSC	7,11
A. L. Kroeber	paradigm rationalizer	C
Theodora Kroeber	biographer	C
Brian Kruger	psychologist	3,C
Rishi Kumar	Assoc. Dean, College of Business	11
Charles Larkowski	Dept. of Music	4
Louis Laux	Workshop presenter	9
David Leach	artist, Community Life Comm.	9
Russel Leng	political scientist, ISA	7
Glenn Leupold	Associate Minister, Westminster Presbyterian Church	11
Jack Levy	political scientist, ISA	7
Vicky Lewis	student	6
Bob Light	neighbor	10
Henrietta Light	neighbor	10
Terri Limbert	student	6
Henry Limouze	English Dept.	4,9
Susan Lippencott	student	6
Paul Lockhart	historian	4
Bob Lowry	Senior Minister, Westminster Presbyterian Church	6,10,11
Harold Macmillan	former U.K. Prime Minister	9
Fritz Magg	cellist	9
Susan Makowski	student	6,C
Barbara Marshall	incoming CLC Chair	9
Billy Martin	baseball manager	11
Rhonda Matthews-Hunter	student	6
Gwen Mattison	University Attorney	6
Ross Maxwell	civilizationist, ISCSC	7
J. Vernon McGee	radio preacher	11
Jerry McDowell	Chair, Dept. of Art and Art History	4

Monica McLendon	student	6
Ellen Melko	student, Northwestern	4,7,10, 11,C
Helen Melko	dedicatee, home maker	7,10
Julie Melko	artist	7,10,11,C
Matthew Melko	sociologist	passim.
Matthew F. Melko	attorney	10,11
Nelle Melko	Community Geriatric Nurse	passim.
Peter Melko	explorer and paver	4,7,10
Lou Menand	former Dean, Bradford Jr. College	5
Phil Messner	College of Education	4
Pat Miche	COPRED presenter	9
Carl Mirre	Presbywed	10
Ruth Mirre	Presbywed	10
Don Moloney	adjunct, all subjects	4
Roberta Monnin	University photographer	8,C
Lynn Morgan	secretary	7,C
Allen Moore	Executive Secretary, American Recorder Society	9
Perry Moore	Dean of Liberal Arts	2,3,4,8,11
Vernon Moore	social worker	4
Louise Morrow	Director, Family Services Grandview Hospital	10,11
Paige Mulhollan	President of Wright State	2,3,4,8,C
Ellen Murray	sociologist	2.5,6
Patti Myers	graduate student	6
Jesus of Nazareth	rabbi, social worker	9
John U. Nef	author, international relations	7
Beth Neher	Church Life Committee	9
Benjamin Nelson	former President, ISCSC	7
Michael Netzley	student	6
Herb Neve	historian	3,C
Sted Noble	civilizationist, ISCSC	7
Paul Ogg	student	4
Dennis O'Grady	consulting psychologist	6,8
Pat Olds	Director, Early Music Center	9,11
Mark Olsen	Theatre Dept.	11
David Orenstein	sociologist	passim.
Francis Padinjarekara	graduate student	4,6,11
Ed Page	editor, Paragon House	7
Michael Palencia-Roth	president, ISCSC	7
Beth Patterson	student	6
Melissa Peltier	student	6
Wayne Peterson	Director, Institutional Research	4
Dave Petreman	Modern Language Dept.	6,11
George Pollack	New Jersey attorney	7

Ellen Jane Porter	composer	7
Pat Porter	Chair, Community Life Comm.	9
Scott Porter	member, Community Life Comm.	9
Denise Potosky	Dept. of Communication	C
Virginia Preston	Elder, Westminster Presby. Church	10
Bob Pruett	Dept. of Communication	4,11
Carroll Quigley	paradigm consolidator	C
Doug Readenauer	contractor	11
Bob Reece	Chair, Dept. of Community Health, religionist	4
Peg Regan	graduate student	6,11
Scott Rice	early music performer	9
Bill Rickert	Associate Dean of Liberal Arts	2,3,4, 6,10,C
Mary Ridgway	graphic artist	4,7,C
Bob Riordan	anthropologist	2,8,C
Phyllis Risner	College of Nursing	11
Dave Robinson	historian	4,6
Judy Roller	director, University Advising	3,4,6
Dennis Rome	sociologist	2,6,11,C
Ellen Rosengarten	sociologist, Sinclair C.C.	4
Heather Rossler	student	6
Ian Rowland	graduate student, COPRED	7
Henry Ruminski	Communication Dept.	6
Jim Runkle	Biologist	4,7,11
Ed Rutter	Chair, Mathematics Dept.	4
Midori Yamanouchi Rynn	sociologist, ISCSC	6
Steve Sanderson	sociologist, editor, ISCSC	7
Jerry Savells	sociologist	2,8,11
Jim Sayer	chair, Communication Dept., Faculty Vice-president	4
Sara Sayer	director, Visiting Nurses	11
Donna Schlagheck	political scientist	4,7,11
Pat Schlaerth	Handicapped Services	6
Herb Schroeder	Church Life Committee	9
Pat Schroeder	Church Life Committee	9
Anna Schultz	student	6
Neil Seeley	officer, American Recorder Soc.	9
Tony Shanahan	spokesman, Media Networks	3
Norma Shepelak	sociologist	2,6,11,C
Walt Shirley	Chair, Sinclair College Sociology Dept.	4
Susan Shoemaker	candidate for sociology position	2
David Singer	political scientist, ISA	7,10
Mark Sirkin	political scientist, Associate Dean of Graduate School	4

Aimee Slocumb	student	6
Al Smith	mathematician, past faculty vice president	4
Reed Smith	political scientist	4,9
Tye Rome Smith	student	6
Mark Smutney	Assoc. Minister, Westminster Presbyterian Church	9
Betty Snow	secretary emeritus	7
Lee Snyder	historian, ISCSC	7
Pitirim Sorokin	paradigm challenger	11,C
In Soo Son	candidate for sociology position	2
Ed Spanier	Vice President for Finance	4
Oswald Spengler	paradigm founder	C
Al Spetter	historian	6
Scott Stemley	student	6
Carolyn Stephens	historian	4,6
Hugh Stevenson	computer consult., Presbywed	10
Mike Stewart	student	6
Bill Stoesz	Chair, Religion Dept.	3,11
Dan Stump	builder	10
Robert Sumser	historian	4
Don Swanson	English Dept.	4,6
Alice Swinger	College of Education	4
Cynthia Swinger	student	6
Chuck Taylor	philosopher	4,5,C
Peter Taylor	historian	4,6
John Thatcher	anthropologist	10
Bob Thobaben	emeritus political scientist	4,7,8
Arnold Toynbee	paradigm expander	C
Pam Trimble	student	C
Chevy Trucks	mythical ballplayer	4
Jim Uphoff	College of Education	11
John Vasquez	political scientist, ISA	7
Jeff Vernooy	Handicapped Services	4
Chris Viola	student	6
Jim Walker	political scientist	4
Veronica Watkins	Student Services, Sinclair College	4
Juanita Wehrle-Einhorn	Affirmative Action Director	2
Gordon Welty	sociologist	2,8,11
Win Wenger	ISCSC, workshop presenter	11
Roger Wescott	anthropologist, ISCSC	11
Tom Whissen	English Dept.	C
Martin Wight	British international relationist	7
John Williams	student	2
Larry Wolf	geographer, ISCSC,	6

Tim Wood	biologist	2,C
Katie Workman	historian	4,5
Li Xue	student	6
Gene Young	Rutgers computer admin.	7,10,11
Tsing Yuan	Chair of History Dept.	2,3,4
Kurt Zeller	baritone, counter tenor	9

References

Andrew Abbott, 1988, *The System of Professionals*, University of Chicago Press.

Charles Addams, 1970, *My Crowd*, Simon and Schuster.

Richard Balzer, 1976, *Clockwork*, Doubleday.

Carl Becker and Robert Thobaben, 1992, *Common Warfare: Parallel Memoirs by Two World War II GIs in the Pacific*, McFarland.

Howard Becker *et al.*, 1961, *Boys in White*, University of Chicago Press.

Jessie Bernard, 1984, "The Good Provider Role: Its Rise and Fall," in Voydanoff q.v., 43-60.

Richard Berendzen, 1986, *Is My Armor on Straight? A Year in the Life of a University President*, Adler and Adler.

Allan Bloom, 1987, *The Closing of the American Mind*, Simon & Schuster.

Catherine Drinker Bowen, 1949, *John Adams and the American Revolution*, Grosset & Dunlap.

Howard Bowen and Jack Schuster, 1986, *American Professors*, Oxford University Press.

Burton Clark, 1987, *The Academic Life: Small Worlds, Different Worlds*, Carnegie Foundation.

Dinesh D'Souza, 1991, *Illiberal Education*, Free Press.

Peter Drucker, 1986, *The Frontiers of Management*, Harper and Row.

———, 1989, *The New Realities*, HarperCollins.

Desiderius Erasmus and Martin Luther, 1988 (1524, 1525), *Discourse on Free Will*, translated and edited by Martin Winter, Continuum.

Henry Fairlie, 1989, "The Great Hesitator," *The New Republic*, July 17-24: 25-30.

Jonathan Franzen, 1988, *The Twenty-Seventh City*, Farrar, Strauss, Giroux.

Robert Georges and Michael Jones, 1980, *People Studying People*, University of California Press.

Langston Gilkey, 1975, *Shantung Compound*, Harper.

John Gray, 1992, *Men are From Mars, Women are From Venus*, Harper-Collins.

Edward G. Hall, 1977, *Beyond Culture*, Anchor.

Sandra Harding, 1986, *The Feminist Question in Science*, Cornell University Press.

Stephen Hawking, 1988, *A Brief History of Time*, Bantam.

Randy Hodson and Teresa Sullivan, 1990, *Social Organization of Work*, Wadsworth.

Maureen Howard, 1982, *Grace Abounding*, Little Brown.

Richard Huber, 1992, *How Professors Play the Cat Guarding the Cream*, University Press of America.

Jane Jacobs, 1961, *The Death and Life of the Great American City*, Random House.

Roger Kimball, 1988, *Tenured Radicals*, Harper & Row.

Thomas Kuhn, 1962, *The Structure of Scientific Revolutions*, University of Chicago Press.

J. Jiddu Krishnamurti, 1967, *Commentaries on Living*, Wheaton IL, Theosophical Publishing House

William Langer, 1948, *Encyclopedia of World History*, Houghton Mifflin.

Sar Levitan and Clifford Johnson, 1982, *Second Thoughts on Work*, Upjohn.

Jack Levy, 1985, "Theories of General War," *World Politics*, 37: 344-374.

Evan Luard, 1987, *War in International Society*, Yale University Press.

Nicholo Machiavelli, 1981 (1513), *The Prince*, Bantam.

Paule Marshall, 1984, *Praisesong for the Widow*, Dutton.

Matthew Melko, 1990, *Peace in Our Time*, Paragon House.

Melko and John Hord, 1984, *Peace in the Western World*, McFarland.

Melko, Thomas Koebernick and David Michael Orenstein, 1994, *Millfield on Saturday*, Wright State University Press.

Melko and Leighton R. Scott, 1987, *The Boundaries of Civilizations In Space and Time*, University Press of America.

Herman Melville, 1967 (1851), *Moby Dick*, Norton.

John Nef, 1968, *War and Human Progress*, Norton.

Friedrich Nietzsche, 1957 (1874), *The Use and Abuse of History*, tr. Adrian Collins, Bobbs-Merrill.

Octavio Paz, 1989, *Labyrinth of Solitude*, Grove Weidenfeld.

Ronald M. Pavalko, 1988, *Sociology of Occupations and Professions*, 2nd ed., Peacock.

Jed Perl, 1990, "The Obscure of Desire," *The New Republic*, April 16: 30-35.

James Phelan, 1989, *Beyond the Tenure Track*, Ohio State University Press.

Carroll Quigley, 1979 (1961), *The Evolution of Civilizations*, Liberty Press.

Charles Sabel, 1982, *Work and Politics*, Cambridge University Press.

Stephen K. Sanderson, editor, 1994, *Comparative Civilizations Review*, n. 30, Spring.

Sanderson, editor, 1996, *Civilizations and World Systems*, Walnut Creek CA, Altamira.

William Shakespeare, 1967 (1597-99), *Henry IV and Henry V*, Airmont.

————, 1971 (c. 1600), *Julius Caesar*, Pelican.

Michael Shanesfelt, 1990, "My Turn," *Newsweek*, March 11: 10-11.

Mansfield Spurrier, n.d., *Suburbia*, C & J.

Ellen Stark, 1989, "Rx: 2 Self Help Books and Call Me in the Morning," *Psychology Today*, June 23: 26.

Willis Stoesz, 1989, "Pre-Mauryan Lay Buddhism" ISCSC Meeting.

Tom Stoppard, 1983, *The Real Thing*, Faber & Faber

Charles Sykes, 1988, *ProfScam*, Regnery Gateway.

Tzvetan Todorov, 1989, "Crimes Against Humanities" *The New Republic*, July 3: 26-30.

Patricia Voydanoff, 1984, *Work and the Family*, Mayfield.

Tony Watson, 1980, *Sociology: Work and Industry*, Routledge.

Max Weber, 1958 (1920), *The Protestant Ethic*, Tr. Talcott Parsons, Scribner.

Jim Williams, 1943, *Out Our Way*, Scribner's.

Bruce Wilshire, 1990, *The Moral Collapse of the University*, SUNY Press.

About the Author

Matthew Melko is Professor Emeritus of Sociology at Wright State University, where he taught for the last 19 of his 36 years on a college or university faculty. He is the author of several books on civilizations, peace, family and community.

His previous books are:

Millfield On Saturday
      (with Thomas E. Koebernick and David Michael Orenstein)
Peace in Our Time
The Boundaries of Civilizations in Space and Time
      (with Leighton Scott)
Peace in the Western World
      (with John Hord)
Singles: Myths and Realities
      (with Leonard Cargan)
Peace in the Ancient World
      (with Richard Weigel, Sally Katary and Michael McKenny)
Fifty-Two Peaceful Societies
The Nature of Civilizations